5 STEPS TO A 5

500

AP English Language Questions
to know by test day

Allyson Ambrose

New York   Chicago   San Francisco   Lisbon   London   Madrid   Mexico City
Milan   New Delhi   San Juan   Seoul   Singapore   Sydney   Toronto

ISBN 978-0-07-175368-5
MHID   0-07-175368-0

Library of Congress Control Number 2010935996

Also in the 5 Steps Series:
5 Steps to a 5: AP English Language
5 Steps to a 5: AP English Language with CD-ROM

Also in the 500 AP Questions to Know by Test Day series:
5 Steps to a 5: 500 AP English Literature Questions to Know by Test Day
5 Steps to a 5: 500 AP Psychology Questions to Know by Test Day
5 Steps to a 5: 500 AP U.S. History Questions to Know by Test Day
5 Steps to a 5: 500 AP World History Questions to Know by Test Day
5 Steps to a 5: 500 AP Biology Questions to Know by Test Day

CONTENTS

PREFACE

The goal of this book is to provide passages and multiple-choice questions for you to become a skilled close reader who will have success on the AP English Language and Composition exam. By practicing your close-reading skills, you can become the type of reader who is able to think like a writer, one who understands that writers make many choices that depend on the purposes of their texts. The questions in this book will help you put yourself in the mind of a writer who thoughtfully chooses which words to use, what sentence types, what rhetorical techniques, what structure, what tone, etc. If you work through these passages and questions, I am confident you will do well on the exam.

Throughout my years of teaching AP English Language, I have asked my students what was most difficult about the exam and with what they would have liked more practice. Without fail, each year the answer is older texts and more multiple-choice questions. Because of their feedback, that is what this book provides—older texts (some from as early as the 1500s) and lots of multiple-choice questions—five hundred, to be exact! You can use this book as extra practice before the exam, perhaps in those last weeks or months, to feel and be well prepared.

This book is organized into ten chapters, six based on genre and four based on time period. Each chapter is set up like one multiple-choice section of the exam, with five passages and a total of fifty questions. Give yourself one hour to do one chapter, and you can practice your timing along with your close-reading skills.

The wonderful thing about practicing your close-reading skills is that these skills also translate to improved writing skills. Working through these chapters will help you analyze passages for their purposes and the techniques that achieve those purposes. This is the same process that you will need to follow for the rhetorical-analysis essay on the exam. Working through these chapters will also help you to think like a writer and to understand the choices writers make. This understanding of writers' choices also will bring you success on the essay portion, which requires you to make choices and to think about your purpose and the best ways to achieve it. These skills are also crucial to your success in college.

I wish you success on the exam and beyond, and I'm confident that by working through this book you will be ready to meet the challenges of the AP English Language and Composition exam.

Thank you to Dan Ambrose, whose continued love and support helped me to write this book. And thank you to my colleagues, whose professional support and faith in me have been invaluable. I'd also like to thank all of my past and current students; they make my work a joy and constantly delight me with their insight, diligence, and humor.

ABOUT THE AUTHOR

Allyson L. Ambrose has taught AP English Language and Composition for several years. She is a National Board certified teacher and a teacher of English language arts. A teacher leader, Allyson has written curricula, facilitated professional development workshops, and mentored teachers of AP English Language and Composition. Due in large part to Allyson's instructional leadership, more than 90 percent of students at her school taking the AP English Language and Composition exam over the past three years have earned at least a 3 on the exam, and more than 50 percent have earned at least a 4. Allyson has also been a College Board SAT essay reader. Allyson Ambrose's passion for scholarship and commitment to education make her a leading pedagogue in the field of English language arts education.

INTRODUCTION

Congratulations! You've taken a big step toward AP success by purchasing *5 Steps to a 5: 500 AP English Language Questions to Know by Test Day*. We are here to help you take the next step and score high on your AP Exam so you can earn college credits and get into the college or university of your choice.

This book gives you 500 AP-style multiple-choice questions that cover all the most essential course material. Each question has a detailed answer explanation. These questions will give you valuable independent practice to supplement your regular textbook and the groundwork you are already doing in your AP classroom.

This and the other books in this series were written by expert AP teachers who know your exam inside out and can identify the crucial exam information as well as questions that are most likely to appear on the exam.

You might be the kind of student who takes several AP courses and needs to study extra questions a few weeks before the exam for a final review. Or you might be the kind of student who puts off preparing until the last weeks before the exam. No matter what your preparation style is, you will surely benefit from reviewing these 500 questions, which closely parallel the content, format, and degree of difficulty of the questions on the actual AP exam. These questions and their answer explanations are the ideal last-minute study tool for those final few weeks before the test.

Remember the old saying "Practice makes perfect." If you practice with all the questions and answers in this book, we are certain you will build the skills and confidence needed to do great on the exam. Good luck!

—Editors of McGraw-Hill Education

CHAPTER 1

Autobiographers and Diarists

Passage 1a: Thomas De Quincey, *Confessions of an English Opium-Eater*

I here present you, courteous reader, with the record of a remarkable period in my life: according to my application of it, I trust that it will prove not merely an interesting record, but in a considerable degree useful and instructive. In that hope it is that I have drawn it up; and that must be my apology for breaking through that delicate and honourable reserve which, for the most part, restrains us from   5
the public exposure of our own errors and infirmities. Nothing, indeed, is more revolting to English feelings than the spectacle of a human being obtruding on our notice his moral ulcers or scars, and tearing away that "decent drapery" which time or indulgence to human frailty may have drawn over them; accordingly, the greater part of our confessions (that is, spontaneous and extra-judicial confessions) proceed   10
from demireps, adventurers, or swindlers: and for any such acts of gratuitous self-humiliation from those who can be supposed in sympathy with the decent and self-respecting part of society, we must look to French literature, or to that part of the German which is tainted with the spurious and defective sensibility of the French. All this I feel so forcibly, and so nervously am I alive to reproach of this tendency,   15
that I have for many months hesitated about the propriety of allowing this or any part of my narrative to come before the public eye until after my death (when, for many reasons, the whole will be published); and it is not without an anxious review of the reasons for and against this step that I have at last concluded on taking it.

Guilt and misery shrink, by a natural instinct, from public notice: they court   20
privacy and solitude: and even in their choice of a grave will sometimes sequester themselves from the general population of the churchyard, as if declining to claim fellowship with the great family of man, and wishing (in the affecting language of Mr. Wordsworth):

Humbly to express   25
A penitential loneliness.

It is well, upon the whole, and for the interest of us all, that it should be so: nor would I willingly in my own person manifest a disregard of such salutary feelings, nor in act or word do anything to weaken them; but, on the one hand,

as my self-accusation does not amount to a confession of guilt, so, on the other, 30
it is possible that, if it did, the benefit resulting to others from the record of an
experience purchased at so heavy a price might compensate, by a vast overbalance,
for any violence done to the feelings I have noticed, and justify a breach of the
general rule. Infirmity and misery do not of necessity imply guilt. They approach
or recede from shades of that dark alliance, in proportion to the probable motives 35
and prospects of the offender, and the palliations, known or secret, of the offence;
in proportion as the temptations to it were potent from the first, and the resistance
to it, in act or in effort, was earnest to the last. For my own part, without breach
of truth or modesty, I may affirm that my life has been, on the whole, the life of
a philosopher: from my birth I was made an intellectual creature, and intellectual 40
in the highest sense my pursuits and pleasures have been, even from my schoolboy
days. If opium-eating be a sensual pleasure, and if I am bound to confess that I have
indulged in it to an excess not yet recorded of any other man, it is no less true that
I have struggled against this fascinating enthrallment with a religious zeal, and have
at length accomplished what I never yet heard attributed to any other man—have 45
untwisted, almost to its final links, the accursed chain which fettered me. Such a
self-conquest may reasonably be set off in counterbalance to any kind or degree
of self-indulgence. Not to insist that in my case the self-conquest was unquestion-
able, the self-indulgence open to doubts of casuistry, according as that name shall
be extended to acts aiming at the bare relief of pain, or shall be restricted to such 50
as aim at the excitement of positive pleasure.

1. According to the writer, the purpose of his autobiography is to:
    (A) teach
    (B) inform
    (C) persuade
    (D) entertain
    (E) refute

2. The first two sentences of the passage contribute to the passage's appeal to:
      I. ethos
     II. logos
    III. pathos

    (A) I
    (B) II
    (C) III
    (D) I and III
    (E) I, II, and III

3. In the first paragraph, the writer uses the diction of illness to describe moral failings, with all of the following terms *except*:

(A) infirmities
(B) ulcers
(C) scars
(D) indulgence
(E) frailty

4. In the sentence "Nothing, indeed, is more revolting to English feelings than the spectacle of a human being obtruding on our notice his moral ulcers or scars, and tearing away that 'decent drapery' which time or indulgence to human frailty may have drawn over them . . . ," "decent drapery" is an example of:

(A) metaphor
(B) allusion
(C) simile
(D) analogy
(E) personification

5. In line 10, the pronoun "our" refers to:

(A) demireps
(B) adventurers
(C) swindlers
(D) human beings
(E) the English

6. In context, the word "propriety" in line 16 most nearly means:

(A) immorality
(B) decency
(C) popularity
(D) benefit
(E) profitability

7. In paragraph two, guilt and misery are personified, through all of the terms *except*:

(A) shrink
(B) instinct
(C) notice
(D) court
(E) sequester

8. The primary rhetorical function of the sentence "Infirmity and misery do not of necessity imply guilt" is to:
   (A) refute the conditional claim made in the line before
   (B) present the major claim of the last paragraph
   (C) introduce a claim to be defended with evidence in the following lines
   (D) elucidate the underlying assumption of the paragraph
   (E) provide evidence to support the first sentence of the paragraph

9. The second half of the last paragraph, beginning with the sentence "If opium-eating be a sensual pleasure, and if I am bound to confess that I have indulged in it to an excess not yet recorded of any other man, it is no less true that I have struggled against this fascinating enthrallment with a religious zeal . . ." contributes to the sense that the writer looks on his own past with:
   (A) guilt
   (B) ambivalence
   (C) paranoia
   (D) fascination
   (E) shame

10. The writer's tone in this passage can best be described as:
    (A) apologetic
    (B) forthright
    (C) indifferent
    (D) wry
    (E) effusive

Passage 1b: Frederick Douglass, *Narrative of the Life of Frederick Douglass*

The home plantation of Colonel Lloyd wore the appearance of a country village. All the mechanical operations for all the farms were performed here. The shoe-making and mending, the blacksmithing, cartwrighting, coopering, weaving, and grain-grinding, were all performed by the slaves on the home plantation. The whole place wore a business-like aspect very unlike the neighboring farms. The number of houses, too, conspired to give it advantage over the neighboring farms. It was called by the slaves the Great House Farm. Few privileges were esteemed higher, by the slaves of the out-farms, than that of being selected to do errands at the Great House Farm. It was associated in their minds with greatness. A representative could not be prouder of his election to a seat in the American Congress, than a slave on one of the out-farms would be of his election to do errands at the Great House Farm. They regarded it as evidence of great confidence reposed in them by their overseers;

and it was on this account, as well as a constant desire to be out of the field from under the driver's lash, that they esteemed it a high privilege, one worth careful living for. He was called the smartest and most trusty fellow, who had this honor conferred upon him the most frequently. The competitors for this office sought as diligently to please their overseers, as the office-seekers in the political parties seek to please and deceive the people. The same traits of character might be seen in Colonel Lloyd's slaves, as are seen in the slaves of the political parties.

The slaves selected to go to the Great House Farm, for the monthly allowance for themselves and their fellow-slaves, were peculiarly enthusiastic. While on their way, they would make the dense old woods, for miles around, reverberate with their wild songs, revealing at once the highest joy and the deepest sadness. They would compose and sing as they went along, consulting neither time nor tune. The thought that came up, came out—if not in the word, in the sound;—and as frequently in the one as in the other. They would sometimes sing the most pathetic sentiment in the most rapturous tone, and the most rapturous sentiment in the most pathetic tone. Into all of their songs they would manage to weave something of the Great House Farm. Especially would they do this, when leaving home. They would then sing most exultingly the following words:—

"I am going away to the Great House Farm!
O, yea! O, yea! O!"

This they would sing, as a chorus, to words which to many would seem unmeaning jargon, but which, nevertheless, were full of meaning to themselves. I have sometimes thought that the mere hearing of those songs would do more to impress some minds with the horrible character of slavery, than the reading of whole volumes of philosophy on the subject could do.

I did not, when a slave, understand the deep meaning of those rude and apparently incoherent songs. I was myself within the circle; so that I neither saw nor heard as those without might see and hear. They told a tale of woe which was then altogether beyond my feeble comprehension; they were tones loud, long, and deep; they breathed the prayer and complaint of souls boiling over with the bitterest anguish. Every tone was a testimony against slavery, and a prayer to God for deliverance from chains. The hearing of those wild notes always depressed my spirit, and filled me with ineffable sadness. I have frequently found myself in tears while hearing them. The mere recurrence to those songs, even now, afflicts me; and while I am writing these lines, an expression of feeling has already found its way down my cheek. To those songs I trace my first glimmering conception of the dehumanizing character of slavery. I can never get rid of that conception. Those songs still follow me, to deepen my hatred of slavery, and quicken my sympathies for my brethren in bonds. If any one wishes to be impressed with the soul-killing effects of slavery, let him go to Colonel Lloyd's plantation, and, on allowance-day, place himself in the deep pine woods, and there let him, in silence, analyze the sounds that shall pass through the chambers of his soul,—and if he is not thus impressed, it will only be because "there is no flesh in his obdurate heart."

I have often been utterly astonished, since I came to the north, to find persons who could speak of the singing, among slaves, as evidence of their contentment and happiness. It is impossible to conceive of a greater mistake. Slaves sing most when they are most unhappy. The songs of the slave represent the sorrows of his heart; and he is relieved by them, only as an aching heart is relieved by its tears. At 60 least, such is my experience. I have often sung to drown my sorrow, but seldom to express my happiness. Crying for joy, and singing for joy, were alike uncommon to me while in the jaws of slavery. The singing of a man cast away upon a desolate island might be as appropriately considered as evidence of contentment and happiness, as the singing of a slave; the songs of the one and of the other are prompted 65 by the same emotion.

11. The first two paragraphs of the passage contain all of the following *except*:
  (A) enumeration
  (B) analogy
  (C) parallelism
  (D) metaphor
  (E) allusion

12. The primary mode of composition of paragraph two is:
  (A) narration
  (B) description
  (C) definition
  (D) cause and effect
  (E) comparison and contrast

13. The purpose of this passage is captured in all of the following lines *except*:
  (A) "They would compose and sing as they went along, consulting neither time nor tune."
  (B) "I have sometimes thought that the mere hearing of those songs would do more to impress some minds with the horrible character of slavery, than the reading of whole volumes of philosophy on the subject could do."
  (C) "To those songs I trace my first glimmering conception of the dehumanizing character of slavery."
  (D) "I have often been utterly astonished, since I came to the north, to find persons who could speak of the singing, among slaves, as evidence of their contentment and happiness."
  (E) "Slaves sing most when they are most unhappy."

14. In context, the word "rude" in line 38 most nearly means:
    (A) impolite
    (B) harsh to the ear
    (C) rough or ungentle
    (D) of a primitive simplicity
    (E) tentative

15. An analogy is made between all of the following pairs *except*:
    (A) the relief that songs bring to slaves and the relief that tears bring to the heart
    (B) the songs of a castaway and the songs of a slave
    (C) a representative voted into Congress and a slave sent to the Great Farm
    (D) slaves trying to get to the Great Farm and a politician trying to get into office
    (E) one wishing to be impressed with the soul-killing effects of slavery and one placed into the deep of the woods

16. In line 40, "they" is a pronoun for the antecedent:
    (A) slaves
    (B) complaints
    (C) songs
    (D) souls
    (E) tones

17. The primary example of figurative language in the third paragraph is:
    (A) personification
    (B) metaphor
    (C) simile
    (D) metonymy
    (E) synecdoche

18. The line "I have often sung to drown my sorrow, but seldom to express my happiness," is an example of:
    (A) anaphora
    (B) epistrophe
    (C) asyndeton
    (D) antithesis
    (E) climax

19. The line "there is no flesh in his obdurate heart" is in quotation marks because:

    (A) the writer disagrees with the sentiment
    (B) someone else is speaking
    (C) he is quoting another work of literature
    (D) he wants to make clear his major claim
    (E) he spoke this line to Colonel Lloyd

20. The tone of the passage as a whole can best be described as:

    (A) introspective and wistful
    (B) detached and somber
    (C) pedantic and moralizing
    (D) contemplative and lugubrious
    (E) mirthful and reflective

Passage 1c: Benjamin Franklin, *The Autobiography of Benjamin Franklin*

It was about this time I conceiv'd the bold and arduous project of arriving at moral perfection. I wish'd to live without committing any fault at any time; I would conquer all that either natural inclination, custom, or company might lead me into. As I knew, or thought I knew, what was right and wrong, I did not see why I might not always do the one and avoid the other. But I soon found I had   5
undertaken a task of more difficulty than I had imagined. While my care was employ'd in guarding against one fault, I was often surprised by another; habit took the advantage of inattention; inclination was sometimes too strong for reason. I concluded, at length, that the mere speculative conviction that it was our interest to be completely virtuous, was not sufficient to prevent our slipping; and that the   10
contrary habits must be broken, and good ones acquired and established, before we can have any dependence on a steady, uniform rectitude of conduct. For this purpose I therefore contrived the following method.

In the various enumerations of the moral virtues I had met with in my reading, I found the catalogue more or less numerous, as different writers included more or   15
fewer ideas under the same name. Temperance, for example, was by some confined to eating and drinking, while by others it was extended to mean the moderating of every other pleasure, appetite, inclination, or passion, bodily or mental, even to our avarice and ambition. I propos'd to myself, for the sake of clearness, to use rather more names, with fewer ideas annex'd to each, than a few names with more ideas;   20
and I included under thirteen names of virtues all that at that time occurr'd to me as necessary or desirable, and annexed to each a short precept, which fully express'd the extent I gave to its meaning.

These names of virtues, with their precepts, were:

1. TEMPERANCE. Eat not to dullness; drink not to elevation.
2. SILENCE. Speak not but what may benefit others or yourself; avoid trifling conversation.
3. ORDER. Let all your things have their places; let each part of your business have its time.
4. RESOLUTION. Resolve to perform what you ought; perform without fail what you resolve.
5. FRUGALITY. Make no expense but to do good to others or yourself; i.e., waste nothing.
6. INDUSTRY. Lose no time; be always employ'd in something useful; cut off all unnecessary actions.
7. SINCERITY. Use no hurtful deceit; think innocently and justly, and, if you speak, speak accordingly.
8. JUSTICE. Wrong none by doing injuries, or omitting the benefits that are your duty.
9. MODERATION. Avoid extremes; forbear resenting injuries so much as you think they deserve.
10. CLEANLINESS. Tolerate no uncleanliness in body, cloaths, or habitation.
11. TRANQUILLITY. Be not disturbed at trifles, or at accidents common or unavoidable.
12. CHASTITY. Rarely use venery but for health or offspring, never to dullness, weakness, or the injury of your own or another's peace or reputation.
13. HUMILITY. Imitate Jesus and Socrates.

My intention being to acquire the habitude of all these virtues, I judg'd it would be well not to distract my attention by attempting the whole at once, but to fix it on one of them at a time; and, when I should be master of that, then to proceed to another, and so on, till I should have gone thro' the thirteen; and, as the previous acquisition of some might facilitate the acquisition of certain others, I arrang'd them with that view, as they stand above. Temperance first, as it tends to procure that coolness and clearness of head, which is so necessary where constant vigilance was to be kept up, and guard maintained against the unremitting attraction of ancient habits, and the force of perpetual temptations. This being acquir'd and establish'd, Silence would be more easy; and my desire being to gain knowledge at the same time that I improv'd in virtue, and considering that in conversation it was obtain'd rather by the use of the ears than of the tongue, and therefore wishing to break a habit I was getting into of prattling, punning, and joking, which only made me acceptable to trifling company, I gave Silence the second place. This and the next, Order, I expected would allow me more time for attending to my project and my studies. Resolution, once become habitual, would keep me firm in my endeavors to obtain all the subsequent virtues; Frugality and Industry freeing

me from my remaining debt, and producing affluence and independence, would   65
make more easy the practice of Sincerity and Justice, etc., etc. Conceiving then,
that, agreeably to the advice of Pythagoras in his Golden Verses, daily examination would be necessary, I contrived the following method for conducting that
examination.

21. The main purpose of this passage is to:
   (A) argue for the impossibility of "arriving at moral perfection"
   (B) describe the writer's planned process of "arriving at moral perfection"
   (C) define the concept of "arriving at moral perfection"
   (D) analyze the effects of "arriving at moral perfection"
   (E) classify the ways of "arriving at moral perfection"

22. The primary mode of composition of paragraph two of the passage is:
   (A) narration
   (B) description
   (C) definition
   (D) cause and effect
   (E) process analysis

23. The primary mode of composition of paragraph three of the passage is:
   (A) narration
   (B) description
   (C) definition
   (D) cause and effect
   (E) process analysis

24. In context, the word "precept" in line 22 most nearly means:
   (A) a definition of the virtue
   (B) an example of the virtue in action
   (C) an exception to the rules of the virtues
   (D) a particular course of action to follow the virtues
   (E) a preconceived notion about the virtue

25. The line "Resolve to perform what you ought; perform without fail what
   you resolve" uses:
   (A) anaphora
   (B) epistrophe
   (C) asyndeton
   (D) repetition
   (E) polysyndeton

26. Paragraph three uses several examples of a type of figurative language called:
    (A) personification
    (B) metaphor
    (C) simile
    (D) metonymy
    (E) synecdoche

27. The writer of the passage can best be characterized as someone who is:
    (A) disapproving
    (B) methodical
    (C) disinterested
    (D) unrealistic
    (E) judgmental

28. The style and the organization of the passage mostly appeals to:
    I. ethos
    II. logos
    III. pathos
    (A) I
    (B) II
    (C) III
    (D) I and II
    (E) II and III

29. The line "in conversation it was obtain'd rather by the use of the ears than of the tongue" uses the rhetorical technique of:
    (A) personification
    (B) metaphor
    (C) simile
    (D) metonymy
    (E) synecdoche

30. The tone of the passage as a whole can best be described as:
    (A) self-deprecating
    (B) resolved
    (C) bemused
    (D) reticent
    (E) irreverent

Passage 1d: Harriet Jacobs, *Incidents in the Life of a Slave Girl*

No pen can give an adequate description of the all-pervading corruption produced by slavery. The slave girl is reared in an atmosphere of licentiousness and fear. The lash and the foul talk of her master and his sons are her teachers. When she is fourteen or fifteen, her owner, or his sons, or the overseer, or perhaps all of them, begin to bribe her with presents. If these fail to accomplish their purpose, she is   5
whipped or starved into submission to their will. She may have had religious principles inculcated by some pious mother or grandmother, or some good mistress; she may have a lover, whose good opinion and peace of mind are dear to her heart; or the profligate men who have power over her may be exceedingly odious to her. But resistance is hopeless.   10

> The poor worm
> Shall prove her contest vain. Life's little day
> Shall pass, and she is gone!

The slaveholder's sons are, of course, vitiated, even while boys, by the unclean influences every where around them. Nor do the master's daughters always escape.   15
Severe retributions sometimes come upon him for the wrongs he does to the daughters of the slaves. The white daughters early hear their parents quarrelling about some female slave. Their curiosity is excited, and they soon learn the cause. They are attended by the young slave girls whom their father has corrupted; and they hear such talk as should never meet youthful ears, or any other ears. They   20
know that the woman slaves are subject to their father's authority in all things; and in some cases they exercise the same authority over the men slaves. I have myself seen the master of such a household whose head was bowed down in shame; for it was known in the neighborhood that his daughter had selected one of the meanest slaves on his plantation to be the father of his first grandchild. She did not make   25
her advances to her equals, nor even to her father's more intelligent servants. She selected the most brutalized, over whom her authority could be exercised with less fear of exposure. Her father, half frantic with rage, sought to revenge himself on the offending black man; but his daughter, foreseeing the storm that would arise, had given him free papers, and sent him out of the state.   30

In such cases the infant is smothered, or sent where it is never seen by any who know its history. But if the white parent is the father, instead of the mother, the offspring are unblushingly reared for the market. If they are girls, I have indicated plainly enough what will be their inevitable destiny.

You may believe what I say; for I write only that whereof I know. I was twenty-   35
one years in that cage of obscene birds. I can testify, from my own experience and observation, that slavery is a curse to the whites as well as to the blacks. It makes white fathers cruel and sensual; the sons violent and licentious; it contaminates the daughters, and makes the wives wretched. And as for the colored race, it needs an abler pen than mine to describe the extremity of their sufferings, the depth of their   40
degradation.

Yet few slaveholders seem to be aware of the widespread moral ruin occasioned by this wicked system. Their talk is of blighted cotton crops—not of the blight on their children's souls.

If you want to be fully convinced of the abominations of slavery, go on a south- 45 ern plantation, and call yourself a negro trader. Then there will be no concealment; and you will see and hear things that will seem to you impossible among human beings with immortal souls.

31. The rhetorical function of the personification of the lash and foul talk in paragraph one is to:
   (A) show the cruelty of the masters
   (B) show the viciousness of the master's sons
   (C) show the "all-pervading corruption produced by slavery"
   (D) show the powerlessness of slave girls
   (E) mirror the personification of the pen in the first line

32. In the line "When she is fourteen or fifteen, her owner, or his sons, or the overseer, or perhaps all of them, begin to bribe her with presents," the number of people who can exert power over the slave girl is stressed by:
   (A) asyndeton
   (B) polysyndeton
   (C) allusion
   (D) analogy
   (E) narration

33. The rhetorical function of the syntax of the last two sentences of paragraph one is:
   (A) the short sentence at the end serves as an answer to the question posed in the longer sentence before it
   (B) the longer sentence mirrors the line that listed the men that could exert power over the slave girl
   (C) the longer sentence presents the list of evidence to the claim presented in the final sentence
   (D) the last sentence serves as a transition from discussing the slave girl to discussing the slave owner's children
   (E) the short sentence at the end shows the finality of her conclusion regardless of the options described in the longer sentence before it

34. In context, the word "vitiated" in line 14 most nearly means:
    (A) made ineffective
    (B) invalidated
    (C) corrupted
    (D) devalued
    (E) buoyed

35. The anecdote in paragraph two is mainly meant to illustrate:
    (A) the cruelness of the fathers
    (B) the violence of the sons
    (C) the contamination of the daughters
    (D) the wretchedness of the wives
    (E) the degradation of the slaves

36. The primary mode of composition of paragraph two is:
    (A) cause and effect
    (B) comparison and contrast
    (C) description
    (D) classification
    (E) definition

37. The thesis of the passage is most clearly stated in the following line:
    (A) "No pen can give an adequate description of the all-pervading corruption produced by slavery."
    (B) "The slave girl is reared in an atmosphere of licentiousness and fear."
    (C) "I can testify, from my own experience and observation, that slavery is a curse to the whites as well as to the blacks."
    (D) "And as for the colored race, it needs an abler pen than mine to describe the extremity of their sufferings, the depth of their degradation."
    (E) "Yet few slaveholders seem to be aware of the widespread moral ruin occasioned by this wicked system."

38. All of the following words are used figuratively *except*:
    (A) blight (line 43)
    (B) cage (line 36)
    (C) storm (line 29)
    (D) pen (lines 1 and 40)
    (E) souls (line 44)

39. The tone of the final paragraph can best be described as:
- (A) inflammatory
- (B) condescending
- (C) apprehensive
- (D) ominous
- (E) cynical

40. The appeal to pathos in this passage is achieved by:
- I. provocative diction
- II. figurative language
- III. first-person accounts of experiences and observations
- (A) I
- (B) II
- (C) III
- (D) I and III
- (E) I, II, and III

Passage 1e: Helen Keller, *The Story of My Life*

Even in the days before my teacher came, I used to feel along the square stiff boxwood hedges, and, guided by the sense of smell would find the first violets and lilies. There, too, after a fit of temper, I went to find comfort and to hide my hot face in the cool leaves and grass. What joy it was to lose myself in that garden of flowers, to wander happily from spot to spot, until, coming suddenly upon a 5 beautiful vine, I recognized it by its leaves and blossoms, and knew it was the vine which covered the tumble-down summer-house at the farther end of the garden! Here, also, were trailing clematis, drooping jessamine, and some rare sweet flowers called butterfly lilies, because their fragile petals resemble butterflies' wings. But the roses—they were loveliest of all. Never have I found in the greenhouses of 10 the North such heart-satisfying roses as the climbing roses of my southern home. They used to hang in long festoons from our porch, filling the whole air with their fragrance, untainted by any earthy smell; and in the early morning, washed in the dew, they felt so soft, so pure, I could not help wondering if they did not resemble the asphodels of God's garden. 15

The beginning of my life was simple and much like every other little life. I came, I saw, I conquered, as the first baby in the family always does. There was the usual amount of discussion as to a name for me. The first baby in the family was not to be lightly named, every one was emphatic about that. My father suggested the name of Mildred Campbell, an ancestor whom he highly esteemed, and he 20 declined to take any further part in the discussion. My mother solved the problem by giving it as her wish that I should be called after her mother, whose maiden name was Helen Everett. But in the excitement of carrying me to church my father lost the name on the way, very naturally, since it was one in which he had declined to have a part. When the minister asked him for it, he just remembered that it had been decided to call me after my grandmother, and he gave her name as Helen Adams. 25

I am told that while I was still in long dresses I showed many signs of an eager, self-asserting disposition. Everything that I saw other people do I insisted upon imitating. At six months I could pipe out "How d'ye," and one day I attracted 30 every one's attention by saying "Tea, tea, tea" quite plainly. Even after my illness I remembered one of the words I had learned in these early months. It was the word "water," and I continued to make some sound for that word after all other speech was lost. I ceased making the sound "wah-wah" only when I learned to spell the word. 35

They tell me I walked the day I was a year old. My mother had just taken me out of the bath-tub and was holding me in her lap, when I was suddenly attracted by the flickering shadows of leaves that danced in the sunlight on the smooth floor. I slipped from my mother's lap and almost ran toward them. The impulse gone, I fell down and cried for her to take me up in her arms. 40

These happy days did not last long. One brief spring, musical with the song of robin and mocking-bird, one summer rich in fruit and roses, one autumn of gold and crimson sped by and left their gifts at the feet of an eager, delighted child. Then, in the dreary month of February, came the illness which closed my eyes and ears and plunged me into the unconsciousness of a new-born baby. They called it 45 acute congestion of the stomach and brain. The doctor thought I could not live. Early one morning, however, the fever left me as suddenly and mysteriously as it had come. There was great rejoicing in the family that morning, but no one, not even the doctor, knew that I should never see or hear again.

41. The primary mode of composition of paragraph one is:
   (A) narration
   (B) description
   (C) process analysis
   (D) classification
   (E) cause and effect

42. The imagery of paragraph one appeals to the sense(s) of:
   I. touch
   II. sight
   III. smell

   (A) I
   (B) II
   (C) III
   (D) I and III
   (E) I, II, and III

43. The second sentence of paragraph two uses the rhetorical device(s) of:
   I. anaphora
   II. asyndeton
   III. allusion

(A) I
(B) II
(C) III
(D) I and II
(E) I, II, and III

44. The primary mode of composition of the passage as a whole is:

(A) narration
(B) description
(C) process analysis
(D) classification
(E) cause and effect

45. The purpose of the passage is to:

(A) paint a picture of life before the writer lost her senses of sight and hearing
(B) explain how the writer lost her senses of sight and hearing
(C) compare and contrast life before and after the writer lost her senses of sight and hearing
(D) inform readers of the effects of acute congestion: loss of the senses of sight and hearing
(E) entertain readers with anecdotes of life before the writer lost her senses of sight and hearing

46. The strongest shift in the passage occurs in the following line:

(A) "But the roses—they were loveliest of all."
(B) "The beginning of my life was simple and much like every other little life."
(C) "I am told that while I was still in long dresses I showed many signs of an eager, self-asserting disposition."
(D) "They tell me I walked the day I was a year old."
(E) "These happy days did not last long."

47. The tone of the passage can best be described as:

(A) regretful
(B) whimsical
(C) bittersweet
(D) foreboding
(E) solemn

48. The style of the passage can best be characterized by all of the following *except*:

    (A) understatement
    (B) sensory imagery
    (C) simple sentence structure
    (D) figurative language
    (E) colorful diction

49. The line, "One brief spring, musical with the song of robin and mocking-bird, one summer rich in fruit and roses, one autumn of gold and crimson sped by and left their gifts at the feet of an eager, delighted child," uses all of the following rhetorical devices *except*:

    (A) anaphora
    (B) asyndeton
    (C) personification
    (D) metaphor
    (E) imagery

50. All of the following grammatical changes would be preferable *except*:

    (A) providing a referent for "they" in line 45
    (B) providing a referent for "they" in line 36
    (C) changing "which" to "that" in line 44
    (D) changing "could" to "would" in line 46
    (E) changing "them" to "it" in line 39

CHAPTER 2

Biographers and History Writers

Passage 2a: James Boswell, *Life of Samuel Johnson*

To this may be added the sentiments of the very man whose life I am about to exhibit . . .

But biography has often been allotted to writers, who seem very little acquainted with the nature of their task, or very negligent about the performance. They rarely afford any other account than might be collected from public papers, but imagine themselves writing a life, when they exhibit a chronological series of actions or preferments; and have so little regard to the manners or behaviour of their heroes, that more knowledge may be gained of a man's real character, by a short conversation with one of his servants, than from a formal and studied narrative, begun with his pedigree, and ended with his funeral. . . .

I am fully aware of the objections which may be made to the minuteness on some occasions of my detail of Johnson's conversation, and how happily it is adapted for the petty exercise of ridicule, by men of superficial understanding and ludicrous fancy; but I remain firm and confident in my opinion, that minute particulars are frequently characteristick, and always amusing, when they relate to a distinguished man. I am therefore exceedingly unwilling that any thing, however slight, which my illustrious friend thought it worth his while to express, with any degree of point, should perish. For this almost superstitious reverence, I have found very old and venerable authority, quoted by our great modern prelate, Secker, in whose tenth sermon there is the following passage:

Rabbi David Kimchi, a noted Jewish Commentator, who lived about five hundred years ago, explains that passage in the first Psalm, His leaf also shall not wither, from Rabbis yet older than himself, thus: That even the idle talk, so he expresses it, of a good man ought to be regarded; the most superfluous things he saith are always of some value. And other ancient authours have the same phrase, nearly in the same sense.

Of one thing I am certain, that considering how highly the small portion which we have of the table-talk and other anecdotes of our celebrated writers is valued, and how earnestly it is regretted that we have not more, I am justified in preserving

rather too many of Johnson's sayings, than too few; especially as from the diversity 30
of dispositions it cannot be known with certainty beforehand, whether what may
seem trifling to some and perhaps to the collector himself, may not be most agreeable to many; and the greater number that an authour can please in any degree, the
more pleasure does there arise to a benevolent mind.

　　To those who are weak enough to think this a degrading task, and the time 35
and labour which have been devoted to it misemployed, I shall content myself with
opposing the authority of the greatest man of any age, JULIUS CÆSAR, of whom
Bacon observes, that "in his book of Apothegms which he collected, we see that he
esteemed it more honour to make himself but a pair of tables, to take the wise and
pithy words of others, than to have every word of his own to be made an apothegm 40
or an oracle."

51. The second paragraph begins its argument with the use of:
　　(A) counterargument
　　(B) claim
　　(C) evidence
　　(D) warrant
　　(E) logical fallacy

52. All of the following are displayed as beneficial to the art of biography by
the writer *except*:
　　(A) minute particulars
　　(B) idle talk
　　(C) table talk
　　(D) a chronological series of actions
　　(E) anecdotes

53. In line 12, the pronoun "it" refers to:
　　(A) objections
　　(B) minuteness
　　(C) occasions
　　(D) details
　　(E) conversation

54. The major claim of the passage is best stated in the following line:
    (A) ". . . but I remain firm and confident in my opinion, that minute particulars are frequently characteristick, and always amusing, when they relate to a distinguished man."
    (B) "Of one thing I am certain, that considering how highly the small portion which we have of the table-talk and other anecdotes of our celebrated writers is valued, and how earnestly it is regretted that we have not more, I am justified in preserving rather too many of Johnson's sayings, than too few . . ."
    (C) "But biography has often been allotted to writers, who seem very little acquainted with the nature of their task, or very negligent about the performance."
    (D) "They rarely afford any other account than might be collected from public papers, but imagine themselves writing a life, when they exhibit a chronological series of actions or preferments . . ."
    (E) " . . . more knowledge may be gained of a man's real character, by a short conversation with one of his servants, than from a formal and studied narrative, begun with his pedigree, and ended with his funeral."

55. In context, the word "apothegm" in line 40 most nearly means:
    (A) anecdote
    (B) prophecy
    (C) prediction
    (D) adage
    (E) quotation

56. The tone of the passage can best be described as:
    (A) pedantic
    (B) detached
    (C) confident
    (D) flippant
    (E) grave

57. The passage as a whole relies mostly on an appeal to:
    I. ethos
    II. logos
    III. pathos
    (A) I
    (B) II
    (C) III
    (D) I and II
    (E) I, II, and III

58. The passage as a whole uses the following mode of composition:

(A) narration
(B) description
(C) process analysis
(D) cause and effect
(E) argument

59. The style of the passage can best be described as:

(A) complex and reasoned
(B) descriptive and evocative
(C) allusive and evocative
(D) symbolic and disjointed
(E) abstract and informal

60. The bulk of this argument is made up of:

(A) an explanation of what biography should and should not include
(B) a defense of the writer's choices in writing Samuel Johnson's biography
(C) an appeal to various authorities to justify the writer's choices in writing Samuel Johnson's biography
(D) responses to those who believe that the writer has "misemployed" his time and labor in writing Samuel Johnson's biography
(E) attacks against those who are "negligent" in the task of writing biography

Passage 2b: Thomas Carlyle, *On Heroes, Hero-Worship and the Heroic in History*

We come now to the last form of Heroism; that which we call Kingship. The Commander over Men; he to whose will our wills are to be subordinated, and loyally surrender themselves, and find their welfare in doing so, may be reckoned the most important of Great Men. He is practically the summary for us of all the various figures of Heroism; Priest, Teacher, whatsoever of earthly or of spiritual dignity we   5 can fancy to reside in a man, embodies itself here, to command over us, to furnish us with constant practical teaching, to tell us for the day and hour what we are to do. He is called Rex, Regulator, Roi: our own name is still better; King, Konning, which means Can-ning, Able-man.

Numerous considerations, pointing towards deep, questionable, and indeed   10 unfathomable regions, present themselves here: on the most of which we must resolutely for the present forbear to speak at all. As Burke said that perhaps fair Trial by Jury was the soul of Government, and that all legislation, administration, parliamentary debating, and the rest of it, went on, in "order to bring twelve impar-

tial men into a jury-box;"—so, by much stronger reason, may I say here, that the   15
finding of your Ableman and getting him invested with the symbols of ability, with
dignity, worship (worth-ship), royalty, kinghood, or whatever we call it, so that
he may actually have room to guide according to his faculty of doing it,—is the
business, well or ill accomplished, of all social procedure whatsoever in this world!
Hustings-speeches, Parliamentary motions, Reform Bills, French Revolutions, all   20
mean at heart this; or else nothing. Find in any country the Ablest Man that exists
there; raise him to the supreme place, and loyally reverence him: you have a perfect government for that country; no ballot-box, parliamentary eloquence, voting,
constitution-building, or other machinery whatsoever can improve it a whit. It is
in the perfect state; an ideal country. The Ablest Man; he means also the truest-   25
hearted, justest, the Noblest Man: what he tells us to do must be precisely the wisest, fittest, that we could anywhere or anyhow learn;—the thing which it will in all
ways behoove US, with right loyal thankfulness and nothing doubting, to do! Our
doing and life were then, so far as government could regulate it, well regulated; that
were the ideal of constitutions.   30

Alas, we know very well that Ideals can never be completely embodied in practice. Ideals must ever lie a very great way off; and we will right thankfully content
ourselves with any not intolerable approximation thereto! Let no man, as Schiller
says, too querulously "measure by a scale of perfection the meagre product of reality" in this poor world of ours. We will esteem him no wise man; we will esteem   35
him a sickly, discontented, foolish man. And yet, on the other hand, it is never
to be forgotten that Ideals do exist; that if they be not approximated to at all, the
whole matter goes to wreck! Infallibly. No bricklayer builds a wall perfectly perpendicular, mathematically this is not possible; a certain degree of perpendicular-
ity suffices him; and he, like a good bricklayer, who must have done with his job,   40
leaves it so. And yet if he sway too much from the perpendicular; above all, if he
throw plummet and level quite away from him, and pile brick on brick heedless,
just as it comes to hand—! Such bricklayer, I think, is in a bad way. He has forgotten himself: but the Law of Gravitation does not forget to act on him; he and his
wall rush down into confused welter of ruin—!   45

This is the history of all rebellions, French Revolutions, social explosions in
ancient or modern times. You have put the too Unable Man at the head of affairs!
The too ignoble, unvaliant, fatuous man. You have forgotten that there is any rule,
or natural necessity whatever, of putting the Able Man there. Brick must lie on
brick as it may and can. Unable Simulacrum of Ability, quack, in a word, must   50
adjust himself with quack, in all manner of administration of human things;—
which accordingly lie unadministered, fermenting into unmeasured masses of failure, of indigent misery: in the outward, and in the inward or spiritual, miserable
millions stretch out the hand for their due supply, and it is not there. The "law
of gravitation" acts; Nature's laws do none of them forget to act. The miserable   55
millions burst forth into Sansculottism, or some other sort of madness: bricks and
bricklayer lie as a fatal chaos—!

61. The second sentence of the passage, "The Commander over Men; he to whose will our wills are to be subordinated, and loyally surrender themselves, and find their welfare in doing so, may be reckoned the most important of Great Men," is the following type of sentence:

(A) simple
(B) sentence fragment
(C) interrogative
(D) complex
(E) imperative

62. The primary mode of composition for the first paragraph is:

(A) narration
(B) description
(C) process analysis
(D) definition
(E) classification

63. In context, the word "querulously" in line 34 most nearly means:

(A) in a complaining fashion
(B) forgivingly
(C) in an interrogative fashion
(D) unhappily
(E) unrealistically

64. The style of the passage can be characterized by its use of all of the following *except*:

(A) varied sentence structure
(B) emphatic punctuation
(C) colloquialisms
(D) enumeration
(E) figurative language

65. The rhetorical function of the line "Alas, we know very well that Ideals can never be completely embodied in practice" is best described as:

(A) shifting the passage from a discussion of ideals to a discussion of practice
(B) providing a claim to be supported with data in the rest of the paragraph
(C) articulating a warrant that is an underlying assumption
(D) concluding an argument presented in the previous paragraph
(E) acknowledging and responding to possible counterargument

66. The primary mode of composition used in paragraph four is:
    (A) narration
    (B) description
    (C) definition
    (D) cause and effect
    (E) comparison and contrast

67. The rhetorical function of the extended metaphor of the bricklayer can best be described as:
    (A) illustrating the disastrous results of having an "unable" man as king
    (B) exemplifying the "plummet and level" referred to in line 42
    (C) providing an analogous example contrasting the "able" and "unable" man
    (D) signaling a shift from a discussion of kings to a discussion of revolutions
    (E) defining the "ignoble, unvaliant, fatuous man"

68. The lines "The 'law of gravitation' acts; Nature's laws do none of them forget to act. The miserable millions burst forth into Sansculottism, or some sort of madness: bricks and bricklayers lie as a fatal chaos—!" uses all of the following rhetorical techniques *except*:
    (A) syntactical inversion
    (B) figurative language
    (C) apposition
    (D) allusion
    (E) alliteration

69. The purpose of the passage is twofold; it is to:
    (A) argue that choosing a king is more important than choosing a jury and to classify able men and unable men
    (B) define what a king should be and to display the effects of choosing poorly
    (C) persuade that a king is the greatest of all heroes and to compare ideals and practice
    (D) analyze the process of choosing a king and to analyze the causes of choosing poorly
    (E) describe great kings and narrate the events that follow choosing poorly

70. The major claim of the passage is stated in which of the following line(s)?

(A) "The Commander over Men; he to whose will our wills are to be subordinated, and loyally surrender themselves, and find their welfare in doing so, may be reckoned the most important of Great Men."

(B) "And yet, on the other hand, it is never to be forgotten that Ideals do exist; that if they be not approximated to at all, the whole matter goes to wreck!"

(C) "The Ablest Man; he means also the truest-hearted, justest, the Noblest Man: what he tells us to do must be precisely the wisest, fittest, that we could anywhere or anyhow learn;—the thing which it will in all ways behoove US, with right loyal thankfulness and nothing doubting, to do!"

(D) "Ideals must ever lie a very great way off; and we will right thankfully content ourselves with any not intolerable approximation thereto!"

(E) "You have forgotten that there is any rule, or natural necessity whatever, of putting the Able Man there."

Passage 2c: Winston Churchill, *The Approaching Conflict*

We are met together at a time when great exertions and a high constancy are required from all who cherish and sustain the Liberal cause. Difficulties surround us and dangers threaten from this side and from that. You know the position which has been created by the action of the House of Lords. Two great political Parties divide all England between them in their conflicts. Now it is discovered that one of these Parties possesses an unfair weapon—that one of these Parties, after it is beaten at an election, after it is deprived of the support and confidence of the country, after it is destitute of a majority in the representative Assembly, when it sits in the shades of Opposition without responsibility, or representative authority, under the frown, so to speak, of the Constitution, nevertheless possesses a weapon, an instrument, a tool, a utensil—call it what you will—with which it can harass, vex, impede, affront, humiliate, and finally destroy the most serious labours of the other. When it is realised that the Party which possesses this prodigious and unfair advantage is in the main the Party of the rich against the poor, of the classes and their dependants against the masses, of the lucky, the wealthy, the happy, and the strong against the left-out and the shut-out millions of the weak and poor, you will see how serious the constitutional situation has become.

A period of supreme effort lies before you. The election with which this Parliament will close, and towards which we are moving, is one which is different in notable features from any other which we have known. Looking back over the politics of the last thirty years, we hardly ever see a Conservative Opposition approaching an election without a programme, on paper at any rate, of social and democratic reform. There was Lord Beaconsfield with his policy of "health and the laws of health." There was the Tory democracy of Lord Randolph Churchill in 1885 and 1886, with large, far-reaching plans of Liberal and democratic reform, of 25 a generous policy to Ireland, of retrenchment and reduction of expenditure upon naval and military armaments—all promises to the people, and for the sake of which he resigned rather than play them false. Then you have the elections of 1892 and 1895. In each the Conservative Party, whether in office or opposition, was, under the powerful influence of Mr. [Joseph] Chamberlain, committed to most 30 extensive social programmes, of what we should call Liberal and Radical reforms, like the Workmen's Compensation Act and Old-Age Pensions, part of which were carried out by them and part by others.

But what social legislation, what plans of reform do the Conservative Party offer now to the working people of England if they will return them to power? 35 I have studied very carefully the speeches of their leaders—if you can call them leaders—and I have failed to discover a single plan of social reform or reconstruction. Upon the grim and sombre problems of the Poor Law they have no policy whatever. Upon unemployment no policy whatever; for the evils of intemperance no policy whatever, except to make sure of the public-house vote; upon the ques- 40 tion of the land, monopolised as it is in the hands of so few, denied to so many, no policy whatever; for the distresses of Ireland, for the relations between the Irish and British peoples, no policy whatever unless it be coercion. In other directions where they have a policy, it is worse than no policy. For Scotland the Lords' veto, for Wales a Church repugnant to the conscience of the overwhelming majority of 45 the Welsh people, crammed down their throats at their own expense.

71. The first paragraph contains all of the following rhetorical techniques *except*:
    (A) anaphora
    (B) metaphor
    (C) enumeration
    (D) understatement
    (E) asyndeton

72. At the end of the first paragraph, the writer sets up all of the following oppositions *except*:
    (A) rich vs. poor
    (B) weak vs. strong
    (C) lucky vs. unfair
    (D) wealthy vs. left-out
    (E) happy vs. shut-out

73. The passage as a whole mostly appeals to:
    I. ethos
    II. logos
    III. pathos
    (A) I
    (B) II
    (C) III
    (D) I and II
    (E) I and III

74. The purpose of the first paragraph is to:
    (A) inform
    (B) entertain
    (C) persuade
    (D) describe
    (E) narrate

75. The purpose of the second paragraph is to:
    (A) inform
    (B) entertain
    (C) persuade
    (D) describe
    (E) narrate

76. The pronoun "it" in line 11 refers to:
    (A) England
    (B) one of these parties
    (C) an unfair weapon
    (D) the Constitution
    (E) the serious labours of the other

77. The tone of the third paragraph can best be described as:
    (A) rapt
    (B) didactic
    (C) reverent
    (D) condescending
    (E) scornful

78. The tone of the third paragraph is achieved by all of the following techniques *except*:

   (A) imagery
   (B) anaphora
   (C) rhetorical questions
   (D) parenthetical statement
   (E) figurative language

79. The sentence "Now it is discovered that one of these Parties possesses an unfair weapon—that one of these Parties, after it is beaten at an election, after it is deprived of the support and confidence of the country, after it is destitute of a majority in the representative Assembly, when it sits in the shades of Opposition without responsibility, or representative authority, under the frown, so to speak, of the Constitution, nevertheless possesses a weapon, an instrument, a tool, a utensil—call it what you will—with which it can harass, vex, impede, affront, humiliate, and finally destroy the most serious labours of the other," is the following type of sentence:

   (A) fragment
   (B) simple
   (C) cumulative
   (D) compound
   (E) periodic

80. In context, the word "repugnant" in line 45 most nearly means:

   (A) incompatible
   (B) hostile
   (C) offensive
   (D) inconsistent
   (E) provocative

Passage 2d: Thomas Babington Macaulay, *Hallam's History*

History, at least in its state of ideal perfection, is a compound of poetry and philosophy. It impresses general truths on the mind by a vivid representation of particular characters and incidents. But, in fact, the two hostile elements of which it consists have never been known to form a perfect amalgamation; and at length, in our own time, they have been completely and professedly separated. Good histories, in the   5
proper sense of the word, we have not. But we have good historical romances, and good historical essays. The imagination and the reason, if we may use a legal metaphor, have made partition of a province of literature of which they were formerly seized per my et per tout; and now they hold their respective portions in severalty, instead of holding the whole in common.   10

To make the past present, to bring the distant near, to place us in the society of a great man or on the eminence which overlooks the field of a mighty battle, to invest with the reality of human flesh and blood beings whom we are too much inclined to consider as personified qualities in an allegory, to call up our ancestors before us with all their peculiarities of language, manners, and garb, to show us over their houses, to seat us at their tables, to rummage their old-fashioned wardrobes, to explain the uses of their ponderous furniture, these parts of the duty which properly belongs to the historian have been appropriated by the historical novelist. On the other hand, to extract the philosophy of history, to direct on judgment of events and men, to trace the connection of cause and effects, and to draw from the occurrences of former time general lessons of moral and political wisdom, has become the business of a distinct class of writers. 15 20

Of the two kinds of composition into which history has been thus divided, the one may be compared to a map, the other to a painted landscape. The picture, though it places the country before us, does not enable us to ascertain with accuracy the dimensions, the distances, and the angles. The map is not a work of imitative art. It presents no scene to the imagination; but it gives us exact information as to the bearings of the various points, and is a more useful companion to the traveller or the general than the painted landscape could be, though it were the grandest that ever Rosa peopled with outlaws, or the sweetest over which Claude ever poured the mellow effulgence of a setting sun. 25 30

81. The primary mode of composition of the passage is:
   (A) narration
   (B) description
   (C) process analysis
   (D) comparison and contrast
   (E) cause and effect

82. The line "It impresses general truths on the mind by a vivid representation of particular characters and incidents" is an example of:
   (A) analogy
   (B) antithesis
   (C) paradox
   (D) allusion
   (E) metaphor

83. In context, the word "amalgamation" in line 4 most nearly means:
   (A) whole
   (B) product
   (C) portion
   (D) dissolution
   (E) union

84. The two hostile elements introduced in the first paragraph are described as all of the following pairs *except*:
    (A) severalty and the whole
    (B) poetry and philosophy
    (C) imagination and reason
    (D) romances and essays
    (E) general truths and particular characters and incidents

85. The second paragraph consists of two of the following types of sentence:
    (A) simple
    (B) compound
    (C) compound-complex
    (D) periodic
    (E) cumulative

86. In line 29, the pronoun "it" refers to:
    (A) history
    (B) composition
    (C) the picture
    (D) the map
    (E) the companion

87. The style of the passage can be characterized by its use of all of the following *except*:
    (A) figurative language
    (B) paradox
    (C) complex sentence structure
    (D) analogy
    (E) allegory

88. The purpose of the second paragraph of the passage is to:
    (A) enumerate all of the details available to us through histories
    (B) describe what historical romances and historical essays each have to offer
    (C) explain the process of making "the past present" and bringing "the distant near"
    (D) argue for the superiority of historical romances and what they can offer
    (E) evaluate which type of history is superior, leaving the answer up to the reader

89. Which of the following sentences best expresses the major claim of this passage?

   (A) "History, at least in its state of ideal perfection, is a compound of poetry and philosophy."
   (B) "It impresses general truths on the mind by a vivid representation of particular characters and incidents."
   (C) "But, in fact, the two hostile elements of which it consists have never been known to form a perfect amalgamation; and at length, in our own time, they have been completely and professedly separated."
   (D) "Good histories, in the proper sense of the word, we have not."
   (E) "But we have good historical romances, and good historical essays."

90. The tone of the second paragraph can best be described as:

   (A) bewildered
   (B) placid
   (C) flippant
   (D) laudatory
   (E) sympathetic

Passage 2e: George Trevelyan, *Life and Letters of Lord Macaulay*

He who undertakes to publish the memoirs of a distinguished man may find a ready apology in the custom of the age. If we measure the effective demand for biography by the supply, the person commemorated need possess but a very moderate reputation, and have played no exceptional part, in order to carry the reader through many hundred pages of anecdote, dissertation, and correspondence. To 5 judge from the advertisements of our circulating libraries, the public curiosity is keen with regard to some who did nothing worthy of special note, and others who acted so continuously in the face of the world that, when their course was run, there was little left for the world to learn about them. It may, therefore, be taken for granted that a desire exists to hear something authentic about the life of a man 10 who has produced works which are universally known, but which bear little or no indication of the private history and the personal qualities of the author.

This was in a marked degree the case with Lord Macaulay. His two famous contemporaries in English literature have, consciously or unconsciously, told their own story in their books. Those who could see between the lines in "David Cop- 15 perfield" were aware that they had before them a delightful autobiography; and all who knew how to read Thackeray could trace him in his novels through every stage in his course, on from the day when as a little boy, consigned to the care of English relatives and schoolmasters, he left his mother on the steps of the landing-place at Calcutta. The dates and names were wanting, but the man was there; while the 20 most ardent admirers of Macaulay will admit that a minute study of his literary productions left them, as far as any but an intellectual knowledge of the writer himself was concerned, very much as it found them. A consummate master of his craft, he turned out works which bore the unmistakable marks of the artificer's hand, but which did not reflect his features. It would be almost as hard to compose 25 a picture of the author from the History, the Essays, and the Lays, as to evolve an idea of Shakespeare from *Henry the Fifth* and *Measure for Measure*.

But, besides being a man of letters, Lord Macaulay was a statesman, a jurist, and a brilliant ornament of society, at a time when to shine in society was a distinction which a man of eminence and ability might justly value. In these several 30 capacities, it will be said, he was known well, and known widely. But in the first place, as these pages will show, there was one side of his life (to him, at any rate, the most important,) of which even the persons with whom he mixed most freely and confidentially in London drawing-rooms, in the Indian Council chamber, and in the lobbies and on the benches of the House of Commons, were only in part 35 aware. And in the next place, those who have seen his features and heard his voice are few already and become yearly fewer; while, by a rare fate in literary annals, the number of those who read his books is still rapidly increasing. For everyone who sat with him in private company or at the transaction of public business,—for every ten who have listened to his oratory in Parliament or from the hustings,—there 40 must be tens of thousands whose interest in history and literature he has awakened and informed by his pen, and who would gladly know what manner of man it was that has done them so great a service.

To gratify that most legitimate wish is the duty of those who have the means at their command. His lifelike image is indelibly impressed upon their minds, (for 45 how could it be otherwise with any who had enjoyed so close relations with such a man?) although the skill which can reproduce that image before the general eye may well be wanting. But his own letters will supply the deficiencies of the biographer. Never did any one leave behind him more copious materials for enabling others to put together a narrative which might be the history, not indeed of his 50 times, but of the man himself. For in the first place he so soon showed promise of being one who would give those among whom his early years were passed reason to be proud, and still more certain assurance that he would never afford them cause for shame, that what he wrote was preserved with a care very seldom bestowed on childish compositions; and the value set upon his letters by those with whom he 55 corresponded naturally enough increased as years went on. And in the next place he was by nature so incapable of affectation or concealment that he could not write otherwise than as he felt, and, to one person at least, could never refrain from writing all that he felt; so that we may read in his letters, as in a clear mirror, his opinions and inclinations, his hopes and affections, at every succeeding period of 60 his existence. Such letters could never have been submitted to an editor not connected with both correspondents by the strongest ties; and even one who stands in that position must often be sorely puzzled as to what he has the heart to publish and the right to withhold.

91. In context, the word "apology" in line 2 most nearly means:

(A) an admission of error
(B) an excuse
(C) an expression of regret
(D) a justification
(E) a poor substitute

92. The major claim of the passage is stated in which of the following lines?

(A) "He who undertakes to publish the memoirs of a distinguished man may find a ready apology in the custom of the age."

(B) "It may, therefore, be taken for granted that a desire exists to hear something authentic about the life of a man who has produced works which are universally known, but which bear little or no indication of the private history and the personal qualities of the author."

(C) "But, besides being a man of letters, Lord Macaulay was a statesman, a jurist, and a brilliant ornament of society, at a time when to shine in society was a distinction which a man of eminence and ability might justly value."

(D) "To gratify that most legitimate wish is the duty of those who have the means at their command."

(E) "Such letters could never have been submitted to an editor not connected with both correspondents by the strongest ties; and even one who stands in that position must often be sorely puzzled as to what he has the heart to publish and the right to withhold."

93. The purpose of the passage is to:

(A) justify the writer's writing a biography of Lord Macaulay
(B) describe the taste for biographies in the writer's era
(C) analyze the appropriate reasons for writing a biography
(D) define the genre of biography
(E) narrate the accomplishments of Lord Macaulay

94. The line "It would be almost as hard to compose a picture of the author from the History, the Essays, and the Lays, as to evolve an idea of Shakespeare from *Henry the Fifth* and *Measure for Measure*" uses the following rhetorical technique:

(A) personification
(B) metaphor
(C) analogy
(D) metonymy
(E) synecdoche

95. The first line of the second paragraph signals a shift in the passage from:
   (A) public to private
   (B) unknown to known
   (C) concrete to abstract
   (D) general to specific
   (E) demand to supply

96. The primary audience for this passage is:
   (A) "the persons with whom he mixed most freely and confidentially"
   (B) "those who have seen his features and heard his voice"
   (C) "everyone who sat with him"
   (D) "every ten who have listened to his oratory"
   (E) "tens of thousands whose interest in history and literature he has awakened and informed by his pen"

97. The style of the passage can best be characterized by its use of all of the following *except*:
   (A) complicated sentence structure
   (B) parallelism
   (C) analogy
   (D) imagery
   (E) parenthesis

98. The style and content of the passage most appeals to:
   I. ethos
   II. logos
   III. pathos

   (A) I
   (B) II
   (C) III
   (D) I and II
   (E) I, II, and III

99. The primary mode of composition of the passage is:
   (A) definition
   (B) argument
   (C) description
   (D) classification
   (E) narration

100. The writer of the passage characterizes himself in the last paragraph in all of the following ways *except*:

   (A) one who has "means at [his] command"
   (B) one who "enjoyed so close relations with such a man" (as Lord Macaulay)
   (C) one with skill enough to "reproduce that image" (of Lord Macaulay)
   (D) one who is connected "by the strongest ties" (to Lord Macaulay and his correspondent)
   (E) one who is "puzzled as to what he has the heart to publish and the right to withhold"

CHAPTER 3

Critics

Passage 3a: Matthew Arnold, *The Function of Criticism at the Current Time*

It has long seemed to me that the burst of creative activity in our literature, through the first quarter of this century, had about it in fact something premature; and that from this cause its productions are doomed, most of them, in spite of the sanguine hopes which accompanied and do still accompany them, to prove hardly more lasting than the productions of far less splendid epochs. And this prematureness 5 comes from its having proceeded without having its proper data, without sufficient materials to work with. In other words, the English poetry of the first quarter of this century, with plenty of energy, plenty of creative force, did not know enough. This makes Byron so empty of matter, Shelley so incoherent, Wordsworth even, profound as he is, yet so wanting in completeness and variety. Wordsworth cared 10 little for books, and disparaged Goethe. I admire Wordsworth, as he is, so much that I cannot wish him different; and it is vain, no doubt, to imagine such a man different from what he is, to suppose that he "could" have been different. But surely the one thing wanting to make Wordsworth an even greater poet than he is,—his thought richer, and his influence of wider application,—was that he should have 15 read more books, among them, no doubt, those of that Goethe whom he disparaged without reading him.

But to speak of books and reading may easily lead to a misunderstanding here. It was not really books and reading that lacked to our poetry at this epoch: Shelley had plenty of reading, Coleridge had immense reading. Pindar and Sophocles—as 20 we all say so glibly, and often with so little discernment of the real import of what we are saying—had not many books; Shakespeare was no deep reader. True; but in the Greece of Pindar and Sophocles, in the England of Shakespeare, the poet lived in a current of ideas in the highest degree animating and nourishing to the creative power; society was, in the fullest measure, permeated by fresh thought, 25 intelligent and alive. And this state of things is the true basis for the creative power's exercise, in this it finds its data, its materials, truly ready for its hand; all the books and reading in the world are only valuable as they are helps to this. Even when this does not actually exist, books and reading may enable a man to construct a kind of semblance of it in his own mind, a world of knowledge and intelligence 30 in which he may live and work. This is by no means an equivalent to the artist for the nationally diffused life and thought of the epochs of Sophocles or Shakespeare; but, besides that it may be a means of preparation for such epochs, it does really constitute, if many share in it, a quickening and sustaining atmosphere of great value. Such an atmosphere the many-sided learning and the long and widely com- 35 bined critical effort of Germany formed for Goethe, when he lived and worked. There was no national glow of life and thought there as in the Athens of Pericles or the England of Elizabeth. That was the poet's weakness. But there was a sort of equivalent for it in the complete culture and unfettered thinking of a large body of Germans. That was his strength. In the England of the first quarter of this century 40 there was neither a national glow of life and thought, such as we had in the age of Elizabeth, nor yet a culture and a force of learning and criticism such as were to be found in Germany. Therefore the creative power of poetry wanted, for success in the highest sense, materials and a basis; a thorough interpretation of the world was necessarily denied to it. 45

101. The writer uses the word "data" to encompass all of the following *except*:

    (A) materials
    (B) a current of ideas
    (C) creative force
    (D) fresh thought
    (E) a national glow of life

102. In context, the word "sanguine" in line 3 most nearly means:

    (A) optimistic
    (B) inevitable
    (C) exhilarating
    (D) doubtful
    (E) infallible

103. The primary purpose of the passage as a whole is to:

    (A) argue for the inability of reading to compensate for a lack in fresh thought
    (B) argue for the importance of criticism for literature in a time that may lack a "national glow of life"
    (C) argue that Wordsworth is one of the misinformed poets of the epoch
    (D) argue that Greece is superior to England in "national glow of life"
    (E) argue that the literature of Germany is superior to the literature of England

104. In line 30, the pronoun "it" refers to:

    (A) material
    (B) a world of knowledge
    (C) creative power's exercise
    (D) data
    (E) state of things

105. The purpose of the sentence "But to speak of books and reading may easily lead to a misunderstanding here," at the beginning of paragraph 2, is to:

    I. provide a transition from the previous paragraph into the current one
    II. acknowledge and refute possible counterargument
    III. provide an example of the writer's major claim

    (A) I
    (B) II
    (C) III
    (D) I and II
    (E) I, II, and III

106. The phrase "a current of ideas" is an example of:

    (A) simile
    (B) metaphor
    (C) metonymy
    (D) synecdoche
    (E) personification

107. The style of the passage can best be characterized by its use of all of the following *except*:

    (A) parallel structure
    (B) examples
    (C) complicated syntax
    (D) sensory images
    (E) provocative statements

108. The tone of the passage can best be described as:

    (A) melancholy and lugubrious
    (B) confident and polemical
    (C) sardonic and irreverent
    (D) detached and aloof
    (E) somber and grave

109. The major claim of the passage is stated in which of the following lines?

   I. "It has long seemed to me that the burst of creative activity in our literature, through the first quarter of this century, had about it in fact something premature; and that from this cause its productions are doomed, most of them, in spite of the sanguine hopes which accompanied and do still accompany them, to prove hardly more lasting than the productions of far less splendid epochs."

  II. "In other words, the English poetry of the first quarter of this century, with plenty of energy, plenty of creative force, did not know enough."

 III. "In the England of the first quarter of this century there was neither a national glow of life and thought, such as we had in the age of Elizabeth, nor yet a culture and a force of learning and criticism such as were to be found in Germany."

  (A) I
  (B) II
  (C) III
  (D) I and II
  (E) I, II, and III

110. The primary mode of composition of the passage as a whole is:

  (A) narration
  (B) description
  (C) process analysis
  (D) comparison and contrast
  (E) argument

Passage 3b: Ralph Waldo Emerson, *Shakespeare; or, the Poet*

Great men are more distinguished by range and extent, than by originality. If we require the originality which consists in weaving, like a spider, their web from their own bowels; in finding clay, and making bricks, and building the house; no great men are original. Nor does valuable originality consist in unlikeness to other men. The hero is in the press of knights, and the thick of events; and, seeing what men want, and sharing their desire, he adds the needful length of sight and of arm, to   5 come to the desired point. The greatest genius is the most indebted man. A poet is no rattlebrain, saying what comes uppermost and, because he says everything, saying, at last, something good; but a heart in unison with his time and country. There is nothing whimsical and fantastic in his production, but sweet and sad earnest, freighted with the weightiest convictions, and pointed with the most determined   10 aim which any man or class knows of in his times.

The Genius of our life is jealous of individuals and will not have any individual great, except through the general. There is no choice to genius. A great man does not wake up on some fine morning, and say, "I am full of life, I will go to sea, and find an Antarctic continent: to-day I will square the circle: I will ransack botany, and find a new food for man: I have a new architecture in my mind: I foresee a new mechanic power:" no, but he finds himself in the river of the thoughts and events, forced onward by the ideas and necessities of his contemporaries. He stands where all the eyes of men look one way, and their hands all point in the direction in which he should go. The church has reared him amidst rites and pomps, and he carries out the advice which her music gave him, and builds a cathedral needed by her chants and processions. He finds a war raging: it educates him, by trumpet, in barracks, and he betters the instruction. He finds two counties groping to bring coal, or flour, or fish, from the place of production to the place of consumption, and he hits on a railroad. Every master has found his materials collected, and his power lay in his sympathy with his people, and in his love of the materials he wrought in. What an economy of power! and what a compensation for the shortness of life! All is done to his hand. The world has brought him thus far on his way. The human race has gone out before him, sunk the hills, filled the hollows, and bridged the rivers. Men, nations, poets, artisans, women, all have worked for him, and he enters into their labors. Choose any other thing, out of the line of tendency, out of the national feeling and history, and he would have all to do for himself: his powers would be expended in the first preparations. Great genial power, one would almost say, consists in not being original at all; in being altogether receptive; in letting the world do all, and suffering the spirit of the hour to pass unobstructed through the mind.

111. The primary mode of composition of the first paragraph of the passage is:

    (A) narration
    (B) description
    (C) classification
    (D) definition
    (E) cause and effect

112. The sentence "If we require the originality which consists in weaving, like a spider, their web from their own bowels; in finding clay, and making bricks, and building the house; no great men are original" is the following type of sentence:

    (A) simple
    (B) periodic
    (C) cumulative
    (D) compound
    (E) compound-complex

113. The sentence "The greatest genius is the most indebted man" can best be described as an example of:

(A) an allusion
(B) antithesis
(C) a paradox
(D) parallelism
(E) colloquialism

114. In context, the word "rattlebrain" in line 8 most nearly means:

(A) one who is scattered and disorganized
(B) one who is flighty and thoughtless
(C) one who is stubborn and obstinate
(D) one who is creative and free willed
(E) one who is giddy and talkative

115. The sentence "A poet is no rattlebrain, saying what comes uppermost and, because he says everything, saying, at last, something good; but a heart in unison with his time and country," contains an example of:

(A) synecdoche
(B) metonymy
(C) simile
(D) metaphor
(E) personification

116. Paragraph two contains all of the following rhetorical strategies *except*:

(A) metaphor
(B) anaphora
(C) epistrophe
(D) asyndeton
(E) exclamatory remarks

117. The second paragraph is developed through the use of examples to prove the claim that above all else geniuses are:

(A) unoriginal
(B) great
(C) jealous
(D) powerful
(E) receptive

118. The sentence "He finds two counties groping to bring coal, or flour, or fish, from the place of production to the place of consumption, and he hits on a railroad," uses all of the following rhetorical techniques *except*:

    (A) polysyndeton
    (B) parallelism
    (C) asyndeton
    (D) colloquialism
    (E) compound syntax

119. The major claim of the passage is best stated in which of the following lines:

    (A) "Great men are more distinguished by range and extent, than by originality."
    (B) "The greatest genius is the most indebted man."
    (C) "There is no choice to genius."
    (D) "Every master has found his materials collected, and his power lay in his sympathy with his people, and in his love of the materials he wrought in."
    (E) "Great genial power, one would almost say, consists in not being original at all; in being altogether receptive; in letting the world do all, and suffering the spirit of the hour to pass unobstructed through the mind."

120. The tone of the passage can best be described as:

    (A) reflective
    (B) fervent
    (C) nostalgic
    (D) optimistic
    (E) bemused

Passage 3c: William Hazlitt, *On Poetry in General*

Poetry is the language of the imagination and the passions. It relates to whatever gives immediate pleasure or pain to the human mind. It comes home to the bosoms and businesses of men; for nothing but what so comes home to them in the most general and intelligible shape, can be a subject for poetry. Poetry is the universal language which the heart holds with nature and itself. He who has a contempt for 5 poetry, cannot have much respect for himself, or for any thing else. It is not a mere frivolous accomplishment, (as some persons have been led to imagine) the trifling amusement of a few idle readers or leisure hours—it has been the study and delight of mankind in all ages. Many people suppose that poetry is something to be found only in books, contained in lines of ten syllables, with like endings: but wherever 10 there is a sense of beauty, or power, or harmony, as in the motion of a wave of the sea, in the growth of a flower that "spreads its sweet leaves to the air, and dedicates its beauty to the sun,"—there is poetry, in its birth. If history is a grave study, poetry may be said to be a graver: its materials lie deeper, and are spread wider. History treats, for the most part, of the cumbrous and unwieldly masses of things, 15 the empty cases in which the affairs of the world are packed, under the heads of intrigue or war, in different states, and from century to century: but there is no thought or feeling that can have entered into the mind of man, which he would be eager to communicate to others, or which they would listen to with delight, that is not a fit subject for poetry. It is not a branch of authorship: it is "the stuff of which 20 our life is made." The rest is "mere oblivion," a dead letter: for all that is worth remembering in life, is the poetry of it. Fear is poetry, hope is poetry, love is poetry, hatred is poetry; contempt, jealousy, remorse, admiration, wonder, pity, despair, or madness, are all poetry. Poetry is that fine particle within us, that expands, rarefies, refines, raises our whole being: without it "man's life is poor as beast's." Man is 25 a poetical animal: and those of us who do not study the principles of poetry, act upon them all our lives, like Molière's "Bourgeois Gentilhomme", who had always spoken prose without knowing it. The child is a poet in fact, when he first plays at hide-and-seek, or repeats the story of Jack the Giant-killer; the shepherd-boy is a poet, when he first crowns his mistress with a garland of flowers; the countryman, 30 when he stops to look at the rainbow; the city-apprentice, when he gazes after the Lord-Mayor's show; the miser, when he hugs his gold; the courtier, who builds his hopes upon a smile; the savage, who paints his idol with blood; the slave, who worships a tyrant, or the tyrant, who fancies himself a god;—the vain, the ambitious, the proud, the choleric man, the hero and the coward, the beggar and the 35 king, the rich and the poor, the young and the old, all live in a world of their own making; and the poet does no more than describe what all the others think and act. If his art is folly and madness, it is folly and madness at second hand. "There is warrant for it." Poets alone have not "such seething brains, such shaping fantasies, that apprehend more than cooler reason" can. 40

121. The primary mode of composition of the passage is:
    (A) narration
    (B) description
    (C) comparison and contrast
    (D) definition
    (E) argument

122. The passage uses all of the following rhetorical techniques *except*:
    (A) polysyndeton
    (B) personification
    (C) metaphor
    (D) colloquialism
    (E) irony

123. The sentence "Fear is poetry, hope is poetry, love is poetry, hatred is poetry; contempt, jealousy, remorse, admiration, wonder, pity, despair, or madness, are all poetry" uses:
  I. epistrophe
  II. asyndeton
  III. enumeration
  (A) I
  (B) II
  (C) III
  (D) I and II
  (E) I, II, and III

124. In context, the word "grave" in line 13 most nearly means:
  (A) deep
  (B) wide
  (C) dignified
  (D) somber
  (E) momentous

125. All of the following are set up in opposition to one another *except*:
  (A) slave and tyrant
  (B) hero and coward
  (C) beggar and king
  (D) rich and poor
  (E) young and old

126. The passage's major claim is developed by all of the following *except*:
  (A) allusion
  (B) example
  (C) figurative language
  (D) quotations
  (E) anecdote

127. The purpose of the passage can best be characterized as to:
  (A) defend poetry against its harshest critics
  (B) explore what poetry is
  (C) argue that poetry is more important than history
  (D) display the many uses for and types of poetry
  (E) describe the many types of poets

128. The main idea of the last sentence, "Poets alone have not 'such seething brains, such shaping fantasies, that apprehend more than cooler reason' can," can be understood as expressing the thought that:

(A) poets are not the only source of poetry
(B) poets can understand more than the rational man can
(C) poets have imagination and passion above regular men
(D) poets have keen and perceptive brains
(E) poets do not have insight, imagination, and understanding

129. The writer would most likely describe poetry as most importantly:

(A) a product of skill and practice
(B) able to transform people's lives
(C) all that is beautiful and powerful in life
(D) evidence of man's respect for himself
(E) a distinction between us and animals

130. The tone of the passage can best be described as:

(A) benevolent
(B) effusive
(C) whimsical
(D) elated
(E) facetious

Passage 3d: Walter Pater, *Studies in the History of the Renaissance*

To burn always with this hard gem-like flame, to maintain this ecstasy, is success in life. Failure is to form habits; for habit is relative to a stereotyped world; meantime it is only the roughness of the eye that makes any two persons, things, situations, seem alike. While all melts under our feet, we may well catch at any exquisite passion, or any contribution to knowledge that seems, by a lifted horizon, to set the   5
spirit free for a moment, or any stirring of the senses, strange dyes, strange flowers, and curious odours, or work of the artist's hands, or the face of one's friend. Not to discriminate every moment some passionate attitude in those about us, and in the brilliance of their gifts some tragic dividing of forces on their ways is, on this short day of frost and sun, to sleep before evening. With this sense of the splendour   10
of our experience and of its awful brevity, gathering all we are into one desperate effort to see and touch, we shall hardly have time to make theories about the things we see and touch. What we have to do is to be for ever curiously testing new opinions and courting new impressions, never acquiescing in a facile orthodoxy of Comte or of Hegel, or of our own. Theories, religious or philosophical ideas,   15
as points of view, instruments of criticism, may help us to gather up what might otherwise pass unregarded by us. La philosophie, c'est la microscope de la pensée. The theory, or idea, or system, which requires of us the sacrifice of any part of this

experience, in consideration of some interest into which we cannot enter, or some abstract morality we have not identified with ourselves, or what is only conven- 20
tional, has no real claim upon us.

One of the most beautiful places in the writings of Rousseau is that in the sixth book of the *Confessions*, where he describes the awakening in him of the literary sense. An undefinable taint of death had always clung about him, and now in early manhood he believed himself stricken by mortal disease. He asked himself how 25
he might make as much as possible of the interval that remained; and he was not biassed by anything in his previous life when he decided that it must be by intellectual excitement, which he found in the clear, fresh writings of Voltaire. Well, we are all condamnés, as Victor Hugo says: les hommes sont tous condamnés a morte avec des sursis indéfinis: we have an interval, and then our place knows us no 30
more. Some spend this interval in listlessness, some in high passions, the wisest in art and song. For our one chance is in expanding that interval, in getting as many pulsations as possible into the given time. High passions give one this quickened sense of life, ecstasy and sorrow of love, political or religious enthusiasm, or the 'enthusiasm of humanity.' Only, be sure it is passion, that it does yield you this 35
fruit of a quickened, multiplied consciousness. Of this wisdom, the poetic passion, the desire of beauty, the love of art for art's sake has most; for art comes to you professing frankly to give nothing but the highest quality to your moments as they pass, and simply for those moments' sake.

131. The passage begins ("To burn always with this hard gem-like flame, to maintain this ecstasy, is success in life") with:

    (A) a claim
    (B) evidence
    (C) a warrant
    (D) a qualifier
    (E) a rebuttal

132. In context, the word "roughness" in line 3 most nearly means:

    (A) the lack of skill or sophistication
    (B) the lack of smoothness
    (C) the lack of the finish or polish of art or culture
    (D) the lack of attention to details
    (E) a crude and unpolished state

133. Paragraph one contains each of the following *except*:

    (A) metaphor
    (B) simile
    (C) asyndeton
    (D) polysyndeton
    (E) allusion

134. In context, the word "discriminate" in line 8 most nearly means to:
   (A) act with prejudice toward
   (B) differentiate between
   (C) recognize as distinct
   (D) treat with disdain
   (E) have condescending feelings against

135. In the sentence "Not to discriminate every moment some passionate attitude in those about us, and in the brilliance of their gifts some tragic dividing of forces on their ways is, on this short day of frost and sun, to sleep before evening," "to sleep before evening" can best be understood as a metaphor for:
   (A) enjoying the prime of your life
   (B) giving up on the people around you for providing you with comfort
   (C) dying at too young an age
   (D) believing that your best years are yet to come
   (E) missing out on the best life has to offer before it is over

136. In line 27, "it" refers to:
   (A) the interval
   (B) anything
   (C) making as much as possible of the interval that remained
   (D) previous life
   (E) intellectual excitement

137. The passage appeals primarily to:
   I. ethos
   II. logos
   III. pathos
   (A) I
   (B) II
   (C) III
   (D) I and III
   (E) I, II, and III

138. The rhetorical function of the first half of paragraph two, through "fresh writings of Voltaire," is to:
   (A) provide an anecdote of the writer's claim that we should focus on beautiful experiences because of the brevity of life
   (B) provide an example of the writer's claim that we should focus on beautiful experiences because of the brevity of life

(C) acknowledge the counterargument against the claim that we should focus on beautiful experiences because of the brevity of life

(D) refute the claim that we should focus on beautiful experiences because of the brevity of life

(E) qualify the claim that we should focus on beautiful experiences because of the brevity of life

139. The primary mode of composition of the passage as a whole is:

(A) narration
(B) description
(C) cause and effect
(D) definition
(E) argument

140. The tone of the passage can best be described as:

(A) indignant
(B) passionate
(C) flippant
(D) pensive
(E) delighted

Passage 3e: John Ruskin, *Of the Pathetic Fallacy*

Now, therefore, putting these tiresome and absurd words[52] quite out of our way, we may go on at our ease to examine the point in question,—namely, the difference between the ordinary, proper, and true appearances of things to us; and the extraordinary, or false appearances, when we are under the influence of emotion, or contemplative fancy; false appearances, I say, as being entirely unconnected with 5
any real power or character in the object, and only imputed to it by us.

For instance—

The spendthrift crocus, bursting through the mould
Naked and shivering, with his cup of gold.[53]

This is very beautiful, and yet very untrue. The crocus is not a spendthrift, but a 10
hardy plant; its yellow is not gold, but saffron. How is it that we enjoy so much the having it put into our heads that it is anything else than a plain crocus?

It is an important question. For, throughout our past reasonings about art, we have always found that nothing could be good or useful, or ultimately pleasurable,

---

52. Three short sections discussing the use of the terms "Objective" and "Subjective" have been omitted from the beginning of this chapter.

53. Holmes (Oliver Wendell), quoted by Miss Mitford in her *Recollections of a Literary Life*. [Ruskin.] From "Astræa, a Poem" delivered before the Phi Beta Kappa Society of Yale College. The passage in which these lines are found was later published as "Spring."

which was untrue. But here is something pleasurable in written poetry which is   15
nevertheless untrue. And what is more, if we think over our favourite poetry, we
shall find it full of this kind of fallacy, and that we like it all the more for being so.

It will appear also, on consideration of the matter, that this fallacy is of two
principal kinds. Either, as in this case of the crocus, it is the fallacy of wilful fancy,
which involves no real expectation that it will be believed; or else it is a fallacy   20
caused by an excited state of the feelings, making us, for the time, more or less
irrational. Of the cheating of the fancy we shall have to speak presently; but, in
this chapter, I want to examine the nature of the other error, that which the mind
admits when affected strongly by emotion. Thus, for instance, in Alton Locke,—
They rowed her in across the rolling foam—   25

The cruel, crawling foam.[54]

The foam is not cruel, neither does it crawl. The state of mind which attributes to
it these characters of a living creature is one in which the reason is unhinged by
grief. All violent feelings have the same effect. They produce in us a falseness in
all our impressions of external things, which I would generally characterize as the   30
"pathetic fallacy."

Now we are in the habit of considering this fallacy as eminently a character
of poetical description, and the temper of mind in which we allow it, as one eminently poetical, because passionate. But I believe, if we look well into the matter,
that we shall find the greatest poets do not often admit this kind of falseness,—that   35
it is only the second order of poets who much delight in it.[55]

---

54. Kingsley's *Alton Locke*, chap. 26.

55. I admit two orders of poets, but no third; and by these two orders I mean the creative
(Shakspere, Homer, Dante), and Reflective or Perceptive (Wordsworth, Keats, Tennyson). But
both of these must be first-rate in their range, though their range is different; and with poetry
second-rate in quality no one ought to be allowed to trouble mankind. There is quite enough
of the best,—much more than we can ever read or enjoy in the length of a life; and it is a literal
wrong or sin in any person to encumber us with inferior work. I have no patience with apologies
made by young pseudo-poets, "that they believe there is some good in what they have written:
that they hope to do better in time," etc. Some good! If there is not all good, there is no good.
If they ever hope to do better, why do they trouble us now? Let them rather courageously burn
all they have done, and wait for the better days. There are few men, ordinarily educated, who in
moments of strong feeling could not strike out a poetical thought, and afterwards polish it so as
to be presentable. But men of sense know better than so to waste their time; and those who sin-
cerely love poetry, know the touch of the master's hand on the chords too well to fumble among
them after him. Nay, more than this, all inferior poetry is an injury to the good, inasmuch as it
takes away the freshness of rhymes, blunders upon and gives a wretched commonalty to good
thoughts; and, in general, adds to the weight of human weariness in a most woful and culpable
manner. There are few thoughts likely to come across ordinary men, which have not already been
expressed by greater men in the best possible way; and it is a wiser, more generous, more noble
thing to remember and point out the perfect words, than to invent poorer ones, wherewith to
encumber temporarily the world. [Ruskin.]

141. The first sentence of the passage, "Now, therefore, putting these tiresome and absurd words[52] quite out of our way, we may go on at our ease to examine the point in question,—namely, the difference between the ordinary, proper, and true appearances of things to us; and the extraordinary, or false appearances, when we are under the influence of emotion, or contemplative fancy; false appearances, I say, as being entirely unconnected with any real power or character in the object, and only imputed to it by us," is the following type of sentence:

(A) sentence fragment
(B) simple
(C) cumulative
(D) imperative
(E) interrogative

142. The first two paragraphs have all of the following rhetorical techniques *except*:

(A) definition
(B) personification
(C) rhetorical question
(D) sentence variety
(E) metaphor

143. Paragraph three is primarily developed by the mode of:

(A) narration
(B) description
(C) cause and effect
(D) classification
(E) process analysis

144. In context, the word "pathetic" in line 31 most nearly means:

(A) caused by feelings
(B) absurd and laughable
(C) marked by sorrow
(D) having the ability to move to pity
(E) pitifully inferior

145. The major claim of the passage is:

(A) the pathetic fallacy is a character of poetical description
(B) the pathetic fallacy can be classified into two types
(C) the pathetic fallacy is used by the reflective and perceptive poets
(D) the pathetic fallacy is used by inferior poets
(E) the pathetic fallacy is believed by readers overwhelmed by strong feelings

146. The tone of the passage (not including the footnotes) can best be described as:

(A) incredulous
(B) scornful
(C) evasive
(D) didactic
(E) curt

147. According to the passage, the words that the writer refers to in the first sentence are:

  I. "tiresome" and "absurd"
 II. "objective" and "subjective"
III. "ordinary" and "extraordinary"

(A) I
(B) II
(C) III
(D) I and II
(E) I, II, and III

148. The first quoted lines are written by:

(A) Holmes
(B) Oliver
(C) Wendell
(D) Mitford
(E) Ruskin

149. The second quoted lines are written by:

(A) Ruskin
(B) Kingsley
(C) Alton
(D) Locke
(E) Mitford

150. The tone of footnote 55 can be described as:

(A) apprehensive
(B) belligerent
(C) condescending
(D) desperate
(E) fatalistic

CHAPTER 4

Essayists and Fiction Writers

Passage 4a: Joseph Addison, *True and False Humour*

Among all kinds of writing, there is none in which authors are more apt to miscarry than in works of humour, as there is none in which they are more ambitious to excel. It is not an imagination that teems with monsters, a head that is filled with extravagant conceptions, which is capable of furnishing the world with diversions of this nature; and yet, if we look into the productions of several writers, who set up for men of humour, what wild, irregular fancies, what unnatural distortions of thought do we meet with? If they speak nonsense, they believe they are talking humour; and when they have drawn together a scheme of absurd, inconsistent ideas, they are not able to read it over to themselves without laughing. These poor gentlemen endeavour to gain themselves the reputation of wits and humorists, by such monstrous conceits as almost qualify them for Bedlam; not considering that humour should always lie under the check of reason, and that it requires the direction of the nicest judgment, by so much the more as it indulges itself in the most boundless freedoms. There is a kind of nature that is to be observed in this sort of compositions, as well as in all other; and a certain regularity of thought which must discover the writer to be a man of sense, at the same time that he appears altogether given up to caprice. For my part, when I read the delirious mirth of an unskilful author, I cannot be so barbarous as to divert myself with it, but am rather apt to pity the man, than to laugh at anything he writes.

The deceased Mr. Shadwell, who had himself a great deal of the talent which I am treating of, represents an empty rake, in one of his plays, as very much surprised to hear one say that breaking of windows was not humour; and I question not but several English readers will be as much startled to hear me affirm, that many of those raving, incoherent pieces, which are often spread among us, under odd chimerical titles, are rather the offsprings of a distempered brain than works of humour.

It is, indeed, much easier to describe what is not humour than what is; and very difficult to define it otherwise than as Cowley has done wit, by negatives. Were I to give my own notions of it, I would deliver them after Plato's manner, in a kind of allegory, and, by supposing Humour to be a person, deduce to him all his qualifications, according to the following genealogy. Truth was the founder of the family, and the father of Good Sense. Good Sense was the father of Wit, who married a lady of a collateral line called Mirth, by whom he had issue Humour. Humour therefore being the youngest of this illustrious family, and descended from parents of such different dispositions, is very various and unequal in his temper; sometimes 35 you see him putting on grave looks and a solemn habit, sometimes airy in his behaviour and fantastic in his dress; insomuch that at different times he appears as serious as a judge, and as jocular as a merry-andrew. But, as he has a great deal of the mother in his constitution, whatever mood he is in, he never fails to make his company laugh. 40

But since there is an impostor abroad, who takes upon him the name of this young gentleman, and would willingly pass for him in the world; to the end that well-meaning persons may not be imposed upon by cheats, I would desire my readers, when they meet with this pretender, to look into his parentage, and to examine him strictly, whether or no he be remotely allied to Truth, and lineally 45 descended from Good Sense; if not, they may conclude him a counterfeit. They may likewise distinguish him by a loud and excessive laughter, in which he seldom gets his company to join with him. For as True Humour generally looks serious while everybody laughs about him, False Humour is always laughing whilst everybody about him looks serious. I shall only add, if he has not in him a mixture of 50 both parents—that is, if he would pass for the offspring of Wit without Mirth, or Mirth without Wit, you may conclude him to be altogether spurious and a cheat.

151. According to the claim in the first sentence of the passage:

(A) authors are ambitious to excel in all kinds of writing
(B) authors are likely to fail when writing humor
(C) authors are not likely to fail when writing humor
(D) there is no kind of writing in which authors are more likely to fail than any other
(E) there is no kind of writing in which authors are more ambitious than any other

152. According to the first paragraph, humor is:

(A) filled with extravagant conceptions
(B) the product of wild, irregular fancies
(C) from unnatural distortions of thought
(D) absurd and inconsistent
(E) required to be reasonable

153. The first paragraph contains all of the following rhetorical techniques *except*:

(A) allusion
(B) rhetorical question
(C) oxymoron
(D) personification
(E) complicated syntax

154. In paragraph three, the writer seeks to prove his claim with the use of:

    (A) literary example
    (B) inductive reasoning
    (C) deductive reasoning
    (D) allegory
    (E) anecdote

155. In context, the word "barbarous" in line 18 most nearly means:

    (A) aggressive
    (B) cruel
    (C) violent
    (D) uncivilized
    (E) ignorant

156. The second "him" of the last paragraph, in line 42, refers to:

    (A) an impostor
    (B) humor
    (C) wit
    (D) good sense
    (E) truth

157. In context, the word "spurious" in line 52 most nearly means:

    (A) counterfeit
    (B) facetious
    (C) deceptive
    (D) authentic
    (E) artless

158. The primary mode of composition of the passage as a whole is:

    (A) narration
    (B) description
    (C) classification
    (D) definition
    (E) cause and effect

159. The tone of the passage can best be described as:

    (A) self-assured
    (B) sympathetic
    (C) acerbic
    (D) somber
    (E) frantic

160. According to the passage as a whole, humor must be all of the following *except*:

(A) rational and truthful
(B) amusing to the writer
(C) amusing to the reader
(D) clear and cohesive
(E) both serious and jovial

Passage 4b: Francis Bacon, *Of Marriage and Single Life*

He that hath wife and children hath given hostages to fortune; for they are impediments to great enterprises, either of virtue or mischief. Certainly the best works, and of greatest merit for the public, have proceeded from the unmarried or childless men; which both in affection and means, have married and endowed the public. Yet it were great reason that those that have children, should have greatest care 5 of future times; unto which they know they must transmit their dearest pledges. Some there are, who though they lead a single life, yet their thoughts do end with themselves, and account future times impertinences. Nay, there are some other, that account wife and children, but as bills of charges. Nay more, there are some foolish rich covetous men, that take a pride, in having no children, because they 10 may be thought so much the richer. For perhaps they have heard some talk, Such an one is a great rich man, and another except to it, Yea, but he hath a great charge of children; as if it were an abatement to his riches. But the most ordinary cause of a single life, is liberty, especially in certain self-pleasing and humorous minds, which are so sensible of every restraint, as they will go near to think their girdles and gar- 15 ters, to be bonds and shackles. Unmarried men are best friends, best masters, best servants; but not always best subjects; for they are light to run away; and almost all fugitives, are of that condition. A single life doth well with churchmen; for charity will hardly water the ground, where it must first fill a pool. It is indifferent for judges and magistrates; for if they be facile and corrupt, you shall have a servant, 20 five times worse than a wife. For soldiers, I find the generals commonly in their hortatives, put men in mind of their wives and children; and I think the despising of marriage amongst the Turks, maketh the vulgar soldier more base. Certainly wife and children are a kind of discipline of humanity; and single men, though they may be many times more charitable, because their means are less exhaust, 25 yet, on the other side, they are more cruel and hardhearted (good to make severe inquisitors), because their tenderness is not so oft called upon. Grave natures, led by custom, and therefore constant, are commonly loving husbands, as was said of Ulysses, vetulam suam praetulit immortalitati. Chaste women are often proud and froward, as presuming upon the merit of their chastity. It is one of the best 30 bonds, both of chastity and obedience, in the wife, if she think her husband wise; which she will never do, if she find him jealous. Wives are young men's mistresses; companions for middle age; and old men's nurses. So as a man may have a quarrel to marry, when he will. But yet he was reputed one of the wise men, that made answer to the question, when a man should marry,—A young man not yet, an elder ₃₅ man not at all. It is often seen that bad husbands, have very good wives; whether it be, that it raiseth the price of their husband's kindness, when it comes; or that the wives take a pride in their patience. But this never fails, if the bad husbands were of their own choosing, against their friends' consent; for then they will be sure to make good their own folly. ₄₀

161. The primary mode of composition of the passage is:

(A) narration
(B) description
(C) classification
(D) definition
(E) cause and effect

162. The following idea is ironic:

(A) "He that hath wife and children hath given hostages to fortune; for they are impediments to great enterprises, either of virtue or mischief."
(B) "Certainly the best works, and of greatest merit for the public, have proceeded from the unmarried or childless men; which both in affection and means, have married and endowed the public. Yet it were great reason that those that have children, should have greatest care of future times; unto which they know they must transmit their dearest pledges."
(C) "Some there are, who though they lead a single life, yet their thoughts do end with themselves, and account future times impertinences."
(D) "Nay, there are some other, that account wife and children, but as bills of charges."
(E) "Unmarried men are best friends, best masters, best servants; but not always best subjects; for they are light to run away; and almost all fugitives, are of that condition."

163. In the sentence "But the most ordinary cause of a single life, is liberty, especially in certain self-pleasing and humorous minds, which are so sensible of every restraint, as they will go near to think their girdles and garters, to be bonds and shackles," "girdles and garters" are used as the following for restraint:

(A) similes
(B) metaphors
(C) personification
(D) symbols
(E) analogies

164. In context, the word "impertinences" in line 8 most nearly means:

(A) acts of disrespect
(B) acts of inappropriateness
(C) acts of rudeness
(D) incongruities
(E) irrelevancies

165. In line 15, "their" refers to:

(A) men
(B) women
(C) married men
(D) single men
(E) children

166. The portion of the sentence "Unmarried men are best friends, best masters, best servants; but not always best subjects" uses the rhetorical technique of:

(A) anaphora
(B) epistrophe
(C) climax
(D) simile
(E) personification

167. According to the passage, single men are best fit for the occupation(s) of:

   I. churchmen
  II. judges
 III. soldiers
 IV. inquisitors

(A) I
(B) II
(C) III
(D) IV
(E) I and IV

168. The purpose of the sentence "Wives are young men's mistresses; companions for middle age; and old men's nurses" is primarily to illustrate:

(A) the chauvinism of men who take their wives for granted
(B) the changing roles of wives through the years
(C) the constancy of wives through good and bad times
(D) the suffering of women at the hands of cruel husbands
(E) the fickle nature of men who change their wants and needs

169. The reader can infer from the last sentence, "But this never fails, if the bad husbands were of their own choosing, against their friends' consent; for then they will be sure to make good their own folly," that women who choose bad husbands against the advice of their friends will keep them to avoid:
    (A) making the same mistake again
    (B) proving their friends wrong
    (C) making fools of themselves
    (D) losing all of their property
    (E) having to be single again

170. The tone of the passage can best be described as:
    (A) antagonistic
    (B) conciliatory
    (C) foreboding
    (D) jovial
    (E) pedantic

Passage 4c: G. K. Chesterton, *A Defence of Baby-Worship*

The two facts which attract almost every normal person to children are, first, that they are very serious, and, secondly, that they are in consequence very happy. They are jolly with the completeness which is possible only in the absence of humour. The most unfathomable schools and sages have never attained to the gravity which dwells in the eyes of a baby of three months old. It is the gravity of astonishment 5 at the universe, and astonishment at the universe is not mysticism, but a transcendent common-sense. The fascination of children lies in this: that with each of them all things are remade, and the universe is put again upon its trial. As we walk the streets and see below us those delightful bulbous heads, three times too big for the body, which mark these human mushrooms, we ought always primarily to 10 remember that within every one of these heads there is a new universe, as new as it was on the seventh day of creation. In each of those orbs there is a new system of stars, new grass, new cities, a new sea.

There is always in the healthy mind an obscure prompting that religion teaches us rather to dig than to climb; that if we could once understand the common clay 15 of earth we should understand everything. Similarly, we have the sentiment that if we could destroy custom at a blow and see the stars as a child sees them, we should need no other apocalypse. This is the great truth which has always lain at the back of baby-worship, and which will support it to the end. Maturity, with its endless energies and aspirations, may easily be convinced that it will find new things to 20 appreciate; but it will never be convinced, at bottom, that it has properly appreciated what it has got. We may scale the heavens and find new stars innumerable, but there is still the new star we have not found—that on which we were born.

But the influence of children goes further than its first trifling effort of remaking heaven and earth. It forces us actually to remodel our conduct in accordance   25
with this revolutionary theory of the marvellousness of all things. We do (even
when we are perfectly simple or ignorant)—we do actually treat talking in children
as marvellous, walking in children as marvellous, common intelligence in children
as marvellous. The cynical philosopher fancies he has a victory in this matter—that
he can laugh when he shows that the words or antics of the child, so much admired   30
by its worshippers, are common enough. The fact is that this is precisely where
baby-worship is so profoundly right. Any words and any antics in a lump of clay
are wonderful, the child's words and antics are wonderful, and it is only fair to say
that the philosopher's words and antics are equally wonderful.

171. The sentence "They are jolly with the completeness which is possible only
     in the absence of humour" uses the rhetorical technique of:
     (A) allusion
     (B) analogy
     (C) paradox
     (D) anaphora
     (E) antithesis

172. The sentence "As we walk the streets and see below us those delightful
     bulbous heads, three times too big for the body, which mark these human
     mushrooms, we ought always primarily to remember that within every one
     of these heads there is a new universe, as new as it was on the seventh day
     of creation" uses the rhetorical technique of:
     (A) allusion
     (B) analogy
     (C) paradox
     (D) anaphora
     (E) antithesis

173. The last line of the first paragraph, "In each of those orbs there is a new
     system of stars, new grass, new cities, a new sea," underlines the wonder of
     the baby's astonishment with the use of:
      I. anaphora
     II. asyndeton
     III. allusion
     (A) I
     (B) II
     (C) III
     (D) I and II
     (E) I, II, and III

174. Which of the following merely contributes to the reasons we worship babies, and is not worthy of worship as an isolated characteristic?

(A) they are very serious
(B) they are very happy
(C) in them, everything is new
(D) they help us treat simple actions as marvelous
(E) they are capable of appreciating everything

175. In context, the word "custom" in line 17 most nearly means:

(A) a practice followed by a particular group of people
(B) a ritual performed at certain times
(C) a habitual practice
(D) a routine done with monotony
(E) an inherited tradition

176. The sentence "But the influence of children goes further than its first trifling effort of remaking heaven and earth" uses the rhetorical technique of:

(A) paradox
(B) allusion
(C) antithesis
(D) analogy
(E) irony

177. The sentence "We do (even when we are perfectly simple or ignorant)—we do actually treat talking in children as marvellous, walking in children as marvellous, common intelligence in children as marvelous," uses the rhetorical technique of:

(A) paradox
(B) epistrophe
(C) anaphora
(D) allusion
(E) polysyndeton

178. The sentence "The cynical philosopher fancies he has a victory in this matter—that he can laugh when he shows that the words or antics of the child, so much admired by its worshippers, are common enough" serves as:

(A) example
(B) expert testimony
(C) counterargument
(D) anecdote
(E) qualification

179. The primary purpose of the passage is to:
  (A) defend the worship of babies
  (B) apologize for the worship of babies
  (C) persuade people to worship babies
  (D) explain why people worship babies
  (E) dissuade people from worshipping babies

180. The tone of the passage can best be described as:
  (A) irreverent and sarcastic
  (B) moralistic and restrained
  (C) sentimental and poignant
  (D) contentious and irate
  (E) thoughtful and jocular

Passage 4d: Charles Lamb, *The Two Races of Men*

The human species, according to the best theory I can form of it, is composed of two distinct races, the men who borrow, and the men who lend. To these two original diversities may be reduced all those impertinent classifications of Gothic and Celtic tribes, white men, black men, red men. All the dwellers upon earth, "Parthians, and Medes, and Elamites," flock hither, and do naturally fall in with 5 one or other of these primary distinctions. The infinite superiority of the former, which I choose to designate as the great race, is discernible in their figure, port, and a certain instinctive sovereignty. The latter are born degraded. "He shall serve his brethren." There is something in the air of one of this cast, lean and suspicious; contrasting with the open, trusting, generous manners of the other. 10

Observe who have been the greatest borrowers of all ages—Alcibiades, Falstaff, Sir Richard Steele—our late incomparable Brinsley what a family likeness in all four!

What a careless, even deportment hath your borrower! what rosy gills! what a beautiful reliance on Providence doth he manifest,—taking no more thought 15 than lilies! What contempt for money,—accounting it (yours and mine especially) no better than dross. What a liberal confounding of those pedantic distinctions of meum and tuum! or rather, what a noble simplification of language (beyond Tooke), resolving these supposed opposites into one clear, intelligible pronoun adjective! What near approaches doth he make to the primitive community, to the 20 extent of one half of the principle at least!

He is the true taxer who "calleth all the world up to be taxed;" and the distance is as vast between him and one of us, as subsisted betwixt the Augustan Majesty and the poorest obolary Jew that paid it tribute-pittance at Jerusalem!—His exactions, too, have such a cheerful, voluntary air! So far removed from your sour parochial or 25 state-gatherers,—those ink-horn varlets, who carry their want of welcome in their faces! He cometh to you with a smile, and troubleth you with no receipt; confining himself to no set season. Every day is his Candlemas, or his Feast of Holy Michael. He applieth the lene tormentum of a pleasant look to your purse, which to that gentle warmth expands her silken leaves, as naturally as the cloak of the traveller, for which sun and wind contended! He is the true Propontic which never ebbeth! The sea which taketh handsomely at each man's hand. In vain the victim, whom he delighteth to honour, struggles with destiny; he is in the net. Lend therefore cheerfully, O man ordained to lend—that thou lose not in the end, with thy worldly penny, the reversion promised. Combine not preposterously in thine own person the penalties of Lazarus and of Dives!—but, when thou seest the proper authority coming, meet it smilingly, as it were half-way. Come, a handsome sacrifice! See how light he makes of it! Strain not courtesies with a noble enemy.

181. The primary mode of composition of the passage is:
   (A) narration
   (B) description
   (C) cause and effect
   (D) classification
   (E) definition

182. In context, the word "impertinent" in line 3 most nearly means:
   (A) important
   (B) insolent
   (C) irrelevant
   (D) impudent
   (E) inappropriate

183. In line 7, the pronoun "their" refers to:
   (A) the human species
   (B) men who borrow
   (C) men who lend
   (D) dwellers upon earth
   (E) distinctions

184. All of the following terms are used to describe lenders *except*:
   (A) degraded
   (B) lean
   (C) suspicious
   (D) latter
   (E) generous

185. The dominant syntactical construction of the third paragraph is:
    (A) simple sentences
    (B) compound sentences
    (C) complex sentences
    (D) imperative sentences
    (E) sentence fragments

186. The writer claims that borrowers have been able to simplify language into "one clear, intelligible pronoun adjective!" This one pronoun adjective is most probably:
    (A) yours
    (B) mine
    (C) he
    (D) one
    (E) their

187. The first sentence of paragraph four, "He is the true taxer who 'calleth all the world up to be taxed;' and the distance is as vast between him and one of us, as subsisted betwixt the Augustan Majesty and the poorest obolary Jew that paid it tribute-pittance at Jerusalem!" uses the rhetorical technique of:
    (A) anaphora
    (B) asyndeton
    (C) anecdote
    (D) analogy
    (E) apostrophe

188. The tone of the passage can best be described as:
    (A) ironic
    (B) pedantic
    (C) conciliatory
    (D) effusive
    (E) deferential

189. The purpose of the passage as a whole is to:
    (A) celebrate the superiority of the borrowers
    (B) satirize the nobility of borrowers
    (C) admonish the lenders for their suspicious ways
    (D) persuade lenders to lend more cheerfully
    (E) evaluate the advantages and disadvantages of being a borrower or lender

190. The style of the passage as a whole can best be described as:
- (A) allegorical
- (B) objective
- (C) allusive
- (D) disjointed
- (E) terse

Passage 4e: Michel de Montaigne, *Of the Punishment of Cowardice*

I once heard of a prince, and a great captain, having a narration given him as he sat at table of the proceeding against Monsieur de Vervins, who was sentenced to death for having surrendered Boulogne to the English,—[To Henry VIII, in 1544]—openly maintaining that a soldier could not justly be put to death for want of courage. And, in truth, 'tis reason that a man should make a great difference 5 betwixt faults that merely proceed from infirmity, and those that are visibly the effects of treachery and malice: for, in the last, we act against the rules of reason that nature has imprinted in us; whereas, in the former, it seems as if we might produce the same nature, who left us in such a state of imperfection and weakness of courage, for our justification. Insomuch that many have thought we are not 10 fairly questionable for anything but what we commit against our conscience; and it is partly upon this rule that those ground their opinion who disapprove of capital or sanguinary punishments inflicted upon heretics and misbelievers; and theirs also who advocate or a judge is not accountable for having from mere ignorance failed in his administration. 15

But as to cowardice, it is certain that the most usual way of chastising it is by ignominy and it is supposed that this practice brought into use by the legislator Charondas; and that, before his time, the laws of Greece punished those with death who fled from a battle; whereas he ordained only that they be for three days exposed in the public dressed in woman's attire, hoping yet for some service from 20 them, having awakened their courage by this open shame:

"Suffundere malis homims sanguinem, quam effundere."
["Rather bring the blood into a man's cheek than let it out of his body."
Tertullian in his *Apologetics*.]

It appears also that the Roman laws did anciently punish those with death who had 25 run away; for Ammianus Marcellinus says that the Emperor Julian commanded ten of his soldiers, who had turned their backs in an encounter against the Parthians, to be first degraded, and afterward put to death, according, says he, to the ancient laws,—[Ammianus Marcellinus, xxiv. 4; xxv. i.]—and yet elsewhere for the like offence he only condemned others to remain amongst the prisoners under the bag- 30 gage ensign. The severe punishment the people of Rome inflicted upon those who fled from the battle of Cannae, and those who ran away with Aeneius Fulvius at his defeat, did not extend to death. And yet, methinks, 'tis to be feared, lest disgrace should make such delinquents desperate, and not only faint friends, but enemies.

Of late memory,—[In 1523]—the Seigneur de Frauget, lieutenant to the 35
Mareschal de Chatillon's company, having by the Mareschal de Chabannes been
put in government of Fuentarabia in the place of Monsieur de Lude, and having
surrendered it to the Spaniard, he was for that condemned to be degraded from
all nobility, and both himself and his posterity declared ignoble, taxable, and for
ever incapable of bearing arms, which severe sentence was afterwards accordingly 40
executed at Lyons.—[In 1536]—And, since that, all the gentlemen who were in
Guise when the Count of Nassau entered into it, underwent the same punishment,
as several others have done since for the like offence. Notwithstanding, in case of
such a manifest ignorance or cowardice as exceeds all ordinary example, 'tis but
reason to take it for a sufficient proof of treachery and malice, and for such to be 45
punished.

191. The primary mode of composition of the first paragraph is:

    (A) narration

    (B) description

    (C) definition

    (D) classification

    (E) cause and effect

192. In context, the word "questionable" in line 11 most nearly means:

    (A) of doubtful integrity

    (B) uncertain

    (C) debatable

    (D) difficult to decide

    (E) capable of being inquired of

193. According to the first paragraph, cowardice is:

    (A) just cause for capital punishment

    (B) a product of frailty

    (C) a product of ill will

    (D) against nature

    (E) against our conscience

194. In response to the claim of the prince mentioned in the first sentence, "that a soldier could not justly be put to death for want of courage," the writer:

    (A) agrees

    (B) disagrees

    (C) qualifies

    (D) refutes with counterargument

    (E) supports with examples

195. The rhetorical function of the sentence "And, in truth, 'tis reason that a man should make a great difference betwixt faults that merely proceed from infirmity, and those that are visibly the effects of treachery and malice: for, in the last, we act against the rules of reason that nature has imprinted in us; whereas, in the former, it seems as if we might produce the same nature, who left us in such a state of imperfection and weakness of courage, for our justification" is to:

(A) acknowledge the validity of one of the claims of the counterargument
(B) put into words the unspoken assumption shared by the writer and his audience
(C) provide evidence to support the major claim of the passage
(D) qualify the original claim of the passage so that the audience will be persuaded
(E) establish the credibility of the writer as an expert on the subject

196. The use of brackets in the passage do all of the following *except*:

(A) provide more information than given in the body of the passage
(B) provide citations for the material in the passage
(C) provide translations of material presented in Latin
(D) provide dates for when the examples occurred
(E) provide personal commentary on the historical information given

197. The quote in the passage, "Rather bring the blood into a man's cheek than let it out of his body," is an aphorism meaning:

(A) it is better to shame a man than kill him
(B) it is better to momentarily harm a man than kill him
(C) it is better to injure a man's face than his body
(D) it is preferable to be shamed rather than killed
(E) it is preferable to be harmed momentarily rather than be killed

198. In the sentence "And yet, methinks, 'tis to be feared, lest disgrace should make such delinquents desperate, and not only faint friends, but enemies," the pronoun "it," in the contraction "'tis," refers to:

(A) the like offence
(B) severe punishment
(C) the battle of Cannae
(D) death
(E) disgrace

199. The passage appeals to:
   I. ethos
  II. logos
  III. pathos
   (A) I
   (B) II
   (C) III
   (D) I and II
   (E) I, II, and III

200. The tone for the majority of the passage can best be described as:
   (A) incredulous
   (B) ambivalent
   (C) objective
   (D) exasperated
   (E) relieved

CHAPTER 5

Journalists and Science and Nature Writers

Passage 5a: Margaret Fuller, *At Home and Abroad; or, Things and Thoughts in America and Europe*

In the afternoon we went on shore at the Manitou Islands, where the boat stops to wood. No one lives here except wood-cutters for the steamboats. I had thought of such a position, from its mixture of profound solitude with service to the great world, as possessing an ideal beauty. I think so still, even after seeing the wood-cutters and their slovenly huts.   5

In times of slower growth, man did not enter a situation without a certain preparation or adaptedness to it. He drew from it, if not to the poetical extent, at least in some proportion, its moral and its meaning. The wood-cutter did not cut down so many trees a day, that the Hamadryads had not time to make their plaints heard; the shepherd tended his sheep, and did no jobs or chores the while;   10
the idyl had a chance to grow up, and modulate his oaten pipe. But now the poet must be at the whole expense of the poetry in describing one of these positions; the worker is a true Midas to the gold he makes. The poet must describe, as the painter sketches Irish peasant-girls and Danish fishwives, adding the beauty, and leaving out the dirt.   15

I come to the West prepared for the distaste I must experience at its mushroom growth. I know that, where "go ahead" is tire only motto, the village cannot grow into the gentle proportions that successive lives and the gradations of experience involuntarily give. In older countries the house of the son grew from that of the father, as naturally as new joints on a bough, and the cathedral crowned the   20
whole as naturally as the leafy summit the tree. This cannot be here. The march of peaceful is scarce less wanton than that of warlike invasion. The old landmarks are broken down, and the land, for a season, bears none, except of the rudeness of conquest and the needs of the day, whose bivouac-fires blacken the sweetest forest glades. I have come prepared to see all this, to dislike it, but not with stupid nar-   25
rowness to distrust or defame. On the contrary, while I will not be so obliging as to confound ugliness with beauty, discord with harmony, and laud and be contented with all I meet, when it conflicts with my best desires and tastes, I trust by reverent

faith to woo the mighty meaning of the scene, perhaps to foresee the law by which
a new order, a new poetry, is to be evoked from this chaos, and with a curiosity as 30
ardent, but not so selfish, as that of Macbeth, to call up the apparitions of future
kings from the strange ingredients of the witch's caldron. Thus I will not grieve
that all the noble trees are gone already from this island to feed this caldron, but
believe it will have Medea's virtue, and reproduce them in the form of new intellectual growths, since centuries cannot again adorn the land with such as have been 35
removed.

201. The "slovenly huts" (line 5) are used as an example of:
    (A) the profound solitude of the wood-cutters
    (B) the service to the great world done by the wood-cutters
    (C) the beauty added by the poet
    (D) the dirt left out by the poet
    (E) the ideal beauty of the lives of the wood-cutters

202. The writer presents the wood-cutter and the shepherd as examples of all of
    the following *except*:
    (A) men with the time to reflect on their positions
    (B) men that are prepared for and adapted to their situations
    (C) men who drew the moral and meaning from their positions
    (D) men living in a time of slower growth
    (E) men who must be at the full expense in describing their position

203. Because of the rapid growth of the present times, poets must:
    (A) describe the lives of workers because workers don't have the time to
        reflect on their positions
    (B) be prepared for the distaste that they will experience
    (C) see the lives of wood-cutters as possessing an ideal beauty
    (D) trust by faith to be able to make meaning from their surroundings
    (E) reproduce the past with a new form of poetry

204. The primary mode of composition of paragraph two is:
    (A) narration
    (B) description
    (C) cause and effect
    (D) definition
    (E) classification

205. In the first sentence of paragraph three, "mushroom" is used to figuratively modify "growth" as being:

(A) natural
(B) dark
(C) hidden
(D) fast
(E) spreading

206. In context, the word "confound" in line 27 most nearly means:

(A) combine
(B) confuse
(C) distinguish
(D) abash
(E) ruin

207. All of the following rhetorical techniques are present in the last paragraph *except*:

(A) metaphor
(B) simile
(C) alliteration
(D) allusion
(E) anaphora

208. Which of the following lines expresses irony?:

(A) "I come to the West prepared for the distaste I must experience at its mushroom growth."
(B) "The march of peaceful is scarce less wanton than that of warlike invasion."
(C) "I have come prepared to see all this, to dislike it, but not with stupid narrowness to distrust or defame."
(D) "On the contrary, while I will not be so obliging as to confound ugliness with beauty, discord with harmony, and laud and be contented with all I meet, when it conflicts with my best desires and tastes, I trust by reverent faith to woo the mighty meaning of the scene, perhaps to foresee the law by which a new order, a new poetry, is to be evoked from this chaos, and with a curiosity as ardent, but not so selfish, as that of Macbeth, to call up the apparitions of future kings from the strange ingredients of the witch's caldron."
(E) "Thus I will not grieve that all the noble trees are gone already from this island to feed this caldron, but believe it will have Medea's virtue, and reproduce them in the form of new intellectual growths, since centuries cannot again adorn the land with such as have been removed."

209. The style of the passage can best be described as:
- (A) disjointed and complex
- (B) terse and dramatic
- (C) descriptive and allusive
- (D) abstract and informal
- (E) colloquial and evocative

210. The tone of the passage can best be described as:
- (A) bittersweet
- (B) skeptical
- (C) derisive
- (D) curt
- (E) moralistic

Passage 5b: H. L. Mencken, *Europe After 8:15*

For the American professional seeker after the night romance of Paris, the French have a phrase which, be it soever inelegant, retains still a brilliant verity. The phrase is "une belle poire." And its Yankee equivalent is "sucker."

The French, as the world knows, are a kindly, forgiving people; and though they cast the epithet, they do so in manner tolerant and with light arpeggio—of $\quad$ 5 Yankee sneer and bitterness containing not a trace. They cast it as one casts a coin into the hand of some maundering beggar, with commingled oh-wells and philosophical pity. For in the Frenchman of the Paris of to-day, though there run not the blood of Lafayette, and though he detest Americans as he detests the Germans, he yet, detesting, sorrows for them, sees them as mere misled yokels, uncosmopo- $\quad$ 10 lite, obstreperous, of comical posturing in ostensible un-Latin lech, vainglorious and spying—children into whose hands has fallen Zola, children adream, somnambulistic, groping rashly for those things out of life that, groped for, are lost—that may come only as life comes, naturally, calmly, inevitably.

But the Frenchman, he never laughs at us; that would his culture forbid. And, if $\quad$ 15 he smile, his mouth goes placid before the siege. His attitude is the attitude of one beholding a Comstock come to the hill of Hörselberg in Thuringia, there to sniff and snicker in Venus's crimson court. His attitude is the attitude of one beholding a Tristan en voyage for a garden of love and roses he can never reach. His attitude, the attitude of an old and understanding professor, shaking his head musingly as $\quad$ 20 his tender pupils, unmellowed yet in the autumnal fragrances of life, giggle covertly over the pages of Balzac and Flaubert, over the nudes of Manet, over even the innocent yearnings of the bachelor Chopin.

The American, loosed in the streets of Paris by night, however sees in himself another and a worldlier image. Into the crevices of his flat house in his now far- $\quad$ 25 away New York have penetrated from time to time vague whisperings of the laxative deviltries, the bold saucinesses of the city by the Seine. And hither has he come, as comes a jack tar to West Street after protracted cruise upon the celibate seas, to smell out, as a very devil of a fellow, quotation-marked life and its attributes. What is romance to such a soul—even were romance, the romance of this Paris, uncurtained to him? Which, forsooth, the romance seldom is; for though it may go athwart his path, he sees it not, he feels it not, he knows it not, can know it not, for what it is.   30

211. In context, the word "verity" in line 2 most nearly means:

    (A) truth
    (B) beauty
    (C) naivety
    (D) romance
    (E) pride

212. The chief effect of the word "sucker" in line 3 is to:

    (A) provide an objective perspective to the subject
    (B) lend an informal and humorous tone to the discussion
    (C) provide an accurate English translation of the French phrase "une belle poire"
    (D) establish a reverential attitude about the subject
    (E) set up a contrast between the French and English language use

213. The second paragraph contains all of the following techniques *except*:

    (A) syntactical inversion
    (B) simile
    (C) colloquialisms
    (D) allusion
    (E) anecdote

214. In paragraph two, the Frenchman primarily views the American with:

    (A) suspicion
    (B) pity
    (C) contempt
    (D) compassion
    (E) forgiveness

215. In paragraph three, the Frenchman primarily views the American as:

    (A) pathetic
    (B) ignorant
    (C) foolish
    (D) inexperienced
    (E) sneaky

216. In paragraph four, the American primarily views himself as:

    (A) devious

    (B) free

    (C) bold

    (D) adventurous

    (E) sophisticated

217. According to the last two sentences of the passage, to the American, romance is:

    (A) known

    (B) seen

    (C) felt

    (D) not in his path

    (E) hidden

218. The style of the passage can best be described as:

    (A) simplistic

    (B) disjointed

    (C) unorthodox

    (D) abstract

    (E) pedantic

219. The tone of the passage can best be described as:

    (A) ambivalent

    (B) bemused

    (C) contemptuous

    (D) playful

    (E) wistful

220. The primary purpose of the passage is to:

    (A) inform

    (B) entertain

    (C) persuade

    (D) refute

    (E) defend

Passage 5c: Charles Darwin, *On the Origin of Species*

In considering the Origin of Species, it is quite conceivable that a naturalist, reflecting on the mutual affinities of organic beings, on their embryological relations, their geographical distribution, geological succession, and other such facts, might come to the conclusion that each species had not been independently created, but had descended, like varieties, from other species. Nevertheless, such a conclusion, even if well founded, would be unsatisfactory, until it could be shown how the innumerable species inhabiting this world have been modified, so as to acquire that perfection of structure and coadaptation which most justly excites our admiration. Naturalists continually refer to external conditions, such as climate, food, etc., as the only possible cause of variation. In one very limited sense, as we shall hereafter see, this may be true; but it is preposterous to attribute to mere external conditions, the structure, for instance, of the woodpecker, with its feet, tail, beak, and tongue, so admirably adapted to catch insects under the bark of trees. In the case of the misseltoe which draws its nourishment from certain trees, which has seeds that must be transported by certain birds, and which has flowers with separate sexes absolutely requiring the agency of certain insects to bring pollen from one flower to the other, it is equally preposterous to account for the structure of this parasite, with its relations to several distinct organic beings, by the effects of external conditions, or of habit, or of the volition of the plant itself.

The author of the *Vestiges of Creation* would, I presume, say that, after a certain unknown number of generations, some bird had given birth to a woodpecker, and some plant to the misseltoe, and that these had been produced perfect as we now see them; but this assumption seems to me to be no explanation, for it leaves the case of the coadaptations of organic beings to each other and to their physical conditions of life, untouched and unexplained.

It is, therefore, of the highest importance to gain a clear insight into the means of modification and coadaptation. At the commencement of my observations it seemed to me probable that a careful study of domesticated animals and of cultivated plants would offer the best chance of making out this obscure problem. Nor have I been disappointed; in this and in all other perplexing cases I have invariably found that our knowledge, imperfect though it be, of variation under domestication, afforded the best and safest clue. I may venture to express my conviction of the high value of such studies, although they have been very commonly neglected by naturalists.

221. In context, the word "affinities" in line 2 most nearly means:

(A) feelings of kinship
(B) natural attractions
(C) relationships
(D) counterparts
(E) resemblances in structure

222. According to the passage, the problem with the "conclusion that each species had not been independently created, but had descended, like varieties, from other species" is that:

(A) it is begging the question
(B) it is a hasty generalization
(C) it is ad hominem
(D) it is post hoc
(E) it is non sequitur

223. The sentences "Naturalists continually refer to external conditions, such as climate, food, etc., as the only possible cause of variation. In one very limited sense, as we shall hereafter see, this may be true; but it is preposterous to attribute to mere external conditions, the structure, for instance, of the woodpecker, with its feet, tail, beak, and tongue, so admirably adapted to catch insects under the bark of trees," are provided by the writer as:

(A) counterargument
(B) a warrant
(C) a rebuttal
(D) data
(E) claim

224. While discussing the woodpecker and the misseltoe in paragraph one, the writer's tone can best be described as:

(A) jovial
(B) sanguine
(C) awed
(D) conciliatory
(E) nostalgic

225. The subject and predicate of the last sentence of the first paragraph are:

(A) case draws
(B) seeds transported
(C) flowers requiring
(D) it is
(E) relations effects

226. The third paragraph can best be described as:

(A) a reasoned introduction to an argument
(B) an impassioned appeal to the audience
(C) a dramatic narrative
(D) a historical commentary
(E) a personal reflection on a problem

227. In context, the word "obscure" in line 29 most nearly means:

    (A) dark
    (B) faint
    (C) mysterious
    (D) remote
    (E) ambiguous

228. "Coadaptation" in a species refers to:

    (A) the effects of geographical distribution
    (B) the effects of embryological relations
    (C) the effects of geological succession
    (D) the effects of relationships with other organic beings and life
    (E) the effects of having descended from other species

229. The tone of the last paragraph can best be described as:

    (A) forthright
    (B) poignant
    (C) evasive
    (D) acerbic
    (E) ominous

230. The passage mostly appeals to:

    I. ethos
    II. logos
    III. pathos

    (A) I
    (B) II
    (C) III
    (D) I and II
    (E) I, II, and III

Passage 5d: Thomas Henry Huxley, *Science and Culture*

From the time that the first suggestion to introduce physical science into ordinary education was timidly whispered, until now, the advocates of scientific education have met with opposition of two kinds. On the one hand, they have been pooh-poohed by the men of business who pride themselves on being the representatives of practicality; while, on the other hand, they have been excommunicated by the classical scholars, in their capacity of Levites in charge of the ark of culture and monopolists of liberal education.

The practical men believed that the idol whom they worship—rule of thumb—has been the source of the past prosperity, and will suffice for the future welfare of the arts and manufactures. They were of opinion that science is speculative rub- 10
bish; that theory and practice have nothing to do with one another; and that the scientific habit of mind is an impediment, rather than an aid, in the conduct of ordinary affairs.

I have used the past tense in speaking of the practical men—for although they were very formidable thirty years ago, I am not sure that the pure species has not 15
been extirpated. In fact, so far as mere argument goes, they have been subjected to such a feu d'enfer that it is a miracle if any have escaped. But I have remarked that your typical practical man has an unexpected resemblance to one of Milton's angels. His spiritual wounds, such as are inflicted by logical weapons, may be as deep as a well and as wide as a church door, but beyond shedding a few drops of 20
ichor, celestial or otherwise, he is no whit the worse. So, if any of these opponents be left, I will not waste time in vain repetition of the demonstrative evidence of the practical value of science; but knowing that a parable will sometimes penetrate where syllogisms fail to effect an entrance, I will offer a story for their consideration.

Once upon a time, a boy, with nothing to depend upon but his own vigor- 25
ous nature, was thrown into the thick of the struggle for existence in the midst of a great manufacturing population. He seems to have had a hard fight, inasmuch as, by the time he was thirty years of age, his total disposable funds amounted to twenty pounds. Nevertheless, middle life found him giving proof of his compre-hension of the practical problems he had been roughly called upon to solve, by a 30
career of remarkable prosperity.

Finally, having reached old age with its well-earned surroundings of "honour, troops of friends," the hero of my story bethought himself of those who were mak-ing a like start in life, and how he could stretch out a helping hand to them.

After long and anxious reflection this successful practical man of business could 35
devise nothing better than to provide them with the means of obtaining "sound, extensive, and practical scientific knowledge." And he devoted a large part of his wealth and five years of incessant work to this end.

I need not point the moral of a tale which, as the solid and spacious fabric of the Scientific College assures us, is no fable, nor can anything which I could say 40
intensify the force of this practical answer to practical objections.

231. In line 3, the pronoun "they" refers to:
- (A) advocates
- (B) kinds
- (C) men
- (D) representatives
- (E) scholars

232. "Pooh-poohed" is an example of:

(A) metaphorical language
(B) regional dialect
(C) colloquialism
(D) archaic diction
(E) concrete diction

233. In describing the classical scholars at the end of paragraph one, the writer makes use of:

(A) anecdote
(B) biblical allusion
(C) literary allusion
(D) mythological allusion
(E) historical reference

234. In the sentence, "The practical men believed that the idol whom they worship—rule of thumb—has been the source of the past prosperity, and will suffice for the future welfare of the arts and manufactures," rule of thumb is:

I. a simple but inexact means of measurement
II. a symbol of practicality
III. an example of a scientific principle

(A) I
(B) II
(C) III
(D) I and II
(E) I, II, and III

235. In context, the word "extirpated" in line 16 most nearly means:

(A) exalted
(B) extorted
(C) extenuated
(D) extolled
(E) exterminated

236. In describing practical men as "Milton's angels," the writer uses:

(A) anecdote
(B) biblical allusion
(C) literary allusion
(D) mythological allusion
(E) historical reference

237. The sentence "His spiritual wounds, such as are inflicted by logical weapons, may be as deep as a well and as wide as a church door, but beyond shedding a few drops of ichor, celestial or otherwise, he is no whit the worse" uses:
I. simile
II. metaphor
III. personification
(A) I
(B) II
(C) III
(D) I and II
(E) I, II, and III

238. The tone of the sentence "So, if any of these opponents be left, I will not waste time in vain repetition of the demonstrative evidence of the practical value of science; but knowing that a parable will sometimes penetrate where syllogisms fail to effect an entrance, I will offer a story for their consideration," can best be described as:
(A) exasperated
(B) uneasy
(C) ominous
(D) apathetic
(E) despairing

239. The writer views "practical men" with:
(A) sympathy
(B) contempt
(C) reverence
(D) bewilderment
(E) admiration

240. The writer uses all of the following to make his claims *except*:
(A) allusions
(B) foreign language
(C) narrative
(D) figurative language
(E) scientific data

Passage 5e: Charles Lyell, *The Student's Elements of Geology*

Of what materials is the earth composed, and in what manner are these materials arranged? These are the first inquiries with which Geology is occupied, a science which derives its name from the Greek ge, the earth, and logos, a discourse. Previously to experience we might have imagined that investigations of this kind would relate exclusively to the mineral kingdom, and to the various rocks, soils, and metals, which occur upon the surface of the earth, or at various depths beneath it. But, in pursuing such researches, we soon find ourselves led on to consider the successive changes which have taken place in the former state of the earth's surface and interior, and the causes which have given rise to these changes; and, what is still more singular and unexpected, we soon become engaged in researches into the history of the animate creation, or of the various tribes of animals and plants which have, at different periods of the past, inhabited the globe.

All are aware that the solid parts of the earth consist of distinct substances, such as clay, chalk, sand, limestone, coal, slate, granite, and the like; but previously to observation it is commonly imagined that all these had remained from the first in the state in which we now see them—that they were created in their present form, and in their present position. The geologist soon comes to a different conclusion, discovering proofs that the external parts of the earth were not all produced in the beginning of things in the state in which we now behold them, nor in an instant of time. On the contrary, he can show that they have acquired their actual configuration and condition gradually, under a great variety of circumstances, and at successive periods, during each of which distinct races of living beings have flourished on the land and in the waters, the remains of these creatures still lying buried in the crust of the earth.

By the "earth's crust," is meant that small portion of the exterior of our planet which is accessible to human observation. It comprises not merely all of which the structure is laid open in mountain precipices, or in cliffs overhanging a river or the sea, or whatever the miner may reveal in artificial excavations; but the whole of that outer covering of the planet on which we are enabled to reason by observations made at or near the surface. These reasonings may extend to a depth of several miles, perhaps ten miles; and even then it may be said, that such a thickness is no more than 1/400 part of the distance from the surface to the centre. The remark is just: but although the dimensions of such a crust are, in truth, insignificant when compared to the entire globe, yet they are vast, and of magnificent extent in relation to man, and to the organic beings which people our globe. Referring to this standard of magnitude, the geologist may admire the ample limits of his domain, and admit, at the same time, that not only the exterior of the planet, but the entire earth, is but an atom in the midst of the countless worlds surveyed by the astronomer.

241. The primary mode of composition of the first paragraph is:

(A) narration

(B) description

(C) definition

(D) classification

(E) process analysis

242. The major claim of the first paragraph is that:

    (A) although geology was first thought to be a study of minerals, further study shows that animals, plants, and evolution are part of the subject as well

    (B) although geology was first thought to be a study of minerals, further study shows that rocks, soils, and metals are part of the subject as well

    (C) although geology was first thought to be a study of the earth's surface, further study shows that the depths beneath the surface are part of the subject as well

    (D) although geology was first thought to be a study of the changes that have taken place in the earth, further study shows that the history of animals and plants are part of the subject as well

    (E) although geology was first thought to be a study of the history of creation, further study shows that animals and plants are part of the subject as well

243. The first sentence of paragraph two, "All are aware that the solid parts of the earth consist of distinct substances, such as clay, chalk, sand, limestone, coal, slate, granite, and the like; but previously to observation it is commonly imagined that all these had remained from the first in the state in which we now see them—that they were created in their present form, and in their present position," uses:

    I. enumeration
    II. metaphor
    III. parallelism

    (A) I
    (B) II
    (C) III
    (D) I and III
    (E) I, II, and III

244. The last sentence of paragraph two, "On the contrary, he can show that they have acquired their actual configuration and condition gradually, under a great variety of circumstances, and at successive periods, during each of which distinct races of living beings have flourished on the land and in the waters, the remains of these creatures still lying buried in the crust of the earth," is an example of a(n):

    (A) sentence fragment
    (B) interrogative sentence
    (C) imperative sentence
    (D) simple sentence
    (E) cumulative sentence

245. In context, the word "artificial" in line 28 most nearly means:

- (A) produced by humans rather than nature
- (B) made in imitation of something
- (C) feigned
- (D) not genuine
- (E) affected

246. In context, the word "just" in line 33 most nearly means:

- (A) impartial
- (B) morally upright
- (C) equitable; fair
- (D) accurate
- (E) deserved

247. The primary mode of composition of the last paragraph is:

- (A) narration
- (B) description
- (C) definition
- (D) classification
- (E) process analysis

248. According to the last sentence, the geologist views the earth with:

- (A) frustration and bewilderment
- (B) awe and humility
- (C) fervor and hostility
- (D) mirth and irreverence
- (E) elation and skepticism

249. The last paragraph primarily appeals to:

- I. ethos
- II. logos
- III. pathos

- (A) I
- (B) II
- (C) III
- (D) I and III
- (E) I, II, and III

250. The primary purpose of the passage is to:
- (A) inform
- (B) persuade
- (C) entertain
- (D) refute
- (E) defend

CHAPTER 6

Political Writers

Passage 6a: Thomas Jefferson, *Sixth State of the Union Address*

It would have given me, fellow citizens, great satisfaction to announce in the moment of your meeting that the difficulties in our foreign relations existing at the time of your last separation had been amicably and justly terminated. I lost no time in taking those measures which were most likely to bring them to such a termination—by special missions charged with such powers and instructions as in 5 the event of failure could leave no imputation on either our moderation or forbearance. The delays which have since taken place in our negotiations with the British Government appear to have proceeded from causes which do not forbid the expectation that during the course of the session I may be enabled to lay before you their final issue. What will be that of the negotiations for settling our differences with 10 Spain nothing which had taken place at the date of the last dispatches enables us to pronounce. On the western side of the Mississippi she advanced in considerable force, and took post at the settlement of Bayou Pierre, on the Red River. This village was originally settled by France, was held by her as long as she held Louisiana, and was delivered to Spain only as a part of Louisiana. Being small, insulated, and 15 distant, it was not observed at the moment of redelivery to France and the United States that she continued a guard of half a dozen men which had been stationed there. A proposition, however, having been lately made by our commander in chief to assume the Sabine River as a temporary line of separation between the troops of the two nations until the issue of our negotiations shall be known, this has been 20 referred by the Spanish commandant to his superior, and in the mean time he has withdrawn his force to the western side of the Sabine River. The correspondence on this subject now communicated will exhibit more particularly the present state of things in that quarter.

The nature of that country requires indispensably that an unusual proportion 25 of the force employed there should be cavalry or mounted infantry. In order, therefore, that the commanding officer might be enabled to act with effect, I had authorized him to call on the governors of Orleans and Mississippi for a corps of 500 volunteer cavalry. The temporary arrangement he has proposed may perhaps render this unnecessary; but I inform you with great pleasure of the promptitude with 30 which the inhabitants of those Territories have tendered their services in defense of their country. It has done honor to themselves, entitled them to the confidence of their fellow citizens in every part of the Union, and must strengthen the general determination to protect them efficaciously under all circumstances which may occur.

Having received information that in another part of the United States a great number of private individuals were combining together, arming and organizing themselves contrary to law, to carry on a military expedition against the territories of Spain, I thought it necessary, by proclamation as well as by special orders, to take measures for preventing and suppressing this enterprise, for seizing the vessels, arms, and other means provided for it, and for arresting and bringing to justice its authors and abettors. It was due to that good faith which ought ever to be the rule of action in public as well as in private transactions, it was due to good order and regular government, that while the public force was acting strictly on defensive and merely to protect our citizens from aggression the criminal attempts of private individuals to decide for their country the question of peace or war by commencing active and unauthorized hostilities should be promptly and efficaciously suppressed.

251. In line 12, the pronoun "she" refers to:
(A) this village
(B) the Bayou Pierre
(C) Spain
(D) France
(E) Louisiana

252. The primary purpose of paragraph one is to:
(A) inform
(B) persuade
(C) entertain
(D) refute
(E) defend

253. The sentence "In order, therefore, that the commanding officer might be enabled to act with effect, I had authorized him to call on the governors of Orleans and Mississippi for a corps of 500 volunteer cavalry" mostly appeals to:
  I. ethos
 II. logos
III. pathos

(A) I
(B) II
(C) III
(D) I and III
(E) I, II, and III

254. The sentence "It has done honor to themselves, entitled them to the confidence of their fellow citizens in every part of the Union, and must strengthen the general determination to protect them efficaciously under all circumstances which may occur" mostly appeals to:

   I. ethos
  II. logos
 III. pathos

  (A) I
  (B) II
  (C) III
  (D) I and II
  (E) I, II, and III

255. In context, the word "promptitude" in line 30 most nearly means:

  (A) fearlessness
  (B) quickness to respond
  (C) bravery
  (D) fortitude
  (E) selflessness

256. The first sentence of paragraph three is a(n):

  (A) sentence fragment
  (B) imperative sentence
  (C) simple sentence
  (D) interrogative sentence
  (E) compound-complex sentence

257. The last sentence of paragraph three uses:

  (A) anaphora
  (B) alliteration
  (C) apostrophe
  (D) allusion
  (E) epistrophe

258. In context, the word "efficaciously" in lines 34 and 47 most nearly means:

  (A) feasibly
  (B) with futility
  (C) effectively
  (D) expeditiously
  (E) fruitlessly

259. The primary purpose of paragraph three is to:
- (A) inform
- (B) persuade
- (C) entertain
- (D) refute
- (E) defend

260. The tone of paragraph three can best be described as:
- (A) fervent
- (B) tranquil
- (C) compassionate
- (D) introspective
- (E) sentimental

Passage 6b: John Stuart Mill, *Considerations on Representative Government*

All speculations concerning forms of government bear the impress, more or less exclusive, of two conflicting theories respecting political institutions; or, to speak more properly, conflicting conceptions of what political institutions are.

By some minds, government is conceived as strictly a practical art, giving rise to no questions but those of means and an end. Forms of government are assimilated 5 to any other expedients for the attainment of human objects. They are regarded as wholly an affair of invention and contrivance. Being made by man, it is assumed that man has the choice either to make them or not, and how or on what pattern they shall be made. Government, according to this conception, is a problem, to be worked like any other question of business. The first step is to define the purposes 10 which governments are required to promote. The next, is to inquire what form of government is best fitted to fulfill those purposes. Having satisfied ourselves on these two points, and ascertained the form of government which combines the greatest amount of good with the least of evil, what further remains is to obtain the concurrence of our countrymen, or those for whom the institutions are intended, 15 in the opinion which we have privately arrived at. To find the best form of government; to persuade others that it is the best; and, having done so, to stir them up to insist on having it, is the order of ideas in the minds of those who adopt this view of political philosophy. They look upon a constitution in the same light (difference of scale being allowed for) as they would upon a steam plow, or a threshing machine. 20

To these stand opposed another kind of political reasoners, who are so far from assimilating a form of government to a machine, that they regard it as a sort of spontaneous product, and the science of government as a branch (so to speak) of natural history. According to them, forms of government are not a matter of choice. We must take them, in the main, as we find them. Governments can not 25 be constructed by premeditated design. They "are not made, but grow." Our business with them, as with the other facts of the universe, is to acquaint ourselves with their natural properties, and adapt ourselves to them. The fundamental political institutions of a people are considered by this school as a sort of organic growth from the nature and life of that people; a product of their habits, instincts, and 30 unconscious wants and desires, scarcely at all of their deliberate purposes. Their will has had no part in the matter but that of meeting the necessities of the moment by the contrivances of the moment, which contrivances, if in sufficient conformity to the national feelings and character, commonly last, and, by successive aggregation, constitute a polity suited to the people who possess it, but which it would be vain 35 to attempt to superinduce upon any people whose nature and circumstances had not spontaneously evolved it.

It is difficult to decide which of these doctrines would be the most absurd, if we could suppose either of them held as an exclusive theory. But the principles which men profess, on any controverted subject, are usually a very incomplete exponent 40 of the opinions they really hold. No one believes that every people is capable of working every sort of institution. Carry the analogy of mechanical contrivances as far as we will, a man does not choose even an instrument of timber and iron on the sole ground that it is in itself the best. He considers whether he possesses the other requisites which must be combined with it to render its employment advantageous, 45 and, in particular whether those by whom it will have to be worked possess the knowledge and skill necessary for its management. On the other hand, neither are those who speak of institutions as if they were a kind of living organisms really the political fatalists they give themselves out to be. They do not pretend that mankind have absolutely no range of choice as to the government they will live under, or 50 that a consideration of the consequences which flow from different forms of polity is no element at all in deciding which of them should be preferred. But, though each side greatly exaggerates its own theory, out of opposition to the other, and no one holds without modification to either, the two doctrines correspond to a deep-seated difference between two modes of thought; and though it is evident 55 that neither of these is entirely in the right, yet it being equally evident that neither is wholly in the wrong, we must endeavour to get down to what is at the root of each, and avail ourselves of the amount of truth which exists in either.

261. The first paragraph introduces the division between the two _____ of political institutions:

(A) definitions
(B) causes
(C) effects
(D) origins
(E) uses

262. In context, the word "contrivance" in line 7 most nearly means:

(A) mechanical device
(B) clever plan
(C) dispute
(D) gadget
(E) laborious process

263. In the portion of the passage, "The first step . . . privately arrived at," the primary mode of composition is:

(A) narration
(B) description
(C) classification
(D) process analysis
(E) definition

264. Government, according to the first conception presented, is described as all of the following *except*:

(A) practical
(B) man-made
(C) a solution
(D) planned
(E) fated

265. The sentence "To find the best form of government; to persuade others that it is the best; and, having done so, to stir them up to insist on having it, is the order of ideas in the minds of those who adopt this view of political philosophy" is the following type of sentence:

(A) fragment
(B) simple
(C) interrogative
(D) imperative
(E) declarative

266. The last line of paragraph two, "They look upon a constitution in the same light (difference of scale being allowed for) as they would upon a steam plow, or a threshing machine," is developed by:

(A) allusion
(B) analogy
(C) anecdote
(D) antithesis
(E) paradox

267. Government, according to the second conception presented, is described as all of the following *except*:

(A) spontaneous
(B) purposeful
(C) natural
(D) organic
(E) found

268. The primary mode of composition of paragraphs two and three is:

(A) narration
(B) description
(C) classification
(D) cause and effect
(E) argument

269. The primary purpose of the passage is to:

(A) persuade the reader that we must find and use the truth in both of these conceptions of government
(B) persuade the reader that the first conception of government is more idealistic than the second
(C) persuade the reader that the second conception of government is more realistic than the first
(D) persuade the reader that both conceptions of government are equally valid
(E) persuade the reader that both conceptions of government are equally absurd

270. The tone of the passage can best be described as:

(A) critical
(B) indignant
(C) apathetic
(D) impartial
(E) caustic

Passage 6c: Thomas Paine, *Common Sense*

Some writers have so confounded society with government, as to leave little or no distinction between them; whereas they are not only different, but have different origins. Society is produced by our wants, and government by our wickedness; the former promotes our happiness POSITIVELY by uniting our affections, the latter NEGATIVELY by restraining our vices. The one encourages intercourse, the other   5
creates distinctions. The first a patron, the last a punisher.

Society in every state is a blessing, but government even in its best state is but a necessary evil; in its worst state an intolerable one; for when we suffer, or are exposed to the same miseries BY A GOVERNMENT, which we might expect in a country WITHOUT GOVERNMENT, our calamity is heightened by reflecting 10 that we furnish the means by which we suffer. Government, like dress, is the badge of lost innocence; the palaces of kings are built on the ruins of the bowers of paradise. For were the impulses of conscience clear, uniform, and irresistibly obeyed, man would need no other lawgiver; but that not being the case, he finds it necessary to surrender up a part of his property to furnish means for the protection of the 15 rest; and this he is induced to do by the same prudence which in every other case advises him out of two evils to choose the least. WHEREFORE, security being the true design and end of government, it unanswerably follows, that whatever FORM thereof appears most likely to ensure it to us, with the least expense and greatest benefit, is preferable to all others. 20

In order to gain a clear and just idea of the design and end of government, let us suppose a small number of persons settled in some sequestered part of the earth, unconnected with the rest; they will then represent the first peopling of any country, or of the world. In this state of natural liberty, society will be their first thought. A thousand motives will excite them thereto, the strength of one man is so unequal 25 to his wants, and his mind so unfitted for perpetual solitude, that he is soon obliged to seek assistance and relief of another, who in his turn requires the same. Four or five united would be able to raise a tolerable dwelling in the midst of a wilderness, but one man might labour out of the common period of life without accomplishing any thing; when he had felled his timber he could not remove it, nor erect it 30 after it was removed; hunger in the mean time would urge him from his work, and every different want call him a different way. Disease, nay even misfortune would be death, for though neither might be mortal, yet either would disable him from living, and reduce him to a state in which he might rather be said to perish than to die. 35

Thus necessity, like a gravitating power, would soon form our newly arrived emigrants into society, the reciprocal blessings of which, would supersede, and render the obligations of law and government unnecessary while they remained perfectly just to each other; but as nothing but heaven is impregnable to vice, it will unavoidably happen, that in proportion as they surmount the first difficulties 40 of emigration, which bound them together in a common cause, they will begin to relax in their duty and attachment to each other; and this remissness will point out the necessity of establishing some form of government to supply the defect of moral virtue.

271. In context, the word "confounded" in line 1 most nearly means:
    (A) combined
    (B) destroyed
    (C) confused
    (D) refuted
    (E) frustrated

272. The primary mode of composition of paragraphs one and two is:
     (A) narration
     (B) description
     (C) cause and effect
     (D) definition
     (E) process analysis

273. The differences between society and government are presented as all of the following oppositions *except*:
     (A) wants and wickedness
     (B) affections and vices
     (C) intercourse and distinctions
     (D) encourages and creates
     (E) uniting and restraining

274. The last line of paragraph one, "The first a patron, the last a punisher," uses:
     (A) apostrophe
     (B) oxymoron
     (C) simile
     (D) metaphor
     (E) personification

275. According to the writer, the suffering described in paragraph two is made worse by the fact that it is:
     (A) inevitable
     (B) self-inflicted
     (C) surprising
     (D) ceaseless
     (E) expected

276. The sentence, "Government, like dress, is the badge of lost innocence; the palaces of kings are built on the ruins of the bowers of paradise," is an example of:
     (A) biblical allusion
     (B) apostrophe
     (C) antithesis
     (D) paradox
     (E) personification

277. The line "he finds it necessary to surrender up a part of his property to furnish means for the protection of the rest" is an example of:
   (A) biblical allusion
   (B) apostrophe
   (C) antithesis
   (D) paradox
   (E) personification

278. The first sentence of paragraph three, "In order to gain a clear and just idea of the design and end of government, let us suppose a small number of persons settled in some sequestered part of the earth, unconnected with the rest; they will then represent the first peopling of any country, or of the world," is the following type of sentence:
   (A) fragment
   (B) simple
   (C) interrogative
   (D) imperative
   (E) declarative

279. The primary purpose of paragraph three is to:
   (A) define natural liberty
   (B) classify the different types of societies
   (C) analyze the causes of creating governments
   (D) describe the earliest society
   (E) illustrate what men can do together and how they need each other

280. The major claim of the passage as a whole is that:
   (A) government is a necessary evil
   (B) government is avoidable in truly civilized societies
   (C) government robs men of their security
   (D) government is synonymous with society
   (E) government is unnecessary because men are inherently good

Passage 6d: Alexis de Tocqueville, *Democracy in America, Volume 1*

Amongst the novel objects that attracted my attention during my stay in the United States, nothing struck me more forcibly than the general equality of conditions. I readily discovered the prodigious influence which this primary fact exercises on the whole course of society, by giving a certain direction to public opinion, and a certain tenor to the laws; by imparting new maxims to the governing powers, and peculiar habits to the governed. I speedily perceived that the influence of this fact

5

extends far beyond the political character and the laws of the country, and that it has no less empire over civil society than over the Government; it creates opinions, engenders sentiments, suggests the ordinary practices of life, and modifies whatever it does not produce. The more I advanced in the study of American society, the 10 more I perceived that the equality of conditions is the fundamental fact from which all others seem to be derived, and the central point at which all my observations constantly terminated.

I then turned my thoughts to our own hemisphere, where I imagined that I discerned something analogous to the spectacle which the New World presented 15 to me. I observed that the equality of conditions is daily progressing towards those extreme limits which it seems to have reached in the United States, and that the democracy which governs the American communities appears to be rapidly rising into power in Europe. I hence conceived the idea of the book which is now before the reader. 20

It is evident to all alike that a great democratic revolution is going on amongst us; but there are two opinions as to its nature and consequences. To some it appears to be a novel accident, which as such may still be checked; to others it seems irresistible, because it is the most uniform, the most ancient, and the most permanent tendency which is to be found in history. Let us recollect the situation 25 of France seven hundred years ago, when the territory was divided amongst a small number of families, who were the owners of the soil and the rulers of the inhabitants; the right of governing descended with the family inheritance from generation to generation; force was the only means by which man could act on man, and landed property was the sole source of power. Soon, however, the political power 30 of the clergy was founded, and began to exert itself: the clergy opened its ranks to all classes, to the poor and the rich, the villein and the lord; equality penetrated into the Government through the Church, and the being who as a serf must have vegetated in perpetual bondage took his place as a priest in the midst of nobles, and not infrequently above the heads of kings. 35

The different relations of men became more complicated and more numerous as society gradually became more stable and more civilized. Thence the want of civil laws was felt; and the order of legal functionaries soon rose from the obscurity of the tribunals and their dusty chambers, to appear at the court of the monarch, by the side of the feudal barons in their ermine and their mail. Whilst the kings 40 were ruining themselves by their great enterprises, and the nobles exhausting their resources by private wars, the lower orders were enriching themselves by commerce. The influence of money began to be perceptible in State affairs. The transactions of business opened a new road to power, and the financier rose to a station of political influence in which he was at once flattered and despised. Gradually 45 the spread of mental acquirements, and the increasing taste for literature and art, opened chances of success to talent; science became a means of government, intelligence led to social power, and the man of letters took a part in the affairs of the State. The value attached to the privileges of birth decreased in the exact proportion

in which new paths were struck out to advancement. In the eleventh century nobil-   50
ity was beyond all price; in the thirteenth it might be purchased; it was conferred
for the first time in 1270; and equality was thus introduced into the Government
by the aristocracy itself.

281. In context, the word "prodigious" in line 3 most nearly means:
- (A) general
- (B) great in size or force
- (C) producing abundant results
- (D) proceeding in steps
- (E) wastefully lavish

282. The word "it" in line 8 refers to:
- (A) government
- (B) American society
- (C) the influence of this fact
- (D) civil society
- (E) the whole course of society

283. The tone of the first and second paragraphs can best be described as:
- (A) serene
- (B) pedantic
- (C) hostile
- (D) reflective
- (E) grave

284. According to the second paragraph, the writer can best be described as:
- I. American
- II. European
- III. a writer

- (A) I
- (B) II
- (C) III
- (D) I and III
- (E) II and III

285. The most immediate reason why the writer wrote the book being introduced is:

(A) he was struck by the equality of conditions in America
(B) there are two different opinions on democratic revolution
(C) this equality of conditions influences ordinary life as well as government
(D) equality of conditions influences every area of American life
(E) equality of conditions is rising into power in Europe

286. The sentence that begins "Let us recollect the situation of France seven hundred years ago . . . " can best be described as the following type(s) of sentence:

   I. imperative sentence
  II. cumulative sentence
 III. periodic sentence

(A) I
(B) II
(C) III
(D) I and II
(E) I and III

287. The two opinions on the nature and consequences of a "great democratic revolution" can best be summarized in the following opposition:

(A) new vs. ancient
(B) uniform vs. ancient
(C) irresistible vs. permanent
(D) accidental vs. controllable
(E) uniform vs. permanent

288. Paragraph three is mostly developed by:

(A) personal opinion
(B) example
(C) anecdote
(D) statistics
(E) expert testimony

289. The mode of composition of paragraph four is mostly:

(A) narration
(B) description
(C) definition
(D) classification
(E) cause and effect

290. The major claim of the last paragraph is most clearly stated in the following sentence:

(A) "The different relations of men became more complicated and more numerous as society gradually became more stable and more civilized."

(B) "Whilst the kings were ruining themselves by their great enterprises, and the nobles exhausting their resources by private wars, the lower orders were enriching themselves by commerce."

(C) "The influence of money began to be perceptible in State affairs."

(D) "The transactions of business opened a new road to power, and the financier rose to a station of political influence in which he was at once flattered and despised."

(E) "The value attached to the privileges of birth decreased in the exact proportion in which new paths were struck out to advancement."

Passage 6e: Mary Wollstonecraft, *A Vindication on the Rights of Woman*

After considering the historic page, and viewing the living world with anxious solicitude, the most melancholy emotions of sorrowful indignation have depressed my spirits, and I have sighed when obliged to confess, that either nature has made a great difference between man and man, or that the civilization, which has hitherto taken place in the world, has been very partial. I have turned over various books   5
written on the subject of education, and patiently observed the conduct of parents and the management of schools; but what has been the result? a profound conviction, that the neglected education of my fellow creatures is the grand source of the misery I deplore; and that women in particular, are rendered weak and wretched by a variety of concurring causes, originating from one hasty conclusion. The con-   10
duct and manners of women, in fact, evidently prove, that their minds are not in a healthy state; for, like the flowers that are planted in too rich a soil, strength and usefulness are sacrificed to beauty; and the flaunting leaves, after having pleased a fastidious eye, fade, disregarded on the stalk, long before the season when they ought to have arrived at maturity. One cause of this barren blooming I attribute   15
to a false system of education, gathered from the books written on this subject by men, who, considering females rather as women than human creatures, have been more anxious to make them alluring mistresses than rational wives; and the understanding of the sex has been so bubbled by this specious homage, that the civilized women of the present century, with a few exceptions, are only anxious to   20
inspire love, when they ought to cherish a nobler ambition, and by their abilities and virtues exact respect.

In a treatise, therefore, on female rights and manners, the works which have been particularly written for their improvement must not be overlooked; especially when it is asserted, in direct terms, that the minds of women are enfeebled by false   25
refinement; that the books of instruction, written by men of genius, have had the same tendency as more frivolous productions; and that, in the true style of Maho-

metanism, they are only considered as females, and not as a part of the human species, when improvable reason is allowed to be the dignified distinction, which raises men above the brute creation, and puts a natural sceptre in a feeble hand. 30

Yet, because I am a woman, I would not lead my readers to suppose, that I mean violently to agitate the contested question respecting the equality and inferiority of the sex; but as the subject lies in my way, and I cannot pass it over without subjecting the main tendency of my reasoning to misconstruction, I shall stop a moment to deliver, in a few words, my opinion. In the government of the physi- 35 cal world, it is observable that the female, in general, is inferior to the male. The male pursues, the female yields—this is the law of nature; and it does not appear to be suspended or abrogated in favour of woman. This physical superiority cannot be denied—and it is a noble prerogative! But not content with this natural pre-eminence, men endeavour to sink us still lower, merely to render us alluring 40 objects for a moment; and women, intoxicated by the adoration which men, under the influence of their senses, pay them, do not seek to obtain a durable interest in their hearts, or to become the friends of the fellow creatures who find amusement in their society.

291. After reading history and making observations around her, the writer of the passage has concluded the following to be true:
  I. there are differences between people that are attributable to nature
  II. there are differences in treatment that have resulted from civilization
  III. the disparities between people are both saddening and infuriating

  (A) I
  (B) II
  (C) III
  (D) I and III
  (E) I, II, and III

292. In context, the word "solicitude" in line 2 most nearly means:

  (A) attention
  (B) isolation
  (C) unity
  (D) discourse
  (E) petition

293. According to the first paragraph, the primary cause of the disparate conditions of people is:

  (A) government
  (B) parents and family
  (C) civilization
  (D) education
  (E) women

294. The sentence "The conduct and manners of women, in fact, evidently prove, that their minds are not in a healthy state; for, like the flowers that are planted in too rich a soil, strength and usefulness are sacrificed to beauty; and the flaunting leaves, after having pleased a fastidious eye, fade, disregarded on the stalk, long before the season when they ought to have arrived at maturity" is developed by:

(A) allusion
(B) analogy
(C) anecdote
(D) antithesis
(E) apostrophe

295. The writer finds fault with the education of women for all of the following reasons *except*:

(A) it teaches women to please rather than to be useful
(B) it teaches women to value love over respect
(C) it is self-inflicted by women
(D) it does not consider women people
(E) it weakens women's minds

296. What may be considered ironic by current-day readers is the fact that the writer claims:

(A) women are inferior to men
(B) women ought to be taught to have more noble goals
(C) women are enfeebled by the education provided for them
(D) men are not satisfied with their physical dominance
(E) men are responsible for keeping women down

297. In context, the word "society" in line 44 most nearly means:

(A) a group of humans
(B) a group of people with a common culture
(C) a group of people with a common interest
(D) the privileged social class
(E) company or companionship

298. The primary purpose of the passage is to:

(A) inform
(B) entertain
(C) persuade
(D) refute
(E) defend

299. The primary mode of composition of the passage is:

    (A) narration

    (B) description

    (C) process analysis

    (D) argument

    (E) classification

300. The tone of the passage can best be described as:

    (A) measured indignation

    (B) cautious admonition

    (C) incredulous bewilderment

    (D) unapologetic criticism

    (E) irreverent sarcasm

CHAPTER 7

16th and 17th Centuries

Passage 7a: Niccolo Machiavelli, *The Prince*

Commencing then with the first of the above-named characteristics, I say that it would be well to be reputed liberal. Nevertheless, liberality exercised in a way that does not bring you the reputation for it, injures you; for if one exercises it honestly and as it should be exercised, it may not become known, and you will not avoid the reproach of its opposite. Therefore, any one wishing to maintain among men 5 the name of liberal is obliged to avoid no attribute of magnificence; so that a prince thus inclined will consume in such acts all his property, and will be compelled in the end, if he wish to maintain the name of liberal, to unduly weigh down his people, and tax them, and do everything he can to get money. This will soon make him odious to his subjects, and becoming poor he will be little valued by any one; 10 thus, with his liberality, having offended many and rewarded few, he is affected by the very first trouble and imperiled by whatever may be the first danger; recognizing this himself, and wishing to draw back from it, he runs at once into the reproach of being miserly.

Therefore, a prince, not being able to exercise this virtue of liberality in such a 15 way that it is recognized, except to his cost, if he is wise he ought not to fear the reputation of being mean, for in time he will come to be more considered than if liberal, seeing that with his economy his revenues are enough, that he can defend himself against all attacks, and is able to engage in enterprises without burdening his people; thus it comes to pass that he exercises liberality towards all from whom 20 he does not take, who are numberless, and meanness towards those to whom he does not give, who are few.

We have not seen great things done in our time except by those who have been considered mean; the rest have failed. Pope Julius the Second was assisted in reaching the papacy by a reputation for liberality, yet he did not strive afterwards to keep 25 it up, when he made war on the King of France; and he made many wars without imposing any extraordinary tax on his subjects, for he supplied his additional expenses out of his long thriftiness. The present King of Spain would not have undertaken or conquered in so many enterprises if he had been reputed liberal. A prince, therefore, provided that he has not to rob his subjects, that he can defend 30 himself, that he does not become poor and abject, that he is not forced to become rapacious, ought to hold of little account a reputation for being mean, for it is one of those vices which will enable him to govern.

   And if any one should say: Caesar obtained empire by liberality, and many others have reached the highest positions by having been liberal, and by being 35 considered so, I answer: Either you are a prince in fact, or in a way to become one. In the first case this liberality is dangerous, in the second it is very necessary to be considered liberal; and Caesar was one of those who wished to become pre-eminent in Rome; but if he had survived after becoming so, and had not moderated his expenses, he would have destroyed his government. And if any one should reply: 40 Many have been princes, and have done great things with armies, who have been considered very liberal, I reply: Either a prince spends that which is his own or his subjects' or else that of others. In the first case he ought to be sparing, in the second he ought not to neglect any opportunity for liberality. And to the prince who goes forth with his army, supporting it by pillage, sack, and extortion, handling that 45 which belongs to others, this liberality is necessary, otherwise he would not be followed by soldiers. And of that which is neither yours nor your subjects' you can be a ready giver, as were Cyrus, Caesar, and Alexander; because it does not take away your reputation if you squander that of others, but adds to it; it is only squandering your own that injures you. 50

   And there is nothing wastes so rapidly as liberality, for even whilst you exercise it you lose the power to do so, and so become either poor or despised, or else, in avoiding poverty, rapacious and hated. And a prince should guard himself, above all things, against being despised and hated; and liberality leads you to both. Therefore it is wiser to have a reputation for meanness which brings reproach without 55 hatred, than to be compelled through seeking a reputation for liberality to incur a name for rapacity which begets reproach with hatred.

301. In order for being liberal to have positive results for the prince, it must be enacted with:

   (A) consistency
   (B) dishonesty
   (C) honesty
   (D) free will
   (E) obligation

302. The primary mode of composition of the first paragraph is:

   (A) narration
   (B) description
   (C) cause and effect
   (D) argument
   (E) compare and contrast

303. According to the first paragraph, being liberal (as a prince) leads to all of the following results *except*:

(A) being loved
(B) becoming poor
(C) being despised
(D) being in danger
(E) being considered miserly

304. In context, the word "odious" in line 10 most nearly means:

(A) pitied
(B) valued
(C) sympathetic
(D) detestable
(E) patronizing

305. The pronoun "it" in line 13 refers to the antecedent:

(A) subjects
(B) becoming poor
(C) liberality
(D) money
(E) danger

306. The primary mode of composition of the third paragraph is:

(A) narration
(B) description
(C) definition
(D) classification
(E) example

307. Paragraph four is primarily developed by the use of:

(A) counterargument
(B) expert testimony
(C) syllogism
(D) anecdote
(E) warrant

308. The writer's major claim that being liberal is dangerous and disastrous, as presented in the sentence "And a prince should guard himself, above all things, against being despised and hated; and liberality leads you to both," is an example of:

(A) antithesis
(B) paradox
(C) allusion
(D) climax
(E) juxtaposition

309. The passage as a whole primarily appeals to:
   I. ethos
   II. logos
   III. pathos

(A) I
(B) II
(C) III
(D) I and II
(E) I, II, and III

310. The tone of the passage can best be described as:

(A) poignant
(B) solemn
(C) forthright
(D) despairing
(E) aloof

Passage 7b: Thomas More, *Utopia*

They [the residents of Utopia] think it is an evidence of true wisdom for a man to pursue his own advantage as far as the laws allow it, they account it piety to prefer the public good to one's private concerns, but they think it unjust for a man to seek for pleasure by snatching another man's pleasures from him; and, on the contrary, they think it a sign of a gentle and good soul for a man to dispense with his 5
own advantage for the good of others, and that by this means a good man finds as much pleasure one way as he parts with another; for as he may expect the like from others when he may come to need it, so, if that should fail him, yet the sense of a good action, and the reflections that he makes on the love and gratitude of those whom he has so obliged, gives the mind more pleasure than the body could have 10
found in that from which it had restrained itself. They are also persuaded that God will make up the loss of those small pleasures with a vast and endless joy, of which religion easily convinces a good soul.

Thus, upon an inquiry into the whole matter, they reckon that all our actions, and even all our virtues, terminate in pleasure, as in our chief end and greatest happiness; and they call every motion or state, either of body or mind, in which Nature teaches us to delight, a pleasure. Thus they cautiously limit pleasure only to those appetites to which Nature leads us; for they say that Nature leads us only to those delights to which reason, as well as sense, carries us, and by which we neither injure any other person nor lose the possession of greater pleasures, and of such as draw no troubles after them. But they look upon those delights which men by a foolish, though common, mistake call pleasure, as if they could change as easily the nature of things as the use of words, as things that greatly obstruct their real happiness, instead of advancing it, because they so entirely possess the minds of those that are once captivated by them with a false notion of pleasure that there is no room left for pleasures of a truer or purer kind.

There are many things that in themselves have nothing that is truly delightful; on the contrary, they have a good deal of bitterness in them; and yet, from our perverse appetites after forbidden objects, are not only ranked among the pleasures, but are made even the greatest designs, of life. Among those who pursue these sophisticated pleasures they reckon such as I mentioned before, who think themselves really the better for having fine clothes; in which they think they are doubly mistaken, both in the opinion they have of their clothes, and in that they have of themselves. For if you consider the use of clothes, why should a fine thread be thought better than a coarse one? And yet these men, as if they had some real advantages beyond others, and did not owe them wholly to their mistakes, look big, seem to fancy themselves to be more valuable, and imagine that a respect is due to them for the sake of a rich garment, to which they would not have pretended if they had been more meanly clothed, and even resent it as an affront if that respect is not paid them. It is also a great folly to be taken with outward marks of respect, which signify nothing; for what true or real pleasure can one man find in another's standing bare or making legs to him? Will the bending another man's knees give ease to yours? and will the head's being bare cure the madness of yours? And yet it is wonderful to see how this false notion of pleasure bewitches many who delight themselves with the fancy of their nobility, and are pleased with this conceit—that they are descended from ancestors who have been held for some successions rich, and who have had great possessions; for this is all that makes nobility at present. Yet they do not think themselves a whit the less noble, though their immediate parents have left none of this wealth to them, or though they themselves have squandered it away.

311. According to the first paragraph, goodness can be equated with:

   (A) honesty
   (B) selflessness
   (C) charity
   (D) generosity
   (E) gratitude

312. The use of the pronoun "he" in paragraph one refers to:

    (A) a good man

    (B) a resident of Utopia

    (C) a wise man

    (D) a gentle and good soul

    (E) God

313. In paragraph two, "Nature" is an example of:

    (A) a metaphor

    (B) an allusion

    (C) an analogy

    (D) personification

    (E) hyperbole

314. The use of the pronouns "us" and "our" in paragraph two refers to:

    (A) residents of Utopia

    (B) human beings

    (C) men

    (D) women

    (E) minds

315. According to paragraph two, all of the following are reasons that the pursuit of delight obstructs happiness *except*:

    (A) it leaves no room for true pleasure

    (B) it provides a false notion of pleasure

    (C) it is the result of a foolish, though common, mistake

    (D) it entirely possesses the minds of those captivated

    (E) it is a result of us following Nature

316. The primary mode of composition of paragraph two is:

    (A) narration

    (B) description

    (C) process analysis

    (D) definition

    (E) compare and contrast

317. In context, the word "perverse" in line 29 most nearly means:

    (A) open to arguments

    (B) directed away from what is right or good

    (C) relating to a specific manner

    (D) lasting for eternity

    (E) deadly and destructive

318. Paragraph three is developed largely by the rhetorical strategy of:

(A) allusions
(B) anecdotes
(C) rhetorical questions
(D) hyperbole
(E) understatement

319. All of the following pairs are explored as opposites in the passage *except*:

(A) public and private
(B) mind and body
(C) true and false
(D) pursue and dispense
(E) perverse and forbidden

320. The passage as a whole most appeals to:

I. ethos
II. logos
III. pathos

(A) I
(B) II
(C) III
(D) II and III
(E) I, II, and III

Passage 7c: Thomas Hobbes, *Leviathan*

It is true, that certain living creatures, as Bees, and Ants, live sociably one with another, (which are therefore by Aristotle numbered amongst Political creatures;) and yet have no other direction, than their particular judgments and appetites; nor speech, whereby one of them can signify to another, what he thinks expedient for the common benefit: and therefore some man may perhaps desire to know, why   5
Man-kind cannot do the same. To which I answer,

First, that men are continually in competition for Honour and Dignity, which these creatures are not; and consequently amongst men there ariseth on that ground, Envy and Hatred, and finally Warre; but amongst these not so.

Secondly, that amongst these creatures, the Common good different not from   10
the Private; and being by nature inclined to their private, they procure thereby the common benefit. But man, whose Joy consisteth in comparing himselfe with other men, can relish nothing but what is eminent.

Thirdly, that these creatures, having not (as man) the use of reason, do not see, nor think they see any fault, in the administration of their common businesses: 15
whereas amongst men, there are very many, that think themselves wiser, and abler to govern the Publique, better than the rest; and these strive to reforme and inno-

vate, one this way, another that way; and thereby bring it into Distraction and
Civill warre.

Fourthly, that these creatures, though they have some use of voice, in making   20
knowne to one another their desires, and other affections; yet they want that art
of words, by which some men can represent to others, that which is Good, in the
likenesse of Evill; and Evill, in the likenesse of Good; and augment, or diminish
the apparent greatnesse of Good and Evill; discontenting men, and troubling their
Peace at their pleasure.   25

Fiftly, irrationall creatures cannot distinguish betweene Injury, and Dammage;
and therefore as long as they be at ease, they are not offended with their fellowes:
whereas Man is then most troublesome, when he is most at ease: for then it is that
he loves to shew his Wisdome, and controule the Actions of them that governe the
Common-wealth.   30

Lastly, the agreement of these creatures is Naturall; that of men, is by Covenant
only, which is Artificiall: and therefore it is no wonder if there be somewhat else
required (besides Covenant) to make their Agreement constant and lasting; which
is a Common Power, to keep them in awe, and to direct their actions to the Common Benefit.   35

321. According to the first paragraph of the passage, what does it mean that
mankind cannot "do the same"?
(A) mankind cannot live sociably one with another
(B) mankind cannot have direction
(C) mankind cannot be directed by his particular judgments and appetites
(D) mankind cannot signify to another
(E) mankind cannot speak what he feels expedient for the common
benefit

322. In context, the word "want" in line 21 most nearly means to:
(A) require
(B) desire
(C) request
(D) lack
(E) seek

323. The pronouns "their" and "their" in lines 24 and 25 refer to:
(A) men
(B) others
(C) creatures and men, respectively
(D) men and others, respectively
(E) others and men, respectively

324. In paragraph six, the statement "whereas Man is then most troublesome, when he is most at ease," can be described as:

(A) figurative
(B) ironic
(C) antithetical
(D) sarcastic
(E) facetious

325. The creatures capable of living sociably with one another are described as all of the following *except*:

(A) political
(B) ambitious
(C) irrational
(D) communicative
(E) at ease

326. The overall structure of the passage is accomplished by:

(A) chronological sequence
(B) enumeration
(C) general to specific
(D) specific to general
(E) brief to long

327. The primary mode of composition of the passage as a whole is:

(A) narration
(B) description
(C) comparison and contrast
(D) cause and effect
(E) process analysis

328. The structure and mode of the passage appeal mostly to:

I. ethos
II. logos
III. pathos

(A) I
(B) II
(C) III
(D) I and III
(E) I, II, and III

329. The overall purpose of the passage as a whole is to:
- (A) inform readers why men cannot live sociably with one another
- (B) argue that men are incapable of living sociably with one another
- (C) refute the argument that men can live sociably with one another
- (D) describe the ways in which men cannot live sociably with one another
- (E) entertain readers with narrative accounts of men not living sociably with one another

330. The tone of the passage as a whole can best be described as:
- (A) bantering
- (B) indifferent
- (C) patronizing
- (D) poignant
- (E) learned

Passage 7d: John Milton, *Areopagitica*

For books are as meats and viands are; some of good, some of evil substance; and yet God, in that unapocryphal vision, said without exception, RISE, PETER, KILL AND EAT, leaving the choice to each man's discretion. Wholesome meats to a vitiated stomach differ little or nothing from unwholesome; and best books to a naughty mind are not unappliable to occasions of evil. Bad meats will scarce   5
breed good nourishment in the healthiest concoction; but herein the difference is of bad books, that they to a discreet and judicious reader serve in many respects to discover, to confute, to forewarn, and to illustrate. Whereof what better witness can ye expect I should produce, than one of your own now sitting in Parliament, the chief of learned men reputed in this land, Mr. Selden; whose volume of natural and   10
national laws proves, not only by great authorities brought together, but by exquisite reasons and theorems almost mathematically demonstrative, that all opinions, yea errors, known, read, and collated, are of main service and assistance toward the speedy attainment of what is truest. I conceive, therefore, that when God did enlarge the universal diet of man's body, saving ever the rules of temperance, he   15
then also, as before, left arbitrary the dieting and repasting of our minds; as wherein every mature man might have to exercise his own leading capacity.

How great a virtue is temperance, how much of moment through the whole life of man! Yet God commits the managing so great a trust, without particular law or prescription, wholly to the demeanour of every grown man. And therefore when   20
he himself tabled the Jews from heaven, that omer, which was every man's daily portion of manna, is computed to have been more than might have well sufficed the heartiest feeder thrice as many meals. For those actions which enter into a man, rather than issue out of him, and therefore defile not, God uses not to captivate under a perpetual childhood of prescription, but trusts him with the gift of reason   25

to be his own chooser; there were but little work left for preaching, if law and com-
pulsion should grow so fast upon those things which heretofore were governed only
by exhortation. Solomon informs us, that much reading is a weariness to the flesh;
but neither he nor other inspired author tells us that such or such reading is unlawful: yet certainly had God thought good to limit us herein, it had been much more 30
expedient to have told us what was unlawful than what was wearisome. As for the
burning of those Ephesian books by St. Paul's converts; 'tis replied the books were
magic, the Syriac so renders them. It was a private act, a voluntary act, and leaves
us to a voluntary imitation: the men in remorse burnt those books which were
their own; the magistrate by this example is not appointed; these men practised 35
the books, another might perhaps have read them in some sort usefully. Good and
evil we know in the field of this world grow up together almost inseparably; and
the knowledge of good is so involved and interwoven with the knowledge of evil,
and in so many cunning resemblances hardly to be discerned, that those confused
seeds which were imposed upon Psyche as an incessant labour to cull out, and sort 40
asunder, were not more intermixed. It was from out the rind of one apple tasted,
that the knowledge of good and evil, as two twins cleaving together, leaped forth
into the world. And perhaps this is that doom which Adam fell into of knowing
good and evil, that is to say of knowing good by evil. As therefore the state of man
now is; what wisdom can there be to choose, what continence to forbear without 45
the knowledge of evil? He that can apprehend and consider vice with all her baits
and seeming pleasures, and yet abstain, and yet distinguish, and yet prefer that
which is truly better, he is the true warfaring Christian.

I cannot praise a fugitive and cloistered virtue, unexercised and unbreathed,
that never sallies out and sees her adversary but slinks out of the race, where that 50
immortal garland is to be run for, not without dust and heat. Assuredly we bring
not innocence into the world, we bring impurity much rather; that which puri-
fies us is trial, and trial is by what is contrary. That virtue therefore which is but a
youngling in the contemplation of evil, and knows not the utmost that vice promises to her followers, and rejects it, is but a blank virtue, not a pure; her whiteness is 55
but an excremental whiteness. Which was the reason why our sage and serious poet
Spenser, whom I dare be known to think a better teacher than Scotus or Aquinas,
describing true temperance under the person of Guion, brings him in with his
palmer through the cave of Mammon, and the bower of earthly bliss, that he might
see and know, and yet abstain. Since therefore the knowledge and survey of vice is 60
in this world so necessary to the constituting of human virtue, and the scanning of
error to the confirmation of truth, how can we more safely, and with less danger,
scout into the regions of sin and falsity than by reading all manner of tractates and
hearing all manner of reason? And this is the benefit which may be had of books
promiscuously read. 65

331. Paragraph one is developed by use of:

(A) syllogism
(B) analogy
(C) anecdote
(D) understatement
(E) expert testimony

332. According to the first paragraph, the difference between meats and books is that:

(A) some books are good and some are evil while all meat is good
(B) good meats are beneficial to a person while good books cannot help them
(C) God created us as omnivores so that we can eat all meats but has laws as to what we should read
(D) bad books and their errors can lead us to attaining the truth while bad meats cannot offer good nourishment
(E) all books (even the Bible) have questionable material, while some food is not completely wholesome

333. The thesis of the passage, provided at the end of paragraph one, is that:

(A) God created us as eaters with particular tastes and needs but expects us to be omnivorous in mind, reading all that is available to us
(B) God created us as omnivores in both body and mind and leads us to exercise our judgment in making choices
(C) God created us an omnivores in body but not in mind, expecting us to practice temperance
(D) God created us as omnivores in both body and mind, but we as people are not mature enough to follow the rules of temperance
(E) God created us as omnivores in body, expecting us to disregard the rules of temperance, and as omnivores in mind, expecting us to exercise our judgment

334. In discussing temperance, in the first statement of paragraph two, the tone can best be described as:

(A) cynical
(B) sarcastic
(C) fanciful
(D) laudatory
(E) perplexed

335. In context, the word "prescription" in line 25 most nearly means:

(A) a written order for the preparation and administration of medicine
(B) a medicine that is prescribed
(C) having rules set down
(D) a depiction
(E) a formal pronouncement

336. Paragraph three contains all of the following rhetorical techniques *except*:

(A) anaphora
(B) allusion
(C) simile
(D) personification
(E) rhetorical questions

337. Paragraph three primarily appeals to:

  I. ethos
 II. logos
III. pathos

(A) I
(B) II
(C) III
(D) I and III
(E) I, II, and III

338. The writer argues that he cannot praise a virtue that is all of the following *except*:

(A) fleeing
(B) secluded
(C) unused
(D) not living
(E) adversarial

339. The primary purpose of the passage as a whole is to:

(A) define temperance and illustrate its use
(B) argue against the censorship of books
(C) classify books as good or evil
(D) describe virtue in its proper form
(E) narrate the story of the eating from the Tree of Knowledge of Good and Evil

340. The style of the passage as a whole can best be described as:

    (A) complex and allusive
    (B) disjointed and abstract
    (C) terse and concrete
    (D) evocative and humorous
    (E) objective and unbiased

Passage 7e: Samuel Pepys, *Diary of Samuel Pepys*

[August 1665] 16th. Up, and after doing some necessary business about my accounts at home, to the office, and there with Mr. Hater wrote letters, and I did deliver to him my last will, one part of it to deliver to my wife when I am dead. Thence to the Exchange, where I have not been a great while. But, Lord! how sad a sight it is to see the streets empty of people, and very few upon the 'Change. 5 Jealous of every door that one sees shut up, lest it should be the plague; and about us two shops in three, if not more, generally shut up. From the 'Change to Sir G. Smith's with Mr. Fenn, to whom I am nowadays very complaisant, he being under payment of my bills to me, and some other sums at my desire, which he readily do. Mighty merry with Captain Cocke and Fenn at Sir G. Smith's, and 10 a brave dinner, but I think Cocke is the greatest epicure that is, eats and drinks with the greatest pleasure and liberty that ever man did. Very contrary newes to-day upon the 'Change, some that our fleete hath taken some of the Dutch East India ships, others that we did attaque it at Bergen and were repulsed, others that our fleete is in great danger after this attaque by meeting with the great body now 15 gone out of Holland, almost 100 sayle of men of warr. Every body is at a great losse and nobody can tell. Thence among the goldsmiths to get some money, and so home, settling some new money matters, and to my great joy have got home L500 more of the money due to me, and got some more money to help Andrews first advanced. This day I had the ill news from Dagenhams, that my poor lord of 20 Hinchingbroke his indisposition is turned to the small-pox. Poor gentleman! that he should be come from France so soon to fall sick, and of that disease too, when he should be gone to see a fine lady, his mistresse. I am most heartily sorry for it. So late setting papers to rights, and so home to bed.

    17th. Up and to the office, where we sat all the morning, and at noon dined 25 together upon some victuals I had prepared at Sir W. Batten's upon the King's charge, and after dinner, I having dispatched some business and set things in order at home, we down to the water and by boat to Greenwich to the Bezan yacht, where Sir W. Batten, Sir J. Minnes, my Lord Bruneker and myself, with some servants (among others Mr. Carcasse, my Lord's clerk, a very civil gentleman), 30 embarked in the yacht and down we went most pleasantly, and noble discourse I had with my Lord Bruneker, who is a most excellent person. Short of Gravesend it grew calme, and so we come to an anchor, and to supper mighty merry, and after it, being moonshine, we out of the cabbin to laugh and talk, and then, as we grew sleepy, went in and upon velvet cushions of the King's that belong to the yacht 35 fell to sleep, which we all did pretty well till 3 or 4 of the clock, having risen in the night to look for a new comet which is said to have lately shone, but we could see no such thing.

18th. Up about 5 o'clock and dressed ourselves, and to sayle again down to the Soveraigne at the buoy of the *Nore*, a noble ship, now rigged and fitted and 40 manned; we did not stay long, but to enquire after her readinesse and thence to Sheernesse, where we walked up and down, laying out the ground to be taken in for a yard to lay provisions for cleaning and repairing of ships, and a most proper place it is for the purpose. Thence with great pleasure up the Meadeway, our yacht contending with Commissioner Pett's, wherein he met us from Chatham, and he 45 had the best of it. Here I come by, but had not tide enough to stop at Quinbrough, a with mighty pleasure spent the day in doing all and seeing these places, which I had never done before. So to the Hill house at Chatham and there dined, and after dinner spent some time discoursing of business. Among others arguing with the Commissioner about his proposing the laying out so much money upon Sheere- 50 nesse, unless it be to the slighting of Chatham yarde, for it is much a better place than Chatham, which however the King is not at present in purse to do, though it were to be wished he were. Thence in Commissioner Pett's coach (leaving them there). I late in the darke to Gravesend, where great is the plague, and I troubled to stay there so long for the tide. At 10 at night, having supped, I took boat alone, 55 and slept well all the way to the Tower docke about three o'clock in the morning. So knocked up my people, and to bed.

341. In the beginning of the first paragraph (August 16th diary entry), the phrase "But, Lord!" is an example of:

(A) an absolute phrase
(B) a prepositional phrase
(C) an appositive
(D) an exclamation
(E) a conjunction

342. The line "Jealous of every door that one sees shut up, lest it should be the plague" is the following type of sentence:

(A) sentence fragment
(B) simple sentence
(C) imperative sentence
(D) interrogative sentence
(E) cumulative sentence

343. The phrase "mighty merry" in the sentence "Mighty merry with Captain Cocke and Fenn at Sir G. Smith's, and a brave dinner, but I think Cocke is the greatest epicure that is, eats and drinks with the greatest pleasure and liberty that ever man did" is an example of:

(A) allusion
(B) metonymy
(C) synecdoche
(D) alliteration
(E) assonance

344. The portion of the sentence that reads, "but I think Cocke is the greatest epicure that is, eats and drinks with the greatest pleasure and liberty that ever man did" from the same sentence just cited is an example of:

(A) litlotes
(B) hyperbole
(C) anaphora
(D) epistrophe
(E) symbolism

345. In context, the word "repulsed" in line 14 most nearly means:

(A) rejected
(B) rebuffed
(C) disgusted
(D) refused
(E) repelled

346. According to the details provided in the first paragraph (August 16th), the occasion for this diary entry is which of the following:

  I. war
  II. plague
  III. personal turmoil

(A) I
(B) II
(C) III
(D) I and II
(E) I, II, and III

347. In the diary entry for August 17th, the tone of the line "embarked in the yacht and down we went most pleasantly, and noble discourse I had with my Lord Bruneker, who is a most excellent person" can best be described as:

(A) compassionate
(B) complimentary
(C) conciliatory
(D) confident
(E) comic

348. In describing a noble ship as "now rigged and fitted and manned," the writer uses:

(A) anaphora
(B) epistrophe
(C) asyndeton
(D) polysyndeton
(E) antithesis

349. In line 41, the pronoun "her" refers to:

(A) ourselves
(B) the Nore
(C) the Soveraigne
(D) the buoy
(E) Sheernesse

350. The primary mode of composition of the passage as a whole is:

(A) narration
(B) description
(C) classification
(D) definition
(E) argument

CHAPTER 8

18th Century

Passage 8a: Edward Gibbon, *The History of the Decline and Fall of the Roman Empire*

After a diligent inquiry, I can discern four principal causes of the ruin of Rome, which continued to operate in a period of more than a thousand years. I. The injuries of time and nature. II. The hostile attacks of the Barbarians and Christians. III. The use and abuse of the materials. And, IV. The domestic quarrels of the Romans.

    I. The art of man is able to construct monuments far more permanent than the narrow span of his own existence; yet these monuments, like himself, are perishable and frail; and in the boundless annals of time, his life and his labors must equally be measured as a fleeting moment. Of a simple and solid edifice, it is not easy, however, to circumscribe the duration. As the wonders of ancient days, the pyramids[9] attracted the curiosity of the ancients: a hundred generations, the leaves of autumn, have dropped[10] into the grave; and after the fall of the Pharaohs and Ptolemies, the Cæsars and caliphs, the same pyramids stand erect and unshaken above the floods of the Nile. A complex figure of various and minute parts to more accessible to injury and decay; and the silent lapse of time is often accelerated by hurricanes and earthquakes, by fires and inundations. The air and earth have doubtless been shaken; and the lofty turrets of Rome have tottered from their foundations; but the seven hills do not appear to be placed on the great cavities of the globe; nor has the city, in any age, been exposed to the convulsions of nature, which, in the climate of Antioch, Lisbon, or Lima, have crumbled in a few moments the works of ages into dust. Fire is the most powerful agent of life and death: the rapid mischief may be kindled and propagated by the industry or negligence of mankind; and every period of the Roman annals is marked by the repetition of similar calamities. A memorable conflagration, the guilt or misfortune of Nero's reign, continued, though with

9. [The age of the pyramids is remote and unknown, since Diodorus Siculus (tom. i l. i. c. 44, p. 72) is unable to decide whether they were constructed 1000, or 3400, years before the clxxxth Olympiad. Sir John Marsham's contracted scale of the Egyptian dynasties would fix them about 2000 years before Christ, (Canon. *Chronicus*, p. 47.)]

10. [See the speech of Glaucus in the *Iliad*, (Z. 146.) This natural but melancholy image is peculiar to Homer.]

unequal fury, either six or nine days.[11] Innumerable buildings, crowded in close and crooked streets, supplied perpetual fuel for the flames; and when they ceased, four only of the fourteen regions were left entire; three were totally destroyed, and seven were deformed by the relics of smoking and lacerated edifices.[12] In the full meridian of empire, the metropolis arose with fresh beauty from her ashes; yet the memory of the old deplored their irreparable losses, the arts of Greece, the trophies of victory, the monuments of primitive or fabulous antiquity. In the days of distress and anarchy, every wound is mortal, every fall irretrievable; nor can the damage be restored either by the public care of government, or the activity of private interest. Yet two causes may be alleged, which render the calamity of fire more destructive to a flourishing than a decayed city. 1. The more combustible materials of brick, timber, and metals, are first melted or consumed; but the flames may play without injury or effect on the naked walls, and massy arches, that have been despoiled of their ornaments. 2. It is among the common and plebeian habitations, that a mischievous spark is most easily blown to a conflagration; but as soon as they are devoured, the greater edifices, which have resisted or escaped, are left as so many islands in a state of solitude and safety.

351. The first paragraph of the passage is structured by:

    (A) minor causes to major causes
    (B) chronological sequence
    (C) specific to general
    (D) general to specific
    (E) enumeration

352. The paradox of the first sentence of paragraph two is that the art of man is:

    (A) more permanent than his life span
    (B) both more permanent and fleeting
    (C) both perishable and frail
    (D) measured as a fleeting moment
    (E) like himself

---

11. [The learning and criticism of M. des Vignoles (*Histoire Critique de la République des Lettres*, tom. viii. p. 47–118, ix. p. 172–187) dates the fire of Rome from July 19, A.D. 64, and the subsequent persecution of the Christians from November 15 of the same year.]

12. [Quippe in regiones quatuordecim Roma dividitur, quarum quatuor integræ manebant, tres solo tenus dejectæ: septem reliquis pauca testorum vestigia supererant, lacera et semiusta. Among the old relics that were irreparably lost, Tacitus enumerates the temple of the moon of Servius Tullius; the fane and altar consecrated by Evander præsenti Herculi; the temple of Jupiter Stator, a vow of Romulus; the palace of Numa; the temple of Vesta cum Penatibus populi Romani. He then deplores the opes tot victoriis quæsitæ et Græcarum artium decora . . . multa quæ seniores meminerant, quæ reparari nequibant, (*Annal.* xv. 40, 41.)]

353. The purpose of footnote 9 is to:

(A) elaborate on the unknown age of the pyramids
(B) cite Diodorus Siculus
(C) cite Sir John Marsham
(D) argue that the pyramids were constructed 1,000 or 3,400 years before the clxxxth Olympiad
(E) argue that the pyramids were constructed 2,000 years before Christ

354. The discussion of the pyramids is provided as an example of:

(A) permanent monuments
(B) perishable monuments
(C) unknown duration of edifices
(D) wonders of ancient days
(E) curiosity of the ancients

355. The purpose of footnote 10 is to:

(A) cite Glaucus's speech
(B) cite the *Iliad*
(C) cite Homer
(D) cite a direct quotation on page 146
(E) elaborate on the image of the leaves and its allusiveness

356. In context, the word "propagated" in line 21 most nearly means:

(A) spread
(B) caused to multiply
(C) bred
(D) transmitted
(E) made widely known

357. The purpose of footnote 11 is all of the following *except* to:

(A) provide the date of the Roman fire as July 19, A.D. 64
(B) provide the date of the Roman fire as November 15, A.D. 64
(C) provide the author of *Histoire Critique de la République des Lettres* as M. des Vignoles
(D) cite the page ranges of 47 to 118 and 172 to 187
(E) provide the writer's source of information on the major fire during Nero's reign

358. The purpose of footnote 12 is all of the following *except* to:
  (A) provide in Latin the account of the devastation of the fire
  (B) list in English the old relics that were irreparably lost
  (C) cite passages from the *Annal*
  (D) cite passages from *Histoire Critique de la République des Lettres*
  (E) cite passages on pages 40 and 41

359. The final portion of text in the passage (before the footnotes), beginning with "In the full meridian of empire" and ending with "are left as so many islands in a state of solitude and safety," uses all of the following rhetorical techniques *except*:
  (A) personification
  (B) asyndeton
  (C) enumeration
  (D) apostrophe
  (E) alliteration

360. The primary mode of composition of the passage as a whole is:
  (A) narration
  (B) description
  (C) cause and effect
  (D) definition
  (E) classification

Passage 8b: Samuel Johnson, *Preface to a Dictionary of the English Language*

It is the fate of those who toil at the lower employments of life, to be rather driven by the fear of evil, than attracted by the prospect of good; to be exposed to censure, without hope of praise; to be disgraced by miscarriage, or punished for neglect, where success would have been without applause, and diligence without reward.

Among these unhappy mortals is the writer of dictionaries; whom mankind   5
have considered, not as the pupil, but the slave of science, the pionier of literature, doomed only to remove rubbish and clear obstructions from the paths through which Learning and Genius press forward to conquest and glory, without bestowing a smile on the humble drudge that facilitates their progress. Every other author may aspire to praise; the lexicographer can only hope to escape reproach, and even   10
this negative recompense has been yet granted to very few.

I have, notwithstanding this discouragement, attempted a dictionary of the English language, which, while it was employed in the cultivation of every species of literature, has itself been hitherto neglected; suffered to spread, under the direc-

tion of chance, into wild exuberance; resigned to the tyranny of time and fashion; 15
and exposed to the corruptions of ignorance, and caprices of innovation.

When I took the first survey of my undertaking, I found our speech copious
without order, and energetick without rules: wherever I turned my view, there was
perplexity to be disentangled, and confusion to be regulated; choice was to be made
out of boundless variety, without any established principle of selection; adultera- 20
tions were to be detected, without a settled test of purity; and modes of expression
to be rejected or received, without the suffrages of any writers of classical reputation
or acknowledged authority.

Having therefore no assistance but from general grammar, I applied myself
to the perusal of our writers; and noting whatever might be of use to ascertain or 25
illustrate any word or phrase, accumulated in time the materials of a dictionary,
which, by degrees, I reduced to method, establishing to myself, in the progress of
the work, such rules as experience and analogy suggested to me; experience, which
practice and observation were continually increasing; and analogy, which, though
in some words obscure, was evident in others. 30

In adjusting the ORTHOGRAPHY, which has been to this time unsettled and
fortuitous, I found it necessary to distinguish those irregularities that are inherent
in our tongue, and perhaps coeval with it, from others which the ignorance or
negligence of later writers has produced. Every language has its anomalies, which,
though inconvenient, and in themselves once unnecessary, must be tolerated 35
among the imperfections of human things, and which require only to be registered,
that they may not be increased, and ascertained, that they may not be confounded:
but every language has likewise its improprieties and absurdities, which it is the
duty of the lexicographer to correct or proscribe.

As language was at its beginning merely oral, all words of necessary or common 40
use were spoken before they were written; and while they were unfixed by any visible signs, must have been spoken with great diversity, as we now observe those
who cannot read catch sounds imperfectly, and utter them negligently. When this
wild and barbarous jargon was first reduced to an alphabet, every penman endeav-
oured to express, as he could, the sounds which he was accustomed to pronounce 45
or to receive, and vitiated in writing such words as were already vitiated in speech.
The powers of the letters, when they were applied to a new language, must have
been vague and unsettled, and therefore different hands would exhibit the same
sound by different combinations.

361. The first sentence of the passage uses:
- (A) anaphora
- (B) epistrophe
- (C) alliteration
- (D) allusion
- (E) personification

362. In the line "doomed only to remove rubbish and clear obstructions from the paths through which Learning and Genius press forward to conquest and glory, without bestowing a smile on the humble drudge that facilitates their progress," the primary form of figurative language is:

(A) simile
(B) metaphor
(C) personification
(D) metonymy
(E) synecdoche

363. The first two paragraphs are structured by:

(A) specific to general
(B) general to specific
(C) enumeration
(D) chronological sequence
(E) flashback

364. In paragraphs one and two, the job of being a writer of dictionaries is primarily characterized as being:

(A) easy
(B) ambitious
(C) thankless
(D) difficult
(E) honorable

365. In paragraph four, our speech is described using:

(A) sensory imagery
(B) parallel structure
(C) allusion
(D) colloquialisms
(E) jargon

366. The primary mode of composition of paragraph five is:

(A) narration
(B) description
(C) classification
(D) argument
(E) process analysis

367. In context, the word "fortuitous" in line 32 most nearly means:

    (A) occurring by having good fortune

    (B) strengthened and secured

    (C) happening by accident

    (D) capable of forming

    (E) expressed systematically

368. The tone of the sentence "Every language has its anomalies, which, though inconvenient, and in themselves once unnecessary, must be tolerated among the imperfections of human things, and which require only to be registered, that they may not be increased, and ascertained, that they may not be confounded: but every language has likewise its improprieties and absurdities, which it is the duty of the lexicographer to correct or proscribe" can best be described as:

    (A) incredulous

    (B) resigned

    (C) outraged

    (D) irreverent

    (E) bitter

369. "Visible signs" in lines 41 and 42 refer to:

    (A) letters

    (B) words

    (C) sounds

    (D) jargon

    (E) hands

370. The primary purpose of the last paragraph of the passage is to:

    (A) argue for the necessity of having standard spelling

    (B) narrate the history of the English language

    (C) justify the writer's decision to write this English dictionary

    (D) analyze the causes of different spellings in English

    (E) describe the writer's process of arriving at standardized spellings of words

Passage 8c: John Locke, *Second Treatise on Government*

Sect. 22. THE *natural liberty* of man is to be free from any superior power on earth, and not to be under the will or legislative authority of man, but to have only the law of nature for his rule. The liberty of man, in society, is to be under no other legislative power, but that established, by consent, in the commonwealth; nor

under the dominion of any will, or restraint of any law, but what that legislative 5
shall enact, according to the trust put in it. Freedom then is not what *Sir Robert Filmer* tells us, *Observations, A. 55. a liberty for every one to do what he lists, to live as he pleases, and not to be tied by any laws*: but *freedom of men under government* is, to have a standing rule to live by, common to every one of that society, and made by the legislative power erected in it; a liberty to follow my own will in all things, 10
where the rule prescribes not; and not to be subject to the inconstant, uncertain, unknown, arbitrary will of another man: as *freedom of nature* is, to be under no other restraint but the law of nature.

Sect. 23. This *freedom* from absolute, arbitrary power, is so necessary to, and closely joined with a man's preservation, that he cannot part with it, but by what 15
forfeits his preservation and life together: for a man, not having the power of his own life, *cannot*, by compact, or his own consent, *enslave himself* to any one, nor put himself under the absolute, arbitrary power of another, to take away his life, when he pleases. No body can give more power than he has himself; and he that cannot take away his own life, cannot give another power over it. Indeed, having by 20
his fault forfeited his own life, by some act that deserves death; he, to whom he has forfeited it, may (when he has him in his power) delay to take it, and make use of him to his own service, and he does him no injury by it: for, whenever he finds the hardship of his slavery outweigh the value of his life, it is in his power, by resisting the will of his master, to draw on himself the death he desires. 25

Sect. 24. This is the perfect condition of *slavery*, which is nothing else, but *the state of war continued, between a lawful conqueror and a captive*: for, if once *compact* enter between them, and make an agreement for a limited power on the one side, and obedience on the other, the *state of war and slavery ceases*, as long as the compact endures: for, as has been said, no man can, by agreement, pass over to another 30
that which he hath not in himself, a power over his own life.

I confess, we find among the *Jews*, as well as other nations, that men did sell themselves; but, it is plain, this was only to *drudgery, not to slavery*: for, it is evident, the person sold was not under an absolute, arbitrary, despotical power: for the master could not have power to kill him, at any time, whom, at a certain time, he 35
was obliged to let go free out of his service; and the master of such a servant was so far from having an arbitrary power over his life, that he could not, at pleasure, so much as maim him, but the loss of an eye, or tooth, set him free, *Exod*. xxi.

371. The primary mode of composition of paragraph one is:

(A) narration
(B) description
(C) cause and effect
(D) definition
(E) process analysis

372. Paragraph one relies on the following type of evidence:
- (A) anecdote
- (B) statistics
- (C) expert testimony
- (D) direct quotation
- (E) observation

373. The evidence provided in paragraph one is used as:
- (A) the major claim
- (B) a warrant
- (C) a counterargument
- (D) a rebuttal
- (E) a qualification

374. To mirror the overwhelming will of another man on a man's freedom, the writer uses the following rhetorical strategy in the line "and not to be subject to the inconstant, uncertain, unknown, arbitrary will of another man":
- (A) asyndeton
- (B) polysyndeton
- (C) syntax inversion
- (D) anaphora
- (E) epistrophe

375. In context, the first use of the word "arbitrary" in line 12 most nearly means:
- (A) belonging to an earlier time
- (B) determined by impulse
- (C) known to only a few
- (D) having the power to judge
- (E) strenuous and difficult

376. In context, the second and third uses of the word "arbitrary" in lines 14 and 18 most nearly mean:
- (A) inherited
- (B) usurped
- (C) without substance
- (D) not limited by law
- (E) fleeting

377. The following claim of paragraph two is ironic:

(A) a man without power cannot enslave himself to another

(B) a man who is frustrated with the hardship of slavery can bring about his own death

(C) a man who has the power of another man may delay taking his life

(D) a man's preservation is dependent upon his freedom

(E) a man cannot give more power than he has

378. Paragraph three defines the following term:

(A) slavery

(B) war

(C) conqueror

(D) captive

(E) compact

379. The primary purpose of the last paragraph is to provide:

(A) an example of the claims made in paragraphs two and three

(B) a justification of the writer's decision to write this treatise

(C) an exception to the claims made in paragraphs two and three

(D) a narration of the story of one slave-master relationship

(E) a description of the conditions of slavery

380. The italicized word, "*Exod.* xxi," at the end of the passage inform the readers that the content of paragraph four is:

(A) historical research

(B) mythological allusion

(C) biblical reference

(D) personal observation

(E) dictionary citation

Passage 8d: Jonathan Swift, *A Modest Proposal*

It is a melancholy object to those, who walk through this great town, or travel in the country, when they see the streets, the roads and cabbin-doors crowded with beggars of the female sex, followed by three, four, or six children, all in rags, and importuning every passenger for an alms. These mothers instead of being able to work for their honest livelihood, are forced to employ all their time in stroling to beg sustenance for their helpless infants who, as they grow up, either turn thieves for want of work, or leave their dear native country, to fight for the Pretender in Spain, or sell themselves to the Barbadoes.

I think it is agreed by all parties, that this prodigious number of children in the arms, or on the backs, or at the heels of their mothers, and frequently of their fathers, is in the present deplorable state of the kingdom, a very great additional grievance; and therefore whoever could find out a fair, cheap and easy method of making these children sound and useful members of the common-wealth, would deserve so well of the publick, as to have his statue set up for a preserver of the nation.

But my intention is very far from being confined to provide only for the children of professed beggars: it is of a much greater extent, and shall take in the whole number of infants at a certain age, who are born of parents in effect as little able to support them, as those who demand our charity in the streets.

As to my own part, having turned my thoughts for many years, upon this important subject, and maturely weighed the several schemes of our projectors, I have always found them grossly mistaken in their computation. It is true, a child just dropt from its dam, may be supported by her milk, for a solar year, with little other nourishment: at most not above the value of two shillings, which the mother may certainly get, or the value in scraps, by her lawful occupation of begging; and it is exactly at one year old that I propose to provide for them in such a manner, as, instead of being a charge upon their parents, or the parish, or wanting food and raiment for the rest of their lives, they shall, on the contrary, contribute to the feeding, and partly to the cloathing of many thousands.

There is likewise another great advantage in my scheme, that it will prevent those voluntary abortions, and that horrid practice of women murdering their bastard children, alas! too frequent among us, sacrificing the poor innocent babes, I doubt, more to avoid the expence than the shame, which would move tears and pity in the most savage and inhuman breast.

The number of souls in this kingdom being usually reckoned one million and a half, of these I calculate there may be about two hundred thousand couple whose wives are breeders; from which number I subtract thirty thousand couple, who are able to maintain their own children, (although I apprehend there cannot be so many, under the present distresses of the kingdom) but this being granted, there will remain an hundred and seventy thousand breeders. I again subtract fifty thousand, for those women who miscarry, or whose children die by accident or disease within the year. There only remain an hundred and twenty thousand children of poor parents annually born. The question therefore is, How this number shall be reared, and provided for? which, as I have already said, under the present situation of affairs, is utterly impossible by all the methods hitherto proposed. For we can neither employ them in handicraft or agriculture; we neither build houses, (I mean in the country) nor cultivate land: they can very seldom pick up a livelihood by stealing till they arrive at six years old; except where they are of towardly parts, although I confess they learn the rudiments much earlier; during which time they can however be properly looked upon only as probationers: As I have been informed by a principal gentleman in the county of Cavan, who protested to me, that he never knew above one or two instances under the age of six, even in a part of the kingdom so renowned for the quickest proficiency in that art.

I am assured by our merchants, that a boy or a girl before twelve years old, is no saleable commodity, and even when they come to this age, they will not yield above three pounds, or three pounds and half a crown at most, on the exchange; which cannot turn to account either to the parents or kingdom, the charge of nutriments and rags having been at least four times that value. 55

I shall now therefore humbly propose my own thoughts, which I hope will not be liable to the least objection.

I have been assured by a very knowing American of my acquaintance in London, that a young healthy child well nursed, is, at a year old, a most delicious nourishing and wholesome food, whether stewed, roasted, baked, or boiled; and I make no doubt that it will equally serve in a fricasie, or a ragout. 60

381. According to the first paragraph, the chief occasion for writing this piece is:

 (A) that the overwhelming number of poor children begging with their mothers makes observers sad
 (B) that mothers are asking for help in finding better employment
 (C) that policy makers are trying to deter children from a life of crime
 (D) that the Spanish government is seeking children to join their ranks
 (E) that "Barbadoes" is seeking more poor children for its slave trade

382. According to the speaker, the primary purpose of the passage is to:

 (A) convince mothers to stop having children that they cannot care for
 (B) propose a practical solution to the problem of too many poor children
 (C) bring attention to and argue against voluntary abortion
 (D) persuade policy makers to intervene from allowing children to fall into criminal activity
 (E) refute the argument that poor children are not deserving of our charity

383. All of the following descriptions are disparaging toward women *except*:

 (A) "beggars of the female sex"
 (B) "a child just dropt from its dam"
 (C) "may be supported by her milk"
 (D) "that horrid practice of women murdering their bastard children"
 (E) "whose wives are breeders"

384. The primary appeal of paragraph six is:
    I. ethos
    II. logos
    III. pathos

    (A) I
    (B) II
    (C) III
    (D) I and III
    (E) I, II, and III

385. In context, the word "towardly" in line 47 most nearly means:

    (A) dangerous
    (B) pleasant
    (C) advantageous
    (D) fearful
    (E) brazen

386. The speaker of the passage finally proposes:

    (A) employing children in handicraft or agriculture
    (B) building houses in the country for the children
    (C) teaching children to steal
    (D) selling the children into slavery
    (E) cooking and eating the children

387. The tone of the passage as a whole can best be described as:

    (A) blustery
    (B) cynical
    (C) idealistic
    (D) pragmatic
    (E) solemn

388. The passage as a whole can best be described as a:

    (A) polemic
    (B) tirade
    (C) appeal
    (D) satire
    (E) anecdote

389. Different from the speaker's stated purpose, the author's actual purpose is to:

   (A) use humor to bring attention to the very serious problem of poverty
   (B) have the public consider the real benefits of eating children
   (C) convince mothers that they are responsible for taking care of their children
   (D) make fathers feel guilt and finally take responsibility
   (E) scare children into wising up about the dangerous paths that could lay before them

390. The eighth paragraph, which is one sentence that reads, "I shall now therefore humbly propose my own thoughts, which I hope will not be liable to the least objection," is an example of:

   (A) hyperbole
   (B) understatement
   (C) allusion
   (D) figurative language
   (E) concrete diction

Passage 8e: Richard Steele, *The Tatler*

A gentleman has writ to me out of the country a very civil letter, and said things which I suppress with great violence to my vanity. There are many terms in my narratives which he complains want explaining, and has therefore desired, that, for the benefit of my country readers, I would let him know what I mean by a Gentleman, a Pretty Fellow, a Toast, a Coquette, a Critic, a Wit, and all other appellations in   5
the gayer world, who are in present possession of these several characters; together with an account of those who unfortunately pretend to them. I shall begin with him we usually call a Gentleman, or man of conversation.

   It is generally thought, that warmth of imagination, quick relish of pleasure, and a manner of becoming it, are the most essential qualities for forming this sort   10
of man. But any one that is much in company will observe, that the height of good breeding is shown rather in never giving offence, than in doing obliging things. Thus, he that never shocks you, though he is seldom entertaining, is more likely to keep your favour, than he who often entertains, and sometimes displeases you. The most necessary talent therefore in a man of conversation, which is what we ordinar-   15
ily intend by a fine gentleman, is a good judgment. He that has this in perfection, is master of his companion, without letting him see it; and has the same advantage over men of any other qualifications whatsoever, as one that can see would have over a blind man of ten times his strength.

   This is what makes Sophronius the darling of all who converse with him, and   20
the most powerful with his acquaintance of any man in town. By the light of this

faculty, he acts with great ease and freedom among the men of pleasure, and acquits himself with skill and despatch among the men of business. This he performs with so much success, that, with as much discretion in life as any man ever had, he nei- ther is, nor appears, cunning. But as he does a good office, if he ever does it, with 25 readiness and alacrity; so he denies what he does not care to engage in, in a manner that convinces you, that you ought not to have asked it. His judgment is so good and unerring, and accompanied with so cheerful a spirit, that his conversation is a continual feast, at which he helps some, and is helped by others, in such a manner, that the equality of society is perfectly kept up, and every man obliges as much as 30 he is obliged: for it is the greatest and justest skill in a man of superior understand- ing, to know how to be on a level with his companions. This sweet disposition runs through all the actions of Sophronius, and makes his company desired by women, without being envied by men. Sophronius would be as just as he is, if there were no law; and would be as discreet as he is, if there were no such thing as calumny. 35

In imitation of this agreeable being, is made that animal we call a Pretty Fel- low; who being just able to find out, that what makes Sophronius acceptable, is a natural behaviour; in order to the same reputation, makes his own an artificial one. Jack Dimple is his perfect mimic, whereby he is of course the most unlike him of all men living. Sophronius just now passed into the inner room directly forward: 40 Jack comes as fast after as he can for the right and left looking-glass, in which he had but just approved himself by a nod at each, and marched on. He will meditate within for half an hour, till he thinks he is not careless enough in his air, and come back to the mirror to recollect his forgetfulness.

391. The occasion of the passage is:
- (A) a public outcry for clarification
- (B) a letter written by a reader asking for explanation of terms used by the writer
- (C) a letter written by a reader praising the writer of the passage
- (D) a public notice in a competing paper arguing against the writer's views
- (E) a request by the publisher for the writer to be clearer in his writing

392. The intended audience for the passage is:
- (A) country readers
- (B) city readers
- (C) critics
- (D) gentlemen
- (E) pretty fellows

393. In context, the word "appellations" in line 5 most nearly means:

(A) identifying names
(B) nicknames
(C) careers
(D) types of men
(E) country personalities

394. According to the second paragraph, the most important characteristic of a gentleman is:

(A) being consistently entertaining
(B) being inoffensive
(C) being strong
(D) being imaginative
(E) being of good breeding

395. Sophronius is provided in the passage as an example of:

(A) a poor substitute for a Gentleman
(B) a Gentleman
(C) a Pretty Fellow
(D) a Critic
(E) a Wit

396. In context, the word "office" in line 25 most nearly means:

(A) a building in which business is carried out
(B) a building in which medicine is practiced
(C) a function or duty assumed by someone
(D) a public position
(E) a position of authority given to someone

397. The description of Sophronius's conversation as "a continual feast" is an example of:

(A) a simile
(B) personification
(C) sensory imagery
(D) alliteration
(E) metaphor

398. Jack Dimple is provided in the passage as an example of:

  (A) a Gentleman
  (B) a Pretty Fellow
  (C) a Toast
  (D) a Critic
  (E) a Wit

399. The Gentleman is also referred to as:

  I. a man of conversation
  II. an agreeable being
  III. a perfect mimic

  (A) I
  (B) II
  (C) III
  (D) I and II
  (E) I, II, and III

400. The primary mode of composition of the passage is:

  (A) narration
  (B) description
  (C) cause and effect
  (D) definition
  (E) process analysis

CHAPTER 9

19th Century

Passage 9a: Samuel Taylor Coleridge, *Biographia Literaria*

My own conclusions on the nature of poetry, in the strictest use of the word, have been in part anticipated in some of the remarks on the Fancy and Imagination in the early part of this work. What is poetry?—is so nearly the same question with, what is a poet?—that the answer to the one is involved in the solution of the other. For it is a distinction resulting from the poetic genius itself, which sustains and 5 modifies the images, thoughts, and emotions of the poet's own mind.

The poet, described in ideal perfection, brings the whole soul of man into activity, with the subordination of its faculties to each other according to their relative worth and dignity. He diffuses a tone and spirit of unity, that blends, and (as it were) fuses, each into each, by that synthetic and magical power, to which 10 I would exclusively appropriate the name of Imagination. This power, first put in action by the will and understanding, and retained under their irremissive, though gentle and unnoticed, control, laxis effertur habenis, reveals "itself in the balance or reconcilement of opposite or discordant" qualities: of sameness, with difference; of the general with the concrete; the idea with the image; the individual with the 15 representative; the sense of novelty and freshness with old and familiar objects; a more than usual state of emotion with more than usual order; judgment ever awake and steady self-possession with enthusiasm and feeling profound or vehement; and while it blends and harmonizes the natural and the artificial, still subordinates art to nature; the manner to the matter; and our admiration of the poet to our sympa- 20 thy with the poetry. Doubtless, as Sir John Davies observes of the soul—(and his words may with slight alteration be applied, and even more appropriately, to the poetic Imagination)—

Doubtless this could not be, but that she turns
Bodies to spirit by sublimation strange,   25
As fire converts to fire the things it burns,
As we our food into our nature change.

From their gross matter she abstracts their forms,
And draws a kind of quintessence from things;
Which to her proper nature she transforms   30
To bear them light on her celestial wings.

Thus does she, when from individual states
She doth abstract the universal kinds;
Which then re-clothed in divers names and fates
Steal access through the senses to our minds.   35

Finally, Good Sense is the Body of poetic genius, Fancy its Drapery, Motion its Life, and Imagination the Soul that is everywhere, and in each; and forms all into one graceful and intelligent whole.

401. The primary mode of composition of the passage is:
(A) narration
(B) description
(C) cause and effect
(D) definition
(E) process analysis

402. The chief rhetorical strategy in the first paragraph is:
(A) imagery
(B) parallel structure
(C) rhetorical questions
(D) syntax inversion
(E) concrete diction

403. In context, the word "subordination" in line 8 most nearly means:
(A) the treatment of something as less valuable or important
(B) the treatment of something as more valuable or important
(C) the treatment of something as unnecessary or redundant
(D) the treatment of something as exceeding expectations
(E) the treatment of something as equal with another thing

404. According to paragraph two, the poet does the following:
   I. brings the soul to life
  II. separates the different abilities of the soul
 III. brings together the different abilities of the soul
(A) I
(B) II
(C) III
(D) I and II
(E) I, II, and III

405. Imagination is defined as:

(A) ideal perfection
(B) a tone and spirit of unity
(C) synthetic and magical power
(D) will and understanding
(E) the balance or reconcilement of opposite or discordant qualities

406. All of the following pairs are represented as opposites *except*:

(A) sameness and difference
(B) the general and the concrete
(C) the idea and the image
(D) the individual and the representative
(E) novelty and freshness

407. Which of the following is (or are) more valued than its (or their) counterpart(s)?

   I. art
  II. nature
 III. manner

(A) I
(B) II
(C) III
(D) I and III
(E) I, II, and III

408. The poem quoted in the passage uses all of the following literary techniques *except*:

(A) personification
(B) imagery
(C) simile
(D) rhyme scheme
(E) apostrophe

409. The writer of the passage uses the poem to:

(A) define the nature of poetry
(B) characterize imagination
(C) display the poet's perfection
(D) describe the difference between fancy and imagination
(E) explore the soul

410. The last paragraph of the passage relies on the following rhetorical technique to make its claims about poetic genius:

(A) figurative language
(B) syllogism
(C) allusion
(D) varied sentence structure
(E) colloquial diction

Passage 9b: John Henry Newman, *Private Judgment*

There is this obvious, undeniable difficulty in the attempt to form a theory of Private Judgment, in the choice of a religion, that Private Judgment leads different minds in such different directions. If, indeed, there be no religious truth, or at least no sufficient means of arriving at it, then the difficulty vanishes: for where there is nothing to find, there can be no rules for seeking, and contradiction in the result is but a reductio ad absurdum of the attempt. But such a conclusion is intolerable to those who search, else they would not search; and therefore on them the obligation lies to explain, if they can, how it comes to pass, that Private Judgment is a duty, and an advantage, and a success, considering it leads the way not only to their own faith, whatever that may be, but to opinions which are diametrically opposite to it; considering it not only leads them right, but leads others wrong, landing them as it may be in the Church of Rome, or in the Wesleyan Connection, or in the Society of Friends. 5 ... 10

Are exercises of mind, which end so diversely, one and all pleasing to the Divine Author of faith; or rather must they not contain some inherent or some incidental defect, since they manifest such divergence? Must private judgment in all cases be a good per se; or is it a good under circumstances, and with limitations? Or is it a good, only when it is not an evil? Or is it a good and evil at once, a good involving an evil? Or is it an absolute and simple evil? Questions of this sort rise in the mind on contemplating a principle which leads to more than the thirty-two points of the compass, and, in consequence, whatever we may here be able to do, in the way of giving plain rules for its exercise, be it greater or less, will be so much gain. 15 ... 20

Now the first remark which occurs is an obvious one, and, we suppose, will be suffered to pass without much opposition, that whatever be the intrinsic merits of Private Judgment, yet, if it at all exerts itself in the direction of proselytism and conversion, a certain onus probandi lies upon it, and it must show cause why it should be tolerated, and not rather treated as a breach of the peace, and silenced instanter as a mere disturber of the existing constitution of things. Of course it may be safely exercised in defending what is established; and we are far indeed from saying that it is never to advance in the direction of change or revolution, else the Gospel itself could never have been introduced; but we consider that serious religious changes have primâ facie case against them; they have something to get over, and have to prove their admissibility, before it can reasonably be allowed; and their agents may be called upon to suffer, in order to prove their earnestness, 25 ... 30

and to pay the penalty of the trouble they are causing. Considering the special 35
countenance given in Scripture to quiet, unanimity, and contentedness, and the
warnings directed against disorder, insubordination, changeableness, discord, and
division; considering the emphatic words of the Apostle, laid down by him as a
general principle, and illustrated in detail, "Let every man abide in the same calling
wherein he was called"; considering, in a word, that change is really the character- 40
istic of error, and unalterableness the attribute of truth, of holiness, of Almighty
God Himself, we consider that when Private Judgment moves in the direction of
innovation, it may well be regarded at first with suspicion and treated with severity.
Nay, we confess even a satisfaction, when a penalty is attached to the expression
of new doctrines, or to a change of communion. We repeat it, if any men have 45
strong feelings, they should pay for them; if they think it a duty to unsettle things
established, they show their earnestness by being willing to suffer. We shall be the
last to complain of this kind of persecution, even though directed against what
we consider the cause of truth. Such disadvantages do no harm to that cause in
the event, but they bring home to a man's mind his own responsibility; they are a 50
memento to him of a great moral law, and warn him that his private judgment, if
not a duty, is a sin.

An act of private judgment is, in its very idea, an act of individual responsibility; this is a consideration which will come with especial force on a conscientious
mind, when it is to have so fearful an issue as a change of religion. A religious man 55
will say to himself, "If I am in error at present, I am in error by a disposition of
Providence, which has placed me where I am; if I change into an error, this is my
own act. It is much less fearful to be born at disadvantage, than to place myself at
disadvantage."

411. What is the difficulty in forming a theory of Private Judgment?

    (A)   that it leads different people to different conclusions
    (B)   that there is no religious truth
    (C)   that there is no sufficient means of arriving at it
    (D)   that there is nothing to find
    (E)   that there are no rules for seeking it

412. The sentence "If, indeed, there be no religious truth, or at least no sufficient means of arriving at it, then the difficulty vanishes: for where there is
nothing to find, there can be no rules for seeking, and contradiction in the
result is but a reductio ad absurdum of the attempt," serves as:

    (A)   a rebuttal to the claim made in the first sentence
    (B)   an unsatisfactory conclusion to the problem posed in the first sentence
    (C)   an example that illustrates the statement made in the first sentence
    (D)   a counterargument to the claim made in the first sentence
    (E)   a qualification of the claim made in the first sentence

413. The major claim of the passage, as made in the end of the first paragraph, is that:

(A) private judgment leads people to their own faith
(B) a conclusion that states that there is no reason to try to form a theory on private judgment is intolerable
(C) those who search to find a theory on private judgment are obligated to explain how private judgment is a duty, an advantage, and a success
(D) private judgment leads people to diametrically opposed opinions
(E) private judgment leads some right and some wrong

414. Paragraphs one and two use all of the following rhetorical techniques *except*:

(A) polysyndeton
(B) asyndeton
(C) anaphora
(D) rhetorical questions
(E) repetition

415. Despite the good values of private judgment, it must be questioned if it:

(A) proselytizes
(B) converts
(C) tolerates
(D) breaks peace
(E) disturbs things in appearance

416. Agents of change must be willing to suffer to do all of the following *except*:

(A) prove their earnestness
(B) pay penalty for causing trouble
(C) advance change
(D) defend what is established
(E) prove admissibility

417. The sentence that begins "Considering the special countenance" uses which rhetorical technique to praise being content with the way things are:

(A) polysyndeton
(B) asyndeton
(C) anaphora
(D) epistrophe
(E) hyperbole

418. The sentence that begins "Considering the special countenance" is the following type of sentence:

(A) sentence fragment
(B) simple sentence
(C) interrogative sentence
(D) cumulative sentence
(E) periodic sentence

419. In the final sentence of the passage, the individual responsibility of private judgment is discussed using:

(A) polysyndeton
(B) asyndeton
(C) anaphora
(D) epistrophe
(E) hyperbole

420. The passage as a whole primarily appeals to:

   I. ethos
   II. logos
   III. pathos

(A) I
(B) II
(C) III
(D) II and III
(E) I, II, and III

Passage 9c: Francis Parkman, *The Oregon Trail: Sketches of Prairie and Rocky-Mountain Life*

Last spring, 1846, was a busy season in the City of St. Louis. Not only were emigrants from every part of the country preparing for the journey to Oregon and California, but an unusual number of traders were making ready their wagons and outfits for Santa Fe. Many of the emigrants, especially of those bound for California, were persons of wealth and standing. The hotels were crowded, and   5
the gunsmiths and saddlers were kept constantly at work in providing arms and equipments for the different parties of travelers. Almost every day steamboats were leaving the levee and passing up the Missouri, crowded with passengers on their way to the frontier.

   In one of these, the *Radnor*, since snagged and lost, my friend and relative,   10
Quincy A. Shaw, and myself, left St. Louis on the 28th of April, on a tour of curiosity and amusement to the Rocky Mountains. The boat was loaded until the water broke alternately over her guards. Her upper deck was covered with large weapons of a peculiar form, for the Santa Fe trade, and her hold was crammed with goods

for the same destination. There were also the equipments and provisions of a party 15
of Oregon emigrants, a band of mules and horses, piles of saddles and harness, and
a multitude of nondescript articles, indispensable on the prairies. Almost hidden in
this medley one might have seen a small French cart, of the sort very appropriately
called a "mule-killer" beyond the frontiers, and not far distant a tent, together with
a miscellaneous assortment of boxes and barrels. The whole equipage was far from 20
prepossessing in its appearance; yet, such as it was, it was destined to a long and
arduous journey, on which the persevering reader will accompany it.

The passengers on board the *Radnor* corresponded with her freight. In her cabin
were Santa Fe traders, gamblers, speculators, and adventurers of various descriptions, and her steerage was crowded with Oregon emigrants, "mountain men," 25
negroes, and a party of Kansas Indians, who had been on a visit to St. Louis.

Thus laden, the boat struggled upward for seven or eight days against the rapid
current of the Missouri, grating upon snags, and hanging for two or three hours
at a time upon sand-bars. We entered the mouth of the Missouri in a drizzling
rain, but the weather soon became clear, and showed distinctly the broad and 30
turbid river, with its eddies, its sand-bars, its ragged islands, and forest-covered
shores. The Missouri is constantly changing its course; wearing away its banks on
one side, while it forms new ones on the other. Its channel is shifting continually.
Islands are formed, and then washed away; and while the old forests on one side
are undermined and swept off, a young growth springs up from the new soil upon 35
the other. With all these changes, the water is so charged with mud and sand that
it is perfectly opaque, and in a few minutes deposits a sediment an inch thick in
the bottom of a tumbler. The river was now high; but when we descended in the
autumn it was fallen very low, and all the secrets of its treacherous shallows were
exposed to view. It was frightful to see the dead and broken trees, thick-set as a 40
military abatis, firmly imbedded in the sand, and all pointing down stream, ready
to impale any unhappy steamboat that at high water should pass over that dangerous ground.

421. The rhetorical function of the first sentence of the passage is to:
   (A) provide the major claim
   (B) establish the setting
   (C) introduce the narrator
   (D) present the point of view
   (E) establish the tone

422. In context, the word "outfits" in line 4 most nearly means:
   (A) sets of clothing
   (B) associations of people
   (C) the acts of equipping
   (D) sets of equipment with a specific purpose
   (E) shipments of goods

423. In the first sentence of paragraph two, the pronoun "these" refers to:

(A) steamboats
(B) passengers and travelers
(C) hotels
(D) gunsmiths and saddlers
(E) arms and equipments

424. The boat in paragraph two is discussed using:

(A) simile
(B) metaphor
(C) personification
(D) hyperbole
(E) litotes

425. The rhetorical function of the statement "The whole equipage was far from prepossessing in its appearance; yet, such as it was, it was destined to a long and arduous journey, on which the persevering reader will accompany it," is primarily to:

  I. appeal to the reader's sense of adventure
 II. flatter the reader
III. appeal to the reader's patriotism

(A) I
(B) II
(C) III
(D) I and II
(E) I, II, and III

426. In detailing all of the things and people on the *Radnor*, the writer uses:

(A) anaphora
(B) epistrophe
(C) enumeration
(D) asyndeton
(E) polysyndeton

427. The primary mode of composition of paragraph four is:

(A) narration
(B) description
(C) definition
(D) cause and effect
(E) classification

428. The tone of paragraph four can best be described as:

(A) awed
(B) contemptuous
(C) ominous
(D) detached
(E) morose

429. In context, the word "treacherous" in line 39 most nearly means:

(A) providing insecure support
(B) marked by hidden dangers
(C) likely to betray trust
(D) given with assurance
(E) true to the standard

430. The primary mode of composition of the passage is:

(A) narration
(B) description
(C) definition
(D) cause and effect
(E) classification

Passage 9d: Henry David Thoreau, *Civil Disobedience*

I heartily accept the motto, "That government is best which governs least"; and I should like to see it acted up to more rapidly and systematically. Carried out, it finally amounts to this, which also I believe—"That government is best which governs not at all"; and when men are prepared for it, that will be the kind of government which they will have. Government is at best but an expedient; but most   5
governments are usually, and all governments are sometimes, inexpedient. The objections which have been brought against a standing army, and they are many and weighty, and deserve to prevail, may also at last be brought against a standing government. The standing army is only an arm of the standing government. The government itself, which is only the mode which the people have chosen to   10
execute their will, is equally liable to be abused and perverted before the people can act through it. Witness the present Mexican war, the work of comparatively a few individuals using the standing government as their tool; for in the outset, the people would not have consented to this measure.

   This American government—what is it but a tradition, though a recent one,   15
endeavoring to transmit itself unimpaired to posterity, but each instant losing some of its integrity? It has not the vitality and force of a single living man; for a single man can bend it to his will. It is a sort of wooden gun to the people themselves. But it is not the less necessary for this; for the people must have some complicated machinery or other, and hear its din, to satisfy that idea of government which they   20

have. Governments show thus how successfully men can be imposed upon, even impose on themselves, for their own advantage. It is excellent, we must allow. Yet this government never of itself furthered any enterprise, but by the alacrity with which it got out of its way. It does not keep the country free. It does not settle the West. It does not educate. The character inherent in the American people has 25 done all that has been accomplished; and it would have done somewhat more, if the government had not sometimes got in its way. For government is an expedient, by which men would fain succeed in letting one another alone; and, as has been said, when it is most expedient, the governed are most let alone by it. Trade and commerce, if they were not made of india-rubber, would never manage to bounce 30 over obstacles which legislators are continually putting in their way; and if one were to judge these men wholly by the effects of their actions and not partly by their intentions, they would deserve to be classed and punished with those mischievious persons who put obstructions on the railroads.

But, to speak practically and as a citizen, unlike those who call themselves no- 35 government men, I ask for, not at once no government, but at once a better government. Let every man make known what kind of government would command his respect, and that will be one step toward obtaining it.

431. In context, the word "expedient" in line 5 most nearly means:
  (A) a thing used when a usual resource is unavailable
  (B) a means to an end
  (C) a temporary replacement
  (D) a recurrent pattern
  (E) a journey

432. The line "The standing army is only an arm of the standing government" uses:
  (A) simile
  (B) personification
  (C) metaphor
  (D) hyperbole
  (E) litotes

433. The final sentence of the first paragraph, "Witness the present Mexican war, the work of comparatively a few individuals using the standing government as their tool; for in the outset, the people would not have consented to this measure," is the following type of sentence:
  (A) sentence fragment
  (B) simple sentence
  (C) imperative sentence
  (D) interrogative sentence
  (E) declarative sentence

434. The writer uses a rhetorical question in the beginning of the second paragraph to make all of the following claims about the American government *except*:

(A) that the American government is traditional
(B) that the American government is new
(C) that the American government is remaining unimpaired
(D) that the American government is trying to make itself last unchanged
(E) that the American government is losing its integrity

435. In order to underscore what the government does not do, the sentences "It does not keep the country free. It does not settle the West. It does not educate" use:

(A) asyndeton
(B) polysyndeton
(C) irony
(D) anaphora
(E) epistrophe

436. Throughout the passage, the writer uses first-person point of view in order to:

   I. underscore the message of the power of the individual
   II. make clear that these claims are personal in nature
   III. appeal to pathos

(A) I
(B) II
(C) III
(D) I and III
(E) I, II, and III

437. The passage as a whole can best be described as:

(A) an objective report
(B) an impassioned proposal
(C) a detached description
(D) an allusive reflection
(E) an allegorical narrative

438. It can be inferred from the passage that, above all else, the writer values:

(A) tradition
(B) honor
(C) independence
(D) law
(E) religion

439. The writer sees government primarily as:

(A) an obstacle to the American people
(B) a support system for the American people
(C) an enemy of the American people
(D) an ally of the American people
(E) a corrupting force of the American people

440. The tone of the passage as a whole can best be described as:

(A) condescending
(B) flippant
(C) facetious
(D) derisive
(E) zealous

Passage 9e: Oscar Wilde, *De Profundis*

Suffering is one very long moment. We cannot divide it by seasons. We can only record its moods, and chronicle their return. With us time itself does not progress. It revolves. It seems to circle round one centre of pain. The paralyzing immobility of a life every circumstance of which is regulated after an unchangeable pattern, so that we eat and drink and lie down and pray, or kneel at least for prayer, according 5 to the inflexible laws of an iron formula: this immobile quality, that makes each dreadful day in the very minutest detail like its brother, seems to communicate itself to those external forces the very essence of whose existence is ceaseless change. Of seed-time or harvest, of the reapers bending over the corn, or the grape gatherers threading through the vines, of the grass in the orchard made white with broken 10 blossoms or strewn with fallen fruit: of these we know nothing and can know nothing.

For us there is only one season, the season of sorrow. The very sun and moon seem taken from us. Outside, the day may be blue and gold, but the light that creeps down through the thickly-muffled glass of the small iron-barred window 15 beneath which one sits is grey and niggard. It is always twilight in one's cell, as it is always twilight in one's heart. And in the sphere of thought, no less than in the sphere of time, motion is no more. The thing that you personally have long ago forgotten, or can easily forget, is happening to me now, and will happen to me again to-morrow. Remember this, and you will be able to understand a little of why 20 I am writing, and in this manner writing. . . .

A week later, I am transferred here. Three more months go over and my mother dies. No one knew how deeply I loved and honoured her. Her death was terrible to me; but I, once a lord of language, have no words in which to express my anguish and my shame. She and my father had bequeathed me a name they had made noble 25 and honoured, not merely in literature, art, archaeology, and science, but in the public history of my own country, in its evolution as a nation. I had disgraced that name eternally. I had made it a low by-word among low people. I had dragged it through the very mire. I had given it to brutes that they might make it brutal, and to fools that they might turn it into a synonym for folly. What I suffered then, 30 and still suffer, is not for pen to write or paper to record. My wife, always kind and gentle to me, rather than that I should hear the news from indifferent lips, travelled, ill as she was, all the way from Genoa to England to break to me herself the tidings of so irreparable, so irremediable, a loss. Messages of sympathy reached me from all who had still affection for me. Even people who had not known me 35 personally, hearing that a new sorrow had broken into my life, wrote to ask that some expression of their condolence should be conveyed to me. . . .

Three months go over. The calendar of my daily conduct and labour that hangs on the outside of my cell door, with my name and sentence written upon it, tells me that it is May. . . . 40

Prosperity, pleasure and success, may be rough of grain and common in fibre, but sorrow is the most sensitive of all created things. There is nothing that stirs in the whole world of thought to which sorrow does not vibrate in terrible and exquisite pulsation. The thin beaten-out leaf of tremulous gold that chronicles the direction of forces the eye cannot see is in comparison coarse. It is a wound that 45 bleeds when any hand but that of love touches it, and even then must bleed again, though not in pain.

441. In its discussion of sorrow in the first paragraph, the writer uses all of the following rhetorical techniques *except*:

(A) metaphor
(B) personification
(C) synecdoche
(D) polysyndeton
(E) sentence type variety

442. The primary mode of composition of paragraph two is:

(A) narration
(B) description
(C) cause and effect
(D) classification
(E) process analysis

443. In blaming himself and expressing his shame in the sentences "I had disgraced that name eternally. I had made it a low by-word among low people. I had dragged it through the very mire. I had given it to brutes that they might make it brutal, and to fools that they might turn it into a synonym for folly," the writer uses all of the following rhetorical techniques *except*:

(A) anaphora
(B) epistrophe
(C) parallelism
(D) repetition
(E) figurative language

444. The use of the pronoun "it" in line 29 refers to:

(A) the writer's anguish
(B) the writer's shame
(C) the writer's name
(D) the writer's mother's death
(E) the writer's country

445. In context, the word "tremulous" in line 44 most nearly means:

(A) exceedingly sensitive
(B) timid
(C) hesitant
(D) having little substance
(E) uncertain

446. The primary mode of composition of the final paragraph is:

(A) narration
(B) description
(C) definition
(D) comparison and contrast
(E) argument

447. The writer of the passage is which of the following:

   I. a husband
  II. a prisoner
 III. a writer

(A) I
(B) II
(C) III
(D) I and III
(E) I, II, and III

448. The major claim of the passage is expressed in all of the following lines *except*:

    (A) "Suffering is one very long moment."

    (B) "For us there is only one season, the season of sorrow."

    (C) "Messages of sympathy reached me from all who had still affection for me."

    (D) "Prosperity, pleasure and success, may be rough of grain and common in fibre, but sorrow is the most sensitive of all created things."

    (E) "There is nothing that stirs in the whole world of thought to which sorrow does not vibrate in terrible and exquisite pulsation."

449. The passage as a whole primarily appeals to:

    I. ethos

    II. logos

    III. pathos

    (A) I

    (B) II

    (C) III

    (D) I and II

    (E) I, II, and III

450. The tone of the passage as a whole can best be described as:

    (A) plaintive

    (B) mirthful

    (C) sanguine

    (D) indignant

    (E) belligerent

CHAPTER 10

20th Century

Passage 10a: Willa Cather, *On the Art of Fiction*

One is sometimes asked about the "obstacles" that confront young writers who are
trying to do good work. I should say the greatest obstacles that writers today have
to get over, are the dazzling journalistic successes of twenty years ago, stories that
surprised and delighted by their sharp photographic detail and that were really
nothing more than lively pieces of reporting. The whole aim of that school of writ-   5
ing was novelty—never a very important thing in art. They gave us, altogether,
poor standards—taught us to multiply our ideas instead of to condense them. They
tried to make a story out of every theme that occurred to them and to get returns
on every situation that suggested itself. They got returns, of a kind. But their work,
when one looks back on it, now that the novelty upon which they counted so much   10
is gone, is journalistic and thin. The especial merit of a good reportorial story is
that it shall be intensely interesting and pertinent today and shall have lost its point
by tomorrow.

Art, it seems to me, should simplify. That, indeed, is very nearly the whole of
the higher artistic process; finding what conventions of form and what detail one   15
can do without and yet preserve the spirit of the whole—so that all that one has
suppressed and cut away is there to the reader's consciousness as much as if it were
in type on the page. Millet had done hundreds of sketches of peasants sowing grain,
some of them very complicated and interesting, but when he came to paint the
spirit of them all into one picture, *The Sower*, the composition is so simple that it   20
seems inevitable. All the discarded sketches that went before made the picture what
it finally became, and the process was all the time one of simplifying, of sacrificing
many conceptions good in themselves for one that was better and more universal.

Any first rate novel or story must have in it the strength of a dozen fairly good
stories that have been sacrificed to it. A good workman can't be a cheap workman;   25
he can't be stingy about wasting material, and he cannot compromise. Writing
ought either to be the manufacture of stories for which there is a market demand—
a business as safe and commendable as making soap or breakfast foods—or it
should be an art, which is always a search for something for which there is no market demand, something new and untried, where the values are intrinsic and have   30
nothing to do with standardized values. The courage to go on without compromise

does not come to a writer all at once—nor, for that matter, does the ability. Both are phases of natural development. In the beginning the artist, like his public, is wedded to old forms, old ideals, and his vision is blurred by the memory of old delights he would like to recapture.   35

451. The pronoun "one" in the first sentence most probably refers to:
  I. the writer
  II. a writer
  III. a journalist

  (A) I
  (B) II
  (C) III
  (D) I and II
  (E) I, II, and III

452. In context, the word "novelty" in lines 6 and 10 most nearly means:
  (A) newness
  (B) fiction
  (C) nonfiction
  (D) realism
  (E) marketability

453. In line 6, the pronoun "they" refers to:
  (A) young writers
  (B) obstacles
  (C) successes
  (D) standards
  (E) ideas

454. In order to set apart important conclusions in the first paragraph, the writer uses:
  (A) quotation marks
  (B) parentheses
  (C) dashes
  (D) hyphens
  (E) semicolons

455. The tone of the last sentence of the first paragraph, "The especial merit of a good reportorial story is that it shall be intensely interesting and pertinent today and shall have lost its point by tomorrow," can best be described as:

(A) objectively detached
(B) ironically disparaging
(C) sentimentally poignant
(D) indignantly irate
(E) mournfully sad

456. The purpose of mentioning Jean François Millet's *The Sower* in the second paragraph is to:

(A) provide an example of journalistic success
(B) provide an example of a good reportorial story
(C) provide an example of conventions of form
(D) provide an example of simplicity
(E) provide an example of a first-rate story

457. In its treatment of writing, the third paragraph relies primarily on the mode of:

(A) narration
(B) description
(C) classification
(D) definition
(E) process analysis

458. The final sentence of the passage, "In the beginning the artist, like his public, is wedded to old forms, old ideals, and his vision is blurred by the memory of old delights he would like to recapture," uses all of the following rhetorical techniques *except*:

(A) repetition
(B) comparison
(C) metaphor
(D) personification
(E) hyperbole

459. The primary mode of composition of the passage as a whole is:

(A) narration
(B) description
(C) argument
(D) comparison and contrast
(E) classification

460. The writer of the passage most values writing that is:

(A) simple
(B) detailed
(C) novel
(D) interesting
(E) complicated

Passage 10b: W. E. B. DuBois, *The Souls of Black Folk*

It was out in the country, far from home, far from my foster home, on a dark Sunday night. The road wandered from our rambling log-house up the stony bed of a creek, past wheat and corn, until we could hear dimly across the fields a rhythmic cadence of song,—soft, thrilling, powerful, that swelled and died sorrowfully in our ears. I was a country schoolteacher then, fresh from the East, and had never seen a   5
Southern Negro revival. To be sure, we in Berkshire were not perhaps as stiff and formal as they in Suffolk of olden time; yet we were very quiet and subdued, and I know not what would have happened those clear Sabbath mornings had some one punctuated the sermon with a wild scream, or interrupted the long prayer with a loud Amen! And so most striking to me, as I approached the village and the   10
little plain church perched aloft, was the air of intense excitement that possessed that mass of black folk. A sort of suppressed terror hung in the air and seemed to seize us,—a pythian madness, a demoniac possession, that lent terrible reality to song and word. The black and massive form of the preacher swayed and quivered as the words crowded to his lips and flew at us in singular eloquence. The people   15
moaned and fluttered, and then the gaunt-cheeked brown woman beside me suddenly leaped straight into the air and shrieked like a lost soul, while round about came wail and groan and outcry, and a scene of human passion such as I had never conceived before.

Those who have not thus witnessed the frenzy of a Negro revival in the   20
untouched backwoods of the South can but dimly realize the religious feeling of the slave; as described, such scenes appear grotesque and funny, but as seen they are awful. Three things characterized this religion of the slave,—the Preacher, the Music, and the Frenzy. The Preacher is the most unique personality developed by the Negro on American soil. A leader, a politician, an orator, a "boss," an   25
intriguer, an idealist,—all these he is, and ever, too, the centre of a group of men, now twenty, now a thousand in number. The combination of a certain adroitness with deep-seated earnestness, of tact with consummate ability, gave him his preeminence, and helps him maintain it. The type, of course, varies according to time and place, from the West Indies in the sixteenth century to New England in   30
the nineteenth, and from the Mississippi bottoms to cities like New Orleans or New York.

The Music of Negro religion is that plaintive rhythmic melody, with its touching minor cadences, which, despite caricature and defilement, still remains the

most original and beautiful expression of human life and longing yet born on 35
American soil. Sprung from the African forests, where its counterpart can still be
heard, it was adapted, changed, and intensified by the tragic soul-life of the slave,
until, under the stress of law and whip, it became the one true expression of a
people's sorrow, despair, and hope.

Finally the Frenzy of "Shouting," when the Spirit of the Lord passed by, and, 40
seizing the devotee, made him mad with supernatural joy, was the last essential of
Negro religion and the one more devoutly believed in than all the rest. It varied
in expression from the silent rapt countenance or the low murmur and moan to
the mad abandon of physical fervor,—the stamping, shrieking, and shouting, the
rushing to and fro and wild waving of arms, the weeping and laughing, the vision 45
and the trance. All this is nothing new in the world, but old as religion, as Delphi
and Endor. And so firm a hold did it have on the Negro, that many generations
firmly believed that without this visible manifestation of the God there could be
no true communion with the Invisible.

461. The rhetorical function of the first sentence of the passage is to:

(A) provide the major claim
(B) establish the setting
(C) introduce the narrator
(D) present the point of view
(E) establish the tone

462. The first paragraph contains all of the following rhetorical techniques
except:

(A) repetition
(B) asyndeton
(C) shift in pronoun
(D) imagery
(E) simile

463. The function of the sentence "Three things characterized this religion of
the slave,—the Preacher, the Music, and the Frenzy" is to:

(A) provide the structure of the rest of the passage
(B) clarify the occasion
(C) develop an objective tone
(D) characterize the audience
(E) appeal to logos

464. In order to characterize the Preacher in the sentence "A leader, a politician, an orator, a 'boss,' an intriguer, an idealist,—all these he is," the writer uses:

(A) anaphora
(B) epistrophe
(C) asyndeton
(D) polysyndeton
(E) hyperbole

465. In context, the word "plaintive" in line 33 most nearly means:

(A) rhyming
(B) amusing
(C) expressing remorse
(D) expressing joy
(E) expressing sorrow

466. The tone of the sentence "The Music of Negro religion is that plaintive rhythmic melody, with its touching minor cadences, which, despite caricature and defilement, still remains the most original and beautiful expression of human life and longing yet born on American soil," can best be described as:

(A) ambivalent
(B) bemused
(C) conciliatory
(D) laudatory
(E) ecstatic

467. The pronoun "it" in line 37 refers to:

(A) music of Negro religion
(B) expression
(C) American soil
(D) African forests
(E) soul-life of the slave

468. The structure of the passage starting with the second paragraph, just after the introductory paragraph, moves:

(A) chronologically
(B) from specific to general
(C) from general to specific
(D) to the most important part of "Negro religion" (a climax)
(E) from the most important part of "Negro religion" to the least

469. The sentence "It varied in expression from the silent rapt countenance or the low murmur and moan to the mad abandon of physical fervor,—the stamping, shrieking, and shouting, the rushing to and fro and wild waving of arms, the weeping and laughing, the vision and the trance" uses the following rhetorical device to mimic the frenzy of sounds:

   (A) alliteration
   (B) assonance
   (C) onomatopoeia
   (D) anaphora
   (E) epistrophe

470. The tone of the passage as a whole can best be described as:

   (A) impressed and slightly amused
   (B) awed and slightly frightened
   (C) indignant and slightly accusatory
   (D) jovial and slightly lyrical
   (E) fanciful and slightly whimsical

Passage 10c: Charlotte Perkins Gilman, *The Man-Made World; or, Our Androcentric Culture*

When we are offered a "woman's" paper, page, or column, we find it filled with matter supposed to appeal to women as a sex or class; the writer mainly dwelling upon the Kaiser's four K's—Kuchen, Kinder, Kirche, Kleider. They iterate and reiterate endlessly the discussion of cookery, old and new; of the care of children; of the overwhelming subject of clothing; and of moral instruction. All this is recognized as "feminine" literature, and it must have some appeal else the women would not read it. What parallel have we in "masculine" literature?

"None!" is the proud reply. "Men are people! Women, being 'the sex,' have their limited feminine interests, their feminine point of view, which must be provided for. Men, however, are not restricted—to them belongs the world's literature!"

Yes, it has belonged to them—ever since there was any. They have written it and they have read it. It is only lately that women, generally speaking, have been taught to read; still more lately that they have been allowed to write. It is but a little while since Harriet Martineau concealed her writing beneath her sewing when visitors came in—writing was "masculine"—sewing "feminine."

We have not, it is true, confined men to a narrowly construed "masculine sphere," and composed a special literature suited to it. Their effect on literature has been far wider than that, monopolizing this form of art with special favor. It was suited above all others to the dominant impulse of self-expression; and being, as we have seen essentially and continually "the sex;" they have impressed that sex upon this art overwhelmingly; they have given the world a masculized literature.

It is hard for us to realize this. We can readily see, that if women had always written the books, no men either writing or reading them, that would have surely "feminized" our literature; but we have not in our minds the concept, much less the word, for an overmasculized influence.   25

Men having been accepted as humanity, women but a side-issue; (most literally if we accept the Hebrew legend!), whatever men did or said was human—and not to be criticized. In no department of life is it easier to contravert this old belief; to show how the male sex as such differs from the human type; and how this maleness has monopolized and disfigured a great social function.   30

Human life is a very large affair; and literature is its chief art. We live, humanly, only through our power of communication. Speech gives us this power laterally, as it were, in immediate personal contact. For permanent use speech becomes oral tradition—a poor dependence. Literature gives not only an infinite multiplication to the lateral spread of communion but adds the vertical reach. Through it we 35 know the past, govern the present, and influence the future. In its servicable common forms it is the indispensable daily servant of our lives; in its nobler flights as a great art no means of human inter-change goes so far.

In these brief limits we can touch but lightly on some phases of so great a subject; and will rest the case mainly on the effect of an exclusively masculine handling 40 of the two fields of history and fiction. In poetry and the drama the same influence is easily traced, but in the first two it is so baldly prominent as to defy objection.

471. The primary mode of composition of paragraph one is:

(A) narration
(B) description
(C) classification
(D) definition
(E) process analysis

472. The claim of the passage, that literature is predominantly masculine, is made in the first paragraph by means of:

(A) syllogism
(B) inductive reasoning
(C) rhetorical question
(D) anecdote
(E) allusion

473. The second paragraph of the passage functions as:

(A) claim
(B) warrant
(C) data
(D) counterargument
(E) qualifier

474. The words "masculine" and "feminine" at the end of paragraph three are in quotation marks because:

    (A) the writer disagrees with the sentiment
    (B) someone else is speaking
    (C) she is quoting another work of literature
    (D) she wants to make clear his major claim
    (E) she spoke this line to Harriet Martineau

475. In context, the word "construed" in line 16 most nearly means:

    (A) analyzed
    (B) structured
    (C) labored
    (D) expressed
    (E) understood

476. The first sentence of paragraph six, "Men having been accepted as humanity, women but a side-issue; (most literally if we accept the Hebrew legend!), whatever men did or said was human—and not to be criticized," uses the following to make its claim that men are "accepted as humanity":

    (A) syllogism
    (B) inductive reasoning
    (C) rhetorical question
    (D) anecdote
    (E) allusion

477. In the line "how this maleness has monopolized and disfigured a great social function," the writer uses the following in order to show the power that maleness has over literature:

    (A) simile
    (B) metaphor
    (C) personification
    (D) anaphora
    (E) epistrophe

478. The primary mode of composition of paragraph seven is:

    (A) narration
    (B) description
    (C) cause and effect
    (D) argument
    (E) comparison and contrast

479. In the sentence "Through it we know the past, govern the present, and influence the future," the writer uses the following rhetorical technique to make her claim about literature's uses through time:

(A) syntactical inversion
(B) parallelism
(C) colloquialism
(D) asyndeton
(E) polysyndeton

480. The purpose of the last paragraph is to:

(A) address those who would argue against the writer's claims
(B) describe the type of material in feminine literature
(C) introduce the examples to follow of masculine literature
(D) define masculine literature and its genres
(E) argue against the proliferation of feminine literature

Passage 10d: George Santayana, *The Life of Reason*

Progress, far from consisting in change, depends on retentiveness. When change is absolute there remains no being to improve and no direction is set for possible improvement: and when experience is not retained, as among savages, infancy is perpetual. Those who cannot remember the past are condemned to repeat it. In the first stage of life the mind is frivolous and easily distracted; it misses progress 5
by failing in consecutiveness and persistence. This is the condition of children and barbarians, in whom instinct has learned nothing from experience. In a second stage men are docile to events, plastic to new habits and suggestions, yet able to graft them on original instincts, which they thus bring to fuller satisfaction. This is the plane of manhood and true progress. Last comes a stage when retentiveness 10
is exhausted and all that happens is at once forgotten; a vain, because unpractical, repetition of the past takes the place of plasticity and fertile readaptation. In a moving world readaptation is the price of longevity. The hard shell, far from protecting the vital principle, condemns it to die down slowly and be gradually chilled; immortality in such a case must have been secured earlier, by giving birth 15
to a generation plastic to the contemporary world and able to retain its lessons. Thus old age is as forgetful as youth, and more incorrigible; it displays the same inattentiveness to conditions; its memory becomes self-repeating and degenerates into an instinctive reaction, like a bird's chirp.

Not all readaptation, however, is progress, for ideal identity must not be lost. 20
The Latin language did not progress when it passed into Italian. It died. Its amiable heirs may console us for its departure, but do not remove the fact that their parent is extinct. So every individual, nation, and religion has its limit of adaptation; so long as the increment it receives is digestible, so long as the organisation already attained is extended and elaborated without being surrendered, growth goes on; 25
but when the foundation itself shifts, when what is gained at the periphery is lost

at the centre, the flux appears again and progress is not real. Thus a succession of
generations or languages or religions constitutes no progress unless some ideal present at the beginning is transmitted to the end and reaches a better expression there;
without this stability at the core no common standard exists and all comparison of 30
value with value must be external and arbitrary. Retentiveness, we must repeat, is
the condition of progress.

481. The opening claim that progress depends on keeping certain things in
place is an example of:

    (A) hyperbole
    (B) antithesis
    (C) a paradox
    (D) an oxymoron
    (E) understatement

482. In context, the word "plastic" in line 8 most nearly means:

    (A) well formed
    (B) impressionable
    (C) artificial
    (D) superficial
    (E) malleable

483. In making clear his claims about progress and retention, the writer relies
on the following technique in paragraph one:

    (A) visual imagery
    (B) analogy of growing up
    (C) personal anecdote
    (D) biblical allusion
    (E) expert testimony

484. The last sentence of paragraph one, "Thus old age is as forgetful as youth,
and more incorrigible; it displays the same inattentiveness to conditions; its
memory becomes self-repeating and degenerates into an instinctive reaction,
like a bird's chirp," uses the following type(s) of figurative language:

    I. personification
    II. simile
    III. synecdoche

    (A) I
    (B) II
    (C) III
    (D) I and II
    (E) I, II, and III

485. According to the first paragraph, the ideal stage of progress is:

(A) infancy
(B) the first stage of life (childhood)
(C) the second stage of life (manhood)
(D) the last stage of life (old age)
(E) immortality

486. The first sentence of the second paragraph, "Not all readaptation, however, is progress, for ideal identity must not be lost," serves as which of the following for the writer's argument:

(A) claim
(B) warrant
(C) data
(D) qualifier
(E) counterargument

487. The rhetorical function of the simple sentence "It died" in the beginning of the second paragraph is to:

(A) succinctly show the realistic effects of what can occur when readaptation fails
(B) skillfully argue that Latin is superior to Italian
(C) describe the ideal identity of Latin
(D) analyze the stages of the process of Latin turning into Italian
(E) define the boundaries of readaptation and progress

488. The sentence "Thus a succession of generations or languages or religions constitutes no progress unless some ideal present at the beginning is transmitted to the end and reaches a better expression there" uses the following technique to show the options of things that must retain their ideal to make progress:

(A) asyndeton
(B) polysyndeton
(C) anaphora
(D) epistrophe
(E) litotes

489. The style of the passage can be characterized by all of the following *except*:

(A) sentence type variety
(B) analogy
(C) figurative language
(D) paradox
(E) enumeration

490. The tone of the passage as a whole can best be described as:

   (A) apathetic
   (B) caustic
   (C) ribald
   (D) contemplative
   (E) morose

Passage 10e: Olive Schreiner, *Woman and Labour*

In that clamour which has arisen in the modern world, where now this, and then
that, is demanded for and by large bodies of modern women, he who listens carefully may detect as a keynote, beneath all the clamour, a demand which may be
embodied in such a cry as this: Give us labour and the training which fits for
labour! We demand this, not for ourselves alone, but for the race.   5

   If this demand be logically expanded, it will take such form as this: Give us
labour! For countless ages, for thousands, millions it may be, we have laboured.
When first man wandered, the naked, newly-erected savage, and hunted and
fought, we wandered with him: each step of his was ours. Within our bodies we
bore the race, on our shoulders we carried it; we sought the roots and plants for its   10
food; and, when man's barbed arrow or hook brought the game, our hands dressed
it. Side by side, the savage man and the savage woman, we wandered free together
and laboured free together. And we were contented!

   Then a change came.

   We ceased from our wanderings, and, camping upon one spot of earth, again   15
the labours of life were divided between us. While man went forth to hunt, or to
battle with the foe who would have dispossessed us of all, we laboured on the land.
We hoed the earth, we reaped the grain, we shaped the dwellings, we wove the
clothing, we modelled the earthen vessels and drew the lines upon them, which
were humanity's first attempt at domestic art; we studied the properties and uses 20
of plants, and our old women were the first physicians of the race, as, often, its first
priests and prophets.

   We fed the race at our breast, we bore it on our shoulders; through us it was
shaped, fed, and clothed. Labour more toilsome and unending than that of man
was ours; yet did we never cry out that it was too heavy for us. While savage man   25
lay in the sunshine on his skins, resting, that he might be fitted for war or the
chase, or while he shaped his weapons of death, he ate and drank that which our
hands had provided for him; and while we knelt over our grindstone, or hoed in
the fields, with one child in our womb, perhaps, and one on our back, toiling till
the young body was old before its time—did we ever cry out that the labour allot-   30
ted to us was too hard for us? Did we not know that the woman who threw down
her burden was as a man who cast away his shield in battle—a coward and a traitor
to his race? Man fought—that was his work; we fed and nurtured the race—that
was ours. We knew that upon our labours, even as upon man's, depended the life

and well-being of the people whom we bore. We endured our toil, as man bore his   35
wounds, silently; and we were content.

Then again a change came.

Ages passed, and time was when it was no longer necessary that all men should
go to the hunt or the field of war; and when only one in five, or one in ten, or but
one in twenty, was needed continually for these labours. Then our fellow-man, hav-   40
ing no longer full occupation in his old fields of labour, began to take his share in
ours. He too began to cultivate the field, to build the house, to grind the corn (or
make his male slaves do it); and the hoe, and the potter's tools, and the thatching-
needle, and at last even the grindstones which we first had picked up and smoothed
to grind the food for our children, began to pass from our hands into his. The old,   45
sweet life of the open fields was ours no more; we moved within the gates, where
the time passes more slowly and the world is sadder than in the air outside; but we
had our own work still, and were content.

If, indeed, we might no longer grow the food for our people, we were still its
dressers; if we did not always plant and prepare the flax and hemp, we still wove   50
the garments for our race; if we did no longer raise the house walls, the tapestries
that covered them were the work of our hands; we brewed the ale, and the simples
which were used as medicines we distilled and prescribed; and, close about our
feet, from birth to manhood, grew up the children whom we had borne; their
voices were always in our ears. At the doors of our houses we sat with our spinning-   55
wheels, and we looked out across the fields that were once ours to labour in—and
were contented. Lord's wife, peasant's, or burgher's, we all still had our work to do!

491. In context, the word "clamour" in line 3 most nearly means:

   (A) loud continuous noise
   (B) assertion
   (C) something unavoidable
   (D) ignorance
   (E) fear

492. The statement "Give us labour and the training which fits for labour!" is
the following type of sentence:

   (A) sentence fragment
   (B) interrogative sentence
   (C) imperative sentence
   (D) cumulative sentence
   (E) periodic sentence

493. The sentence "We hoed the earth, we reaped the grain, we shaped the
dwellings, we wove the clothing, we modelled the earthen vessels and drew
the lines upon them, which were humanity's first attempt at domestic art;
we studied the properties and uses of plants, and our old women were the

first physicians of the race, as, often, its first priests and prophets" uses the
following rhetorical technique to show the tremendous role of women:

(A) asyndeton
(B) polysyndeton
(C) anaphora
(D) epistrophe
(E) litotes

494. The statement "While savage man lay in the sunshine on his skins, resting,
that he might be fitted for war or the chase, or while he shaped his
weapons of death, he ate and drank that which our hands had provided
for him; and while we knelt over our grindstone, or hoed in the fields,
with one child in our womb, perhaps, and one on our back, toiling till the
young body was old before its time—did we ever cry out that the labour
allotted to us was too hard for us?" uses which of the following techniques:
   I. anaphora
  II. periodic structure
 III. rhetorical question

(A) I
(B) II
(C) III
(D) I and II
(E) I, II, and III

495. Paragraph five, which begins, "We fed at our breast," primarily appeals to:
   I. ethos
  II. logos
 III. pathos

(A) I
(B) II
(C) III
(D) I and III
(E) I, II, and III

496. The purpose of the final sentence of the passage, "Lord's wife, peasant's, or
burgher's, we all still had our work to do!" is to express that:

(A) women of privilege had it easier than poor women
(B) poor women had less work to do in the home
(C) women's husbands controlled them
(D) the constancy of women's labor was not reliant on class
(E) women's labor is dependent on their husband's positions in society

497. The tone of the last paragraph can best be described as:

(A) resilient
(B) derisive
(C) facetious
(D) mirthful
(E) irate

498. The structure of the passage as a whole can best be described as:

(A) moving from specific to general
(B) moving from general to specific
(C) enumerative
(D) providing flashbacks
(E) chronological

499. The primary mode of composition of the passage as a whole is:

(A) narration
(B) description
(C) definition
(D) classification
(E) argument

500. The purpose of the passage as a whole is to:

(A) define what a woman's labor and training are
(B) tell the story of how women's work has changed over time
(C) describe a woman's labor and training in the modern world
(D) analyze the causes of men's taking over the role women once played
(E) argue that men are to blame for the diminishing role of women over time

ANSWERS

Chapter 1

Passage 1a

1. (A) In the third line of the passage, the writer states that he trusts his autobiography will be "useful and instructive," showing that according to him, the purpose of his autobiography is to teach, or instruct.

2. (D) The writer talks directly to the reader in the first sentence of the passage, establishing a connection that appeals both to ethos, making himself a credible and trusted writer, and pathos, complimenting the reader by calling him "courteous." The writer's hopes that the autobiography he's writing will be "useful" and "instructive" also characterize the writer as a man of good intentions, furthering the appeal to ethos.

3. (D) The words "infirmities" (meaning diseases or weaknesses), "ulcers," "scars," and "frailty" (again meaning weakness) can all be used to describe physical ailments and illness. The word "indulgence" is an act for pleasure or comfort and does not refer to illness in any way.

4. (A) "Decent drapery" uses the metaphor of drapes, or curtains, to compare the hiding of "moral ulcers or scars" to the use of drapery to block the vision of outsiders with a thick fabric. It is figurative language, but it does not give the drapery human characteristics nor does it use "like" or "as," and so it is neither personification nor a simile.

5. (E) The pronoun "our," if traced to its antecedent, refers to the English. This can be seen in that the writer is discussing English feelings and uses "our" in the earlier part of that sentence to refer to "our notice," also referring to the English.

6. (B) The word "propriety," used in the line "I have for many months hesitated about the propriety of allowing this or any part of my narrative to come before the public eye until after my death" can best be understood as a synonym for "decency," in that the writer doubted the decency of publishing an autobiography that showed his self-indulgence and moral failings.

7. (C) Guilt and misery are given the human actions of shrinking, courting, and sequestering; and they are also given the human characteristic of having instinct, but the word "notice" is used in the phrase "public notice," something outside of guilt and misery. In other words, "notice" does not describe guilt and misery.

8. (A) In the line before the one quoted in the question, the writer provides a conditional claim, considering a situation in which his self-accusation did constitute a confession of guilt. In the line quoted, he makes clear that his admitting that he was both sick and in pain does not mean that he's accepting guilt; therefore, he's refuting the conditional, or hypothetical, claim made in the line before.

9. **(B)** In the final portion of the passage, the writer looks on his past with ambivalence as he uses positive words such as, "accomplished" and "self-conquest," along with negative words, such as, "accursed" and "self-indulgence." The writer discusses the counterbalance between the positive and negative, showing his ambivalence.

10. **(B)** Because the writer discusses his self-indulgence openly after acknowledging his uncertainty about sharing such private and improper behavior, the tone can best be characterized as forthright, or frank.

Passage 1b

11. **(E)** In the third sentence, the writer enumerates the different operations of the farm. There are two analogies between slaves wanting to get to the Great House Farm and a representative getting a seat in Congress and office-seekers wanting to please and deceive the people. There is parallelism in the phrase "the highest joy and the deepest sadness" in paragraph two. There is also a metaphor of weaving in the second paragraph. There are no allusions present in the first two paragraphs.

12. **(A)** The second paragraph tells the story of the slaves elected to the Great House Farm. The reader is told the story of how the slaves would sing as they walked. This paragraph is primarily developed by narration.

13. **(A)** All of the sentences except the sentence in choice A reflect on the meaning of the slave songs and show the writer's purpose in exploring the nature of slaves' singing. Only sentence A merely tells the story of singing without showing any of the writer's purpose in composing this passage.

14. **(D)** As the writer uses it, the word "rude" most nearly means "of a primitive simplicity" in the sentence "I did not, when a slave, understand the deep meaning of those rude and apparently incoherent songs." These songs seem incoherent because of their simple and unrefined nature. While "harsh to the ear" could fit, it's clear from the content that he doesn't understand the meaning of the songs because they are deceptively simple and he is not commenting on their sound.

15. **(E)** There is no analogy between one wishing to be impressed with the soul-killing effects of slavery and one placed into the deep of the woods because this is the same person. There is no comparison being made because it is only one person.

16. **(C)** "They" refers to songs here. Songs are being personified as telling a tale of woe. "They" refers back to "those rude and apparently incoherent songs."

17. **(A)** In paragraph three, both songs that told a tale of woe and the tear that has found its way down the writer's cheek are personified as performing human actions.

18. **(D)** The sentence provided uses antithesis as it expresses opposite ideas in parallel structure. "Often" is the opposite of "seldom," "drown" is the opposite of "express," and "sorrow" is the opposite of "happiness." These opposite ideas are expressed in the same structures of "I have often sung to drown my sorrow, but seldom to express my happiness."

19. (C) The line in quotation marks is a line from a poem. Even without knowing the source of this line of poetry, it should be clear from the content and tone that the writer is not disagreeing, no one else is speaking, he's not emphasizing his point, and he's not speaking this line to Colonel Lloyd.

20. (D) The passage as a whole is thoughtful, as it reflects on and contemplates the meaning of the singing of slave songs. It is also lugubrious, as it is sorrowful throughout. The writer also describes himself as crying as he is writing this passage, so he is sad.

Passage 1c

21. (B) The writer of the passage describes in detail his planned process of "arriving at moral perfection." Although he does define the virtues he needs to practice (he doesn't classify) and define moral perfection, these are steps along the way of him describing the process. He does not argue in this passage, nor does he analyze the effects, as he just discusses the plan.

22. (C) The second paragraph is developed through definition. The writer defines each virtue by attaching a precept that must be followed to achieve it and so makes clear what it means to practice the virtue. It's also clear that the mode is definition since the writer names each virtue.

23. (E) Once the virtues have been defined, the writer analyzes his process for achieving these virtues in paragraph three. This paragraph goes through the steps and pulls apart the process by detailing how the writer plans to practice and master each virtue. Process analysis walks through a process step-by-step and this can be seen here.

24. (D) Because the writer calls what follows each virtue a precept, it can be seen that precept most nearly means a particular course of action to follow each virtue. What follow each virtue, the precepts, are specific directions, such as "eat not to dullness; drink not to elevation." The imperative sentence shows that these precepts are commands.

25. (D) Repetition is the technique used. The specific type of repetition is called epanalepsis. Here, the word "resolve" is repeated at both the beginning and end of the sentence.

26. (A) There are several examples of personification in paragraph three. For example, in the sentence "This and the next, Order, I expected would allow me more time for attending to my project and my studies," the writer gives Order the human attribute of being able to allow something.

27. (B) Because of his enumeration and process analysis, the writer can be characterized as someone who is methodical, meaning that he is characterized as having systematic behavior or habits. Both the style and content are orderly and mirror the writer's nature.

28. (D) The subject of the passage, arriving at moral perfection, appeals to ethos. As does the writer's comments about his intentions of being wholly virtuous, which makes him seem credible and trustworthy. Aside from that, the orderly structure of the passage appeals to logos as it follows a clear and rational pattern.

29. (D) Metonymy is used in this sentence as ears stand for the action of listening and the tongue stands for the action of speaking. Metonymy is when a word is substituted for another with which it is closely related, such as in the line, "the pen is mightier than the sword." In this example, the pen stands for writing while the sword stands for warfare.

30. (B) The writer's tone can best be described as resolved, as he is committed to his process at arriving at moral perfection. He has made a firm decision and is trying to achieve his goal.

Passage 1d

31. (D) The power of the lash and the foul talk over the slave girls serves to further show their powerlessness. By giving even objects power over slave girls, their powerlessness is further highlighted.

32. (B) The repetition of the conjunction "or" makes this example polysyndeton, which is the repetition of more conjunctions than are grammatically necessary. In this example, the overuse of "or" extends the list of people who can exert power over the slave girl.

33. (E) The long sentence offers many options for the slave girl, but the structure of the simple sentence negates those options with a directness of force, because of its shortness, that expresses truth and finality.

34. (C) The context clues of the sentence in which "vitiated" appears help us understand its meaning to be "corrupted." We are told the slaveholder's sons are "vitiated" by "the unclean influences every where around them." People are often corrupted by bad influences, which is what is occurring here.

35. (C) Although the paragraph begins discussing the sons, the second sentence provides us with the claim "Nor do the daughter's masters always escape." The anecdote that follows is an example to prove this claim and it tells the story of one daughter who has been "contaminated," or more aptly, corrupted.

36. (A) The causal relationship between daughters hearing talk of their fathers' power over female slaves and the effect of daughters exercising this same power over the male slaves is analyzed in this paragraph. The writer provides the reasons for the daughter's "contamination," or more aptly corruption, and follows these causes to their eventual effects.

37. (C) The major claim of the passage is that slavery is a corrupting force to slaveholders as well as, obviously, oppressive to slaves. For example, the writer discusses in detail both the slave girl and the slaveholder's daughters and the curse that slavery is to both.

38. (E) "Souls" is the only word on the list that is used literally. "Blight" and "cage" are metaphors for the effects and conditions of slavery. "Storm" is a metaphor for the impending trouble that was coming to the slave from the slaveholder's father. "Pen" is personified as having the ability to write about slavery, when actually a person does the writing using a pen as a tool.

39. (A) The tone of the last paragraph is inflammatory, meaning that it is arousing anger. The writer uses the second person to challenge readers to see the nature of slavery themselves and she is inciting indignation in the readers.

40. **(E)** The provocative diction, such as "wretched" and "violent," the figurative language, for example, comparing slavery to a cage, and the first-person experiences and observations throughout all contribute to the writer's appeal to pathos. This passage is meant to emotionally persuade the readers of the pervasive corruption caused by slavery.

Passage 1e

41. **(B)** Paragraph 1 is developed by description, through its use of rich sensory imagery. The writer describes the smells of violets and lilies and the comfort of the cool leaves and grass on her hot face, among many other plants and flowers that she encounters outside.

42. **(D)** The images of the first paragraph appeal to touch and smell. For example, she describes the smells of violets and lilies and the comfort of the cool leaves and grass on her hot face. The writer later reveals that she is both blind and deaf.

43. **(E)** The sentence "I came, I saw, I conquered, as the first baby in the family always does," uses anaphora with the repetition of "I" in the successive clauses, asyndeton with its lack of the conjunction "and" between "I saw" and "I conquered," and allusion to the famous quote from Julius Caesar: "Veni, Vidi, Vici," which translates to "I came, I saw, I conquered."

44. **(A)** While the first paragraph of the passage relies on the mode of description, the passage as a whole narrates a story, which is the story of the writer's early life, leading up to the sickness that left her bereft of her sense of sight and hearing.

45. **(A)** The passage begins with a vivid descriptive paragraph and moves on to narrate the writer's early life and because of this development the best description of the purpose is "to paint a picture of life before the writer lost her senses of sight and hearing."

46. **(E)** The sentence "These happy days did not last long" marks a shift from a happier time in the writer's early life to her illness and the loss of her being able to see and hear that resulted from that illness. Words such as "dreary" and "plunged" help mark this transition.

47. **(C)** The passage can best be described as bittersweet in that it expresses feelings of both pleasure and pain that the writer has for her early days.

48. **(A)** The passage is full of sensory imagery, especially in the first paragraph. It has simple sentence structure in lines such as, "They tell me I walked the day I was a year old." It also has colorful diction with lines such as "one autumn of gold and crimson." The passage has figurative language, such as the personification of the seasons as speeding by.

49. **(D)** Anaphora is there with the repetition of "one" at the beginning of the successive phrases; asyndeton with the missing conjunctions; personification of the seasons speeding by; and imagery with the appeals to hearing, smell/taste, and sight.

50. **(E)** "Them" is the correct pronoun choice because it refers to the flickering shadows and not the sunlight or smooth floor that follows the subject in prepositional phrases. All of the other grammatical changes would be preferable.

Chapter 2

Passage 2a

51. (A) The first sentence of the second paragraph contains an admission that the writer is fully aware of the objections (i.e., counterargument), which may be made to "the minuteness on some occasions of [his] detail of Johnson's conversation." The writer acknowledges that some may think that he included too much detail, but he disagrees.

52. (D) The writer argues that some biographers believe themselves to be writing good biographies when they are showing a chronological series of actions, but one of the claims of the passage is that good biographies include personal details, such as minute particulars, idle talk, table talk, and anecdotes.

53. (B) "It" refers to "minuteness" in the sentence "I am fully aware of the objections which may be made to the minuteness on some occasions of my detail of Johnson's conversation, and how happily it is adapted for the petty exercise of ridicule, by men of superficial understanding and ludicrous fancy; but I remain firm and confident in my opinion, that minute particulars are frequently characteristick, and always amusing, when they relate to a distinguished man." It could be restated as ". . . how happily minuteness is adapted for the petty exercise of ridicule."

54. (B) The sentence provided in choice B defends the writer's choice to include as many details and particulars as possible when writing Johnson's biography. The other statements are generally about the genre of biography but do not say anything specific about the writer's claims about Johnson's biography.

55. (D) "Apothegm" is used to mean "adage," or "maxim," or "proverb," or "aphorism." All of these synonyms mean a short, wise saying. The word "apothegm" is defined in the context of the sentence as "the wise and pithy words of others."

56. (C) The tone can be described as confident because the writer speaks with certainty when defending his choice to write Johnson's biography. His confidence is in part due to his special relationship with Johnson, which provides him with access to the intimate details that would make a strong biography. He confidently aligns himself with Julius Caesar, whom he refers to as "the greatest man of any age."

57. (A) The passage relies mostly on ethos, as the writer is seeking to make himself a credible biographer and an expert. He quotes experts on the subject, including a noted rabbi and Francis Bacon.

58. (E) The passage as a whole is developed by the mode of argument. The writer makes claims defending his writing of Johnson's biography, he acknowledges and refutes counterargument, he uses expert testimony as evidence, and he uses a confident tone.

59. (A) The style is complex and reasoned because of his use of complicated syntax, evidence, and argument skills. He creates a reasoned argument with complicated syntax.

60. (C) The passage relies heavily on quotes, beginning with a block quote from Johnson, continuing with a block quote from Secker, and ending with an embedded quote from

Francis Bacon about Julius Caesar. All of this expert testimony is meant to justify the writer's choices in writing Johnson's biography.

Passage 2b

61. (D) The sentence provided is complex because all of the information between the commas is modifying the subject, "the Commander over Men," which is provided at the beginning of the sentence, but the predicate, "may be reckoned the most important of Great Men," is held until the end. Hence it is complex because it has dependent clauses.

62. (D) The first paragraph of the passage relies on the mode of definition. It defines "king," doing so in part by exploring the etymology of the word.

63. (A) In context, "querulously" means "in a complaining fashion," and it is used to describe the discontentedness of men who measure reality against ideals and complain when reality does not measure up to ideals.

64. (C) The passage uses formal diction and does not use colloquialisms. It does vary its sentence structure (uses periodic among other constructions), use emphatic punctuation (the exclamation mark, for example), enumerate (for example, "Husting-speeches, Parliamentary motions, Reform Bills, French Revolution . . ."), and use figurative language (for example, an extended metaphor of a bricklayer).

65. (E) The writer acknowledges the counterargument that others would raise in objection. This counterargument would point out that ideals cannot be fully realized. The writer raises and responds to this possible counterargument.

66. (D) Paragraph four analyzes the causes of rebellions. The writer claims that the cause of all rebellions is the placement of an unable man at the head of affairs. The writer points to this misplacement as the major cause of "madness" and "a fatal chaos."

67. (A) The extended metaphor of the bricklayer begins in the third paragraph and continues into the fourth paragraph and illustrates the disastrous results of having an unable man as king. This is developed through the cause and effect of rebellions in paragraph four.

68. (C) There is no apposition, nor an appositive, in which a noun or noun phrase replaces the preceding noun. There is inversion in the phrase "Nature's laws do none of them forget to act"; there is figurative language in that this sentence is employing an extended metaphor; there is an allusion to "Sansculottism"; and there is alliteration with the phrase "miserable millions."

69. (B) The first portion of the passage defines "king" and the last portion of the passage analyzes the effects of choosing an unable man to be king, when the proper definition of a king is an "able man."

70. (C) This sentence defines the king as the "ablest," "truest-hearted," "justest," and "noblest," and then it discusses how following the able man has the best consequences for us. This sentence is the most complete in terms of the thesis of this passage as it defines and then analyzes the effects of choosing the king.

Passage 2c

71. (D) Anaphora is found in the repetition of "after it is" in three consecutive clauses. Metaphor is found in the line "possesses an unfair weapon," as the writer is not discussing a literal weapon. Enumeration is found when the writer lists "harass, vex, impede, affront, humiliate . . ." Asyndeton is found is the line "a weapon, an instrument, a tool, a utensil . . ." Understatement is not found in the paragraph.

72. (C) All of the listed options are opposites, except "lucky vs. unfair," because "lucky" describes those who are also wealthy, happy, and strong. "Unfair" modifies "advantages," not the "weak and poor."

73. (E) The speech is meant to inspire the crowd and relies on pathos through its moving figurative language, and the passage relies on ethos by asking the audience to consider what is right and wrong in the situation between the two political parties. The passage does not rely heavily on logos to persuade the audience.

74. (C) The speech is meant to persuade the audience, which can be seen in the last sentence, which reads, "When it is realised that the Party which possesses this prodigious and unfair advantage is in the main the Party of the rich against the poor, of the classes and their dependants against the masses, of the lucky, the wealthy, the happy, and the strong against the left-out and the shut-out millions of the weak and poor, you will see how serious the constitutional situation has become." The purpose is to persuade the audience of how serious the situation is.

75. (A) The second paragraph is meant to inform the audience of the particular details of the situation, which includes the names of specific people involved and the dates of specific events. Many declarative sentences inform the audience, such as, "There was the Tory democracy of Lord Randolph Churchill in 1885 and 1886, with large, far-reaching plans of Liberal and democratic reform, of a generous policy to Ireland, of retrenchment and reduction of expenditure upon naval and military armaments . . ."

76. (B) If the word "it" is traced to its antecedent, it refers to "one of these Parties." "It" is repeated many times to point to all of the offenses of the party being blamed.

77. (E) The writer is scorning the Conservative Party in the third paragraph and his tone is clear in the following line, between two dashes, "if you can call them leaders." His tone is harsh and full of contempt. This is also clear in his diction, with choices such as "monopolised" and "coercion" to describe the Conservative Party.

78. (A) The power of the third paragraph of the speech is achieved by its use of anaphora, repeating "upon." It also uses rhetorical questions, such as, "But what social legislation, what plans of reform do the Conservative Party offer now to the working people of England if they will return them to power?" It also uses a parenthetical statement in between dashes, "if you can call them leaders." It also uses figurative language in the closing of "crammed down their throats at their own expense."

79. (C) This sentence is cumulative because the main independent clause is at the beginning of the sentence, reading, "Now it is discovered that one of these Parties possess an unfair weapon," and then tacks on many supporting details.

80. (C) "Repugnant" most nearly means "offensive" in this statement. It is a much harsher word than "incompatible," which seems to be a close fit. The church is described as offensive to the conscience of the Welsh people.

Passage 2d

81. (D) The passage uses the mode of comparison and contrast to develop its point about history. The writer contrasts the two different types of history throughout the passage, namely historical romances and historical essays.

82. (C) The statement is paradoxical because one would not expect it to be true that specific details impress general truths upon the reader. It is seemingly contradictory that specific points would have a general effect.

83. (E) "Amalgamation" most nearly means "union" because the sentence is stating that there has not been a coming together of two hostile elements. The antonym of "separated" is a context clue to help the reader define amalgamation as "union."

84. (A) Although "severalty" and "the whole" are used as opposites, these terms are not used to describe the hostile elements in the first paragraph. All of the other pairs are used to describe the hostile elements.

85. (D) The two sentences in paragraph two are both periodic, in that the main clauses of the sentences are held until the end, near the period. The predicate of the first sentence is "have been appropriated" and the predicate of the second sentence is "has become."

86. (C) "It" refers to "the picture" mentioned above. The reader can determine that "it" refers to the picture because it is grand and Rosa (an artist) peopled (painted people) the picture with outlaws. A map would not be populated nor would it have a setting sun, as mentioned in the last part of the sentence.

87. (E) Although the writer mentions "allegory," he does not employ allegory, which is the representation of abstract ideas with characters that symbolize these ideas.

88. (B) The second paragraph describes in detail what each type of history has to offer. In short, the historical novel provides us details, while the historical essay provides us general truths. But the writer describes these two types in detail.

89. (C) All of the other statements provide claims that lead up to the major claim, but only the sentence provided in answer choice C provides the full claim that the combination of these two hostile elements of history have not been joined in the time period that the writer is writing in.

90. (D) The writer is praising, or lauding, what the two types of history have to offer. He provides long sentences that pile on the details of what historical essays and novels have to offer.

Passage 2e

91. (D) In context, the word "apology" most nearly means "justification," in that the writer who wants to publish a memoir is justified in wanting to do so due to the popularity of the genre at the time.

92. (B) The claim of the passage is that the taste of the age allows for biographies that provide little to no personal information about the subject. The writer makes this claim about the time to prepare his audience for the defense of his own biography of Lord Macaulay.

93. (A) The overall purpose of the passage is for the writer to justify his writing of Macaulay's biography. He describes the era and then defends his choices in writing this biography, for which he has personal knowledge.

94. (C) The line is an analogy in that it compares getting an idea of Macaulay from his works to getting an idea of who Shakespeare is from his plays. The point is that it is difficult to know the writer from his body of work with his personal conversations, letters, etc.

95. (D) In the first paragraph of the essay the writer speaks generally about the subject of biographies in his era and the next paragraph shifts to a specific discussion of Macaulay as not being known through his works, much like Shakespeare, in contrast to Dickens and Thackeray, whose works reflected more of their lives and personal qualities.

96. (E) The primary audience for this passage would be those who were familiar with and interested in Macaulay's work and as a result would want to know more of his personal life and could do so by reading his biography, as written by the writer of the passage.

97. (D) The passage has long complicated sentences throughout, parallel structure, analogy ("It would be almost as hard to compose a picture of the author from the History, the Essays, and the Lays, as to evolve an idea of Shakespeare from *Henry the Fifth* and *Measure for Measure*"), and parenthesis, using both parentheses and dashes to enclose amplifications to the sentences in which they appear. The passage doesn't provide imagery.

98. (D) The argument presented here is reasoned and uses tools such as analogy to make its point clear and persuasive. The writer is trying to present himself as a credible person and expert on the subject. Because of these two reasons, it mostly appeals to ethos and logos.

99. (B) This passage is a defense or justification and so it uses the mode of argument to achieve its purpose. It is arguing for the need for the type of biography that the writer has written about Macaulay and is defending the choices of the writer.

100. (C) In the last paragraph, the writer characterizes himself as not having the skill necessary to write this biography. He is trying to make himself humble in the eyes of the reader.

Chapter 3

Passage 3a

101. (C) The writer refers to the poetry of the first quarter of the century as having creative force, but not having data, which he defines as materials, a current of ideas, fresh thought, and a national glow of life.

102. (A) In context, sanguine means "optimistic" as it is used to describe the hopes that the literature of this time period would last longer than the literature of the time periods before it.

103. (B) Overall, the writer is arguing for the necessity of criticism in a time when there is not a "national glow of life." This is seen in the line "In the England of the first quarter of this century there was neither a national glow of life and thought, such as we had in the age of Elizabeth, nor yet a culture and a force of learning and criticism such as were to be found in Germany." The other answer choices are inaccurate.

104. (E) When the writer refers to "a kind of semblance to it," "it" is referring back to "this state of things." "It" refers to different nouns in other parts of the sentence, but this example of "it" refers to "this state of things."

105. (D) The statement presented does not give an example of the writer's claim. It provides a transition with its shift and use of the word "but," and it acknowledges and refutes the possible counterargument that books and reading were missing from the poets of the first quarter of the 19th century.

106. (B) "A current of ideas" is a metaphor in which a collection of ideas is compared to a part of a body of water that has a definite and powerful force, something that could take over.

107. (D) The passage is reliant on parallel structure, such as in the sentences "In other words, the English poetry of the first quarter of this century, with plenty of energy, plenty of creative force, did not know enough. This makes Byron so empty of matter, Shelley so incoherent, Wordsworth even, profound as he is, yet so wanting in completeness and variety." It also uses examples of different authors and different time periods. It uses complicated sentence structures throughout and provocative statements, such as the writer's harsh judgments about Wordsworth. It does not rely on description or imagery.

108. (B) With its provocative statements and self-praise on the role of criticism, the tone of the passage can best be described as confident and polemical, meaning disputatious and controversial.

109. (E) Each of the provided sentences states the major claim about the lack of "data" in the poetry of the first quarter of the 19th century. This major claim leads the writer to provide his answer to this lack, which is the presence of thoughtful criticism.

110. (E) The passage as a whole is an argument. It doesn't narrate a sequence of events; describe an object, scene, etc.; analyze a process; nor compare and contrast subjects. It makes a provocative claim and provides examples to prove its claim, with a confident and polemical tone.

Passage 3b

111. (D) The first paragraph sets up the writer's argument by defining both "great men" and subsequently "the greatest genius." This can be seen in the construction that clearly defines genius by saying, "The greatest genius is the most indebted man." The mode of definition lays out the boundaries of what is and what is not for a term or concept. Here, the writer defines the greatest man, or genius, by saying he is not the most original, but that he is most in touch with his time and place.

112. (B) The sentence provided is a periodic sentence because its main clause is at the end of the sentence: "no great men are original." It is not simple because it has dependent clauses and it is not compound or compound-complex because there is only one independent clause, which comes at the end, which is the opposite of cumulative.

113. (C) The sentence provided can best be described as a paradox, because the sentiment presented is seemingly contradictory but true (according to the writer) nonetheless. One imagines a genius to be original, but it is the writer's provocative idea that a genius is actually in touch with his surroundings and capable of providing something necessary, which is not necessarily original.

114. (E) Although "rattlebrain" can be defined as "one who is thoughtless and flighty," the context of the sentence provides the definition as used here. The definition is provided in the portion of the sentence that reads, "because he says everything," providing a definition in context that "rattlebrain" is a synonym for "one who is giddy and talkative."

115. (A) The portion of the sentence that reads, "a heart in unison with his time and country," contains an example of synecdoche, because the heart stands for the man. Synecdoche is a type of figurative language in which the part stands for the whole. Here, the heart is a part of the whole, the man or the poet.

116. (C) One metaphor is found in the line "in the river of the thoughts and events"; anaphora is found in the repetition of "He finds"; asyndeton is found in "Men, nations, poets, artisans, women"; one exclamatory remark is found in "What an economy of power!" Epistrophe, or the repetition of a word or group of words at the end of successive phrases, clauses, or sentences, is not found in the paragraph.

117. (E) All of the examples in the second paragraph show situations in which the genius is receptive. The examples show the genius understanding the needs of his time and being open and responsive to filling those needs.

118. (C) Polysyndeton is used in the repetition of "or," colloquialism is used in "hits on a railroad," parallelism is used in "from the place of production to the place of consumption," and the sentence has two independent clauses separated by "and."

119. (E) Although the other sentences all contain claims that lead up to the major claim, only the last sentence contains the major claim that a genius is not original and that he is receptive to his time, filling the needs of his contemporaries.

120. (A) Judging from the paradox of the major claim of the passage and the range of examples provided, "reflective" is the best choice for the tone of the passage. The writer is thoughtful and deliberative as he presents his thoughts on what a genius truly is.

Passage 3c

121. (D) The passage uses the mode of composition of definition to explore what poetry is and is not. For example, poetry is defined as being a "universal language" and is also defined as not being "a mere frivolous accomplishment."

122. (E) The writer is straightforward in his discussion of poetry, not using irony to develop his position. There is polysyndeton in "there is a sense of beauty, or power, or harmony" with the repetition of "or"; there is personification in "there is poetry, in its birth," providing poetry with the human characteristic of being born; there is colloquialism when the writer uses the word "stuff" in the line "'the stuff of which our life is made'"; and metaphor is used in "the empty cases in which the affairs of the world are packed," when the writer is discussing history.

123. (E) The sentence provided uses epistrophe as "is poetry" is repeated at the end of successive clauses; it uses asyndeton as no conjunctions are used between the penultimate and last clause in that same series; and it uses enumeration as the writer lists the many emotions and feelings that are poetry.

124. (C) Although the words "deep" and "wide" are both used in the sentence, they do not encompass all that the word "grave" connotes. Although "somber" is a synonym for "grave," the writer isn't arguing that poetry is dark. "Momentous" is also a synonym for grave, as in a grave decision, but that doesn't fit its use here. Overall, the writer is arguing that poetry is "serious" in that it requires serious thought and has both breadth and depth.

125. (A) Although slaves and tyrants could be considered opposites, there is no textual evidence to make them opposites here. All of the other pairs are set up in the same parallel structure and this form asks us to see them all as pairs of opposites.

126. (E) The author alludes to other literature, quotes throughout, provides many and varied examples of what poetry is, and uses figurative language throughout to make his claim clear to the reader. At no point does the writer tell a short or personal narrative.

127. (B) As stated in question 121, the passage uses a mode of composition of definition. Above all else, the writer is exploring what poetry is, and while he explores the inspirations for and surprising places that poetry exists, he doesn't explore forms or types of poetry and poets.

128. (A) The last sentence of the passage states that poets are not the only ones who have keen insight, wild imagination, and an understanding beyond what rationality can offer. In other words, poets are not the only sources of poetry in the world.

129. (C) The many examples listed in the passage present situations that the writer calls poetry. All show powerful and beautiful moments in life. His main claim is that poetry is not confined to the works of poets; poetry is all of the most poignant of human emotions and experiences.

130. (B) Because of the writer's long and enumerative sentences, long paragraph length, figurative language, and thorough exploration of the definition of poetry, his tone can be described as effusive. In other words, the style and content of the passage leads to the belief that the writer has great enthusiasm and emotion for his subject, poetry.

Passage 3d

131. (A) The first sentence of the passage is a claim, meaning that it states a thesis. A warrant is a shared assumption, a qualification is a modification of a claim, evidence is the providing of examples to prove the validity of the claim, and a rebuttal is an answer to another claim, a counterargument to the argument provided.

132. (D) The context clues provided in the line "meantime it is only the roughness of the eye that makes any two persons, things, situations, seem alike" point to the definition of "The lack of attention to details." Because this eye would make persons, things, and situations seem alike, it is lacking attention to the details that would make distinctions.

133. (B) There are many metaphors, such as "this hard gem-like flame," which compares living a full life to burning brightly. Asyndeton is used in the phrase "persons, things, situations," which doesn't have any conjunctions; and polysyndeton is used in the phrase "theory, or idea, or system," which uses more conjunctions than necessary. There are also allusions to Comte and Hegel.

134. (C) In context, it can be seen that "discriminate" means "to see what is distinct in those around us," and the writer claims that to not do that all of the time is to "sleep before evening"—that is, miss out on life before it is over.

135. (E) "To sleep before evening" is a metaphor for missing out on the best of life before your time is over. In this example of figurative language, "sleep" is to give up or shut down and "evening" is death.

136. (C) When the writer discusses Rousseau, he says he decided that "it" must be by intellectual excitement. If you trace the pronoun use back to its antecedent, you can see that "it" refers to making as much as possible of the interval that remained, and he decides "it" must be done (making as much as possible) by intellectual excitement.

137. (C) With its figurative language, carpe diem message, and ruminations on art above all else, this passage appeals primarily to pathos. The writer hopes readers will be moved emotionally.

138. (B) The beginning of paragraph two provides an example of Rousseau, who when struck by a mortal disease decided to live the rest of his life to the fullest, which meant for him pursuing intellectual excitement, namely reading Voltaire. An anecdote is a personal story and this example comes from the writer's reading not his experiences.

139. (E) Using primarily an appeal to pathos, the passage as a whole is developed by argumentation. The writer makes bold claims, such as "To burn always with this hard gem-like flame, to maintain this ecstasy, is success in life," and, "Failure is to form habits." The writer argues that the best way to live a short life is to immerse one's self in beauty and experience.

140. (B) The writer writes vividly and earnestly using striking metaphors and provocative claims. The tone can best be described as passionate. There is an outpouring of emotion and thoughts, and the writer seems to believe strongly in what he writes. He speaks with passion and fervor.

Passage 3e

141. (C) The sentence quoted is a cumulative sentence because the main clause is stated in the beginning portion of the sentence. The subject is "we" and the predicate is "may go on at our ease to examine the point in question." From there additional clauses are accumulated after the first main, independent clause.

142. (E) The first two paragraphs contain sentence variety, ranging from simple to cumulative; they have a definition for the term "false appearances," as "entirely unconnected with any real power or character in the object;" they have personification in the quote, "The spendthrift crocus, bursting through the mould / Naked and shivering, with his cup of gold," and they have a rhetorical question, "How is it that we enjoy so much the having it put into our heads that it is anything else than a plain crocus?"

143. (D) Paragraph three classifies "this fallacy" into binary groups, those "of wilful fancy" and those "caused by an excited state of the feelings." This paragraph uses the mode of classification to further the writer's claims.

144. (A) When the writer defines "pathetic fallacy," he is using a definition of "pathetic" that is "caused by the feelings," because the fallacy that he is discussing is a "falseness in all our impressions of external things" caused by strong feelings.

145. (C) The last line of the passage states the major claim "But I believe, if we look well into the matter, that we shall find the greatest poets do not often admit this kind of falseness,—that it is only the second order of poets who much delight in it.[55]" Understanding what the writer means by the "second order of poets" requires you to read footnote 55 for his definition.

146. (D) The tone of the passage can best be described as didactic as the passage is intended to instruct. The writer aims to make his topic clear to readers by defining, classifying, and ultimately making a claim about who uses the pathetic fallacy in their poetry.

147. (D) The two words discussed are revealed as being "objective" and "subjective" in footnote 52, and the writer describes the words as "tiresome" and "absurd" in the first sentence.

148. (A) Holmes. The writer's name being quoted is Oliver Wendell Holmes. Footnote 53 provides the name of the author being quoted and his first and middle name in parentheses.

It would be incorrect to provide a first name to cite a quote so it's clear that the author leads with the last name in the footnote.

149. (B) Kingsley. Footnote 54 more clearly provides the author's last name and the title of the work that is being quoted. The title of the work is *Alton Locke*, and these lines are taken from chapter 26 of that work.

150. (C) The writer looks down on "young pseudo-poets" and writes that, "all inferior poetry is an injury to the good." Because of his judgments and lack of patience with those who write bad poetry, his tone can best be described as condescending.

Chapter 4

Passage 4a

151. (B) The first sentence of the passage claims that authors are most likely to fail when writing humor because it is the kind of writing in which they are most ambitious to excel.

152. (E) The first four answer choices state what humor is not. After providing what humor is not, the writer states that humor "should always lie under the check of reason."

153. (C) There is an allusion to Bedlam, a mental hospital; there is personification of humor as indulging itself; there are many complicated sentence structures; and there is a rhetorical question: "who set up for men of humour, what wild, irregular fancies, what unnatural distortions of thought do we meet with?"

154. (D) The writer provides an allegory in which Truth is the father of Good Sense, who is the father of Wit, who marries Mirth, with whom Wit fathered a child named Humor. Allegory uses symbolic fictional actions and figures to reveal truths.

155. (D) When the writer uses the word "barbarous," he is referring to his inability to enjoy false humor and as such, the word is used to mean "uncivilized." He suggests that the false humor is beneath him in terms of his level of sophistication and culture.

156. (B) The second "him" refers to Humor, while the first "him" in that sentence refers to "an impostor." We are told the impostor would try to pass for "him" in this world, which lets us know that the "him" is Humor.

157. (A) "Spurious" is here being used to mean "counterfeit." While "deceptive" is close, the context states that the reader should be looking for signs of a lack of authenticity. Readers are told to look for "an impostor," in other words, a fake or a counterfeit.

158. (D) The passage's primary mode of composition is definition, as the passage seeks to answer the question "what is humor?" The first paragraph primarily enumerates what humor is not, the third paragraph provides an allegory to help define humor and its sources, and the fourth and final paragraph classifies true and false humor to further clarify the definition of humor.

159. (A) The tone is self-assured in that the writer feels certain of his convictions about humor and in his expertise. For example, the writer sees himself as qualified to judge the skill of an author in the sentence, "For my part, when I read the delirious mirth of an unskilful author, I cannot be so barbarous as to divert myself with it, but am rather apt to pity the man, than to laugh at anything he writes."

160. (B) There are two references to the claim that the writer of humor should not be the amused party and that while the reader should laugh, "False Humour is always laughing whilst everybody about him looks serious."

Passage 4b

161. (C) The purpose of the passage is to classify the different types of single men, married men, and married women. The writer discusses the different types of single and married people, ruminating on the characters and the best possible occupations for them.

162. (B) The irony of the two sentences provided is that those with children should care more about the future generations, but they contribute less. This is situational irony because the outcome of the situation is the opposite of what we would expect.

163. (D) Because "girdles and garters" are literal women's undergarments, these two objects are being used as symbols of restraint to certain men who choose to marry.

164. (E) In the line referenced, the word "impertinences" most nearly means "irrelevancies," in the sense that some single men consider future times irrelevancies and allow their thoughts and work to die with them.

165. (B) Because the word "their" modifies "girdles and garters," the only noun that makes sense in this example is "women." Girdles and garters are women's undergarments.

166. (A) The repetition of the word "best" at the beginning of successive phrases makes this sentence an example of anaphora.

167. (E) The writer of the passage claims that single men make better churchmen, as they have the time and resources for charity, and that single men make better inquisitors, because they are more capable of cruelty without the humanizing force of women and children in their lives. Judges can be either married or not, and soldiers are better as married men.

168. (B) The sentence that shows wives as mistresses then companions then nurses is meant to illustrate the changing roles of wives throughout the years based on the age and condition of the husbands.

169. (C) The word choice of "folly" in the last sentence makes it more likely that the women the writer is referring to are likely to make the most of their marriages to avoid looking foolish. They want to "good their own folly," or correct their own foolishness.

170. (D) The tone can best be described as jovial, meaning that the writer's comments are good-natured and convivial. This can be seen in his inclusion of some jokes, such as "But yet he was reputed one of the wise men, that made answer to the question, when a man should marry,—A young man not yet, an elder man not at all," which states that a wise man said it's never a good time to get married. His tone is light and good natured as he ponders the different types of unmarried and married people.

Passage 4c

171. (C) The claim that jolliness in babies is a result of their humorlessness is a paradox in that one would expect jolliness to be a result of humor, but according to the writer, the truth is that their seriousness contributes to their happiness.

172. (A) The allusion in the sentence is to the Bible's story of creation in Genesis. The phrase "the seventh day of creation" would provide an allusion, or indirect reference, to those who are familiar with Genesis.

173. (D) The sentence provided uses both anaphora (by repeating "new" at the beginning of the successive phrases) and asyndeton (by not having any conjunctions) to show the wonder of the newness of the universe in a baby's perspective.

174. (A) The fact that babies are serious is stated as a fact as to why we are drawn to them in the first sentence, but their seriousness is not alone in why we worship them. The rest of the sentence makes it clear that their seriousness is a cause of their happiness, which is a reason to worship them. They are completely happy because of their seriousness and that is worthy of worship.

175. (D) The sentence claims that we believe that if we could destroy custom and see the stars as a child seems them, it would be revolutionary. In this sense, "custom" is used as a routine that we follow without thinking about it, and the context that if we could destroy that monotonous routine we would see the world anew makes that particular meaning clear.

176. (E) The sentence uses irony in its use of "trifling." "Trifling" means lacking in significance or worth, and so the writer's modifying the "effort of remaking heaven and earth" is verbally ironic in that this effort is the opposite of meaningless and insignificant.

177. (B) The repetition of "marvelous" makes this sentence use epistrophe, meaning the repetition of a word or a group of words at the end of successive phrases, clauses, or sentences.

178. (C) The sentence provides counterargument in that some (the cynical philosopher) would say that what babies do is common and not worthy of worship. The writer goes on to argue why that counterargument is incorrect.

179. (A) Although he does explain why people worship babies, the writer's primary purpose in the passage is to defend the practice of worshipping babies. He explains why it happens and why it makes perfect sense. His goal is not to persuade people to worship babies, although that may be a side effect. The primary purpose is to defend baby-worship.

180. (E) The tone is jocular and thoughtful in that the writer is playful with his use of description of babies as "human mushrooms" and his ironic use of "trifling." But besides being playful and joking, the writer is thoughtful in that he is musing big concepts throughout the passage, such as creation, apocalypse, maturity, appreciation, and so on.

Passage 4d

181. (D) The passage primarily uses classification as it classifies the human species into two groups, those who borrow and those who lend. This is an evaluative classification as it makes clear which group of the two is superior. The writer says those who borrow are "the great race."

182. (C) "Impertinent" most nearly means "irrelevant" in the context of the statement. The writer's claim is that men can be classified into two major groups so the other classifications, such as Gothic, Celtic, white, black, etc., are all irrelevant.

183. (B) "Their" is used as a pronoun to refer to the great race, "the men who borrow," and the former. "Their" modifies "figure, port, and a certain instinctive sovereignty," which are all qualities that belong to the men who borrow.

184. (E) Ironically, the term "generous" is used to describe the borrowers, not the lenders.

185. (E) Paragraph three has many sentence fragments, such as "what rosy gills!" Paragraph three is primarily composed of sentences that do not have both a subject and predicate; most of the constructions are lacking a predicate.

186. (B) This paragraph is about the borrower's ability to resolve the two opposite of mine and yours (meum and tuum) into the one pronoun of "mine." In other words, in the eyes of the borrower, everything is "mine."

187. (D) The first sentence includes an analogy, which compares the distance between "him" (a borrower) and "one of us" (lenders) and the distance between the Augustan Majesty and the poorest obolary Jew that paid tribute at Jerusalem. This analogy is ironic in that the borrower is compared to royalty and the lenders are compared to the poor.

188. (A) The passage as a whole is ironic, claiming that borrowers are generous, trusting, and open. The reason that they are generous is that they belong to the group that does not have anything. Borrowers are also ironically described as noble and honorable.

189. (B) The essay is a satire, poking fun at the so-called "generous manners" of borrowers. Borrowers are careless because they have nothing to care for, they have contempt for money because they are without any, and they want to simplify pronouns so that the only pronoun is "mine," so that they can freely borrow what is not theirs.

190. (C) Overall, the passage is very allusive. The writer alludes to Shakespeare with his mention of the character Falstaff. Besides literary allusions, the writer alludes freely to both history and the Bible.

Passage 4e

191. (D) Although the writer does mention a story that he heard in the first sentence, the bulk of the first paragraph is a binary classification of faults. It classifies faults into two groups, those from infirmity and those from treachery and malice.

192. (E) The definition of "questionable" as used in this sentence is obsolete. In context it means capable of being inquired of or capable of being questioned. The statement reads that we are not capable of being questioned for anything not committed against our consciences.

193. (B) The only answer choice that contains a description of cowardice is B, a product of frailty, or infirmity. All of the other descriptions are used to describe faults proceeding from treachery and malice.

194. (C) The writer qualifies the first claim presented. In the last line of the passage, he writes, "Notwithstanding, in case of such a manifest ignorance or cowardice as exceeds all ordinary example, 'tis but reason to take it for a sufficient proof of treachery and malice, and for such to be punished," meaning that if the example of cowardice is not within the realm of the ordinary, it should be treated as evil and should be punished as such. He is qualifying the original claim, stating that if the example is bad enough, it should be punished as if it were treachery or malice.

195. (A) The sentence provided is an acknowledgment of the counterargument because the writer does believe that cowardice should be punished when it is extreme enough. He agrees that there is reason to differentiate between faults, but ultimately his claim is against the claim stated at the beginning of the passage.

196. (E) The first set of brackets provides both amplification (that this surrender referred to was to Henry VIII) and the date. The second set provides a translation. The third set provides a citation, and the fourth and fifth sets provide dates. None provide personal commentary.

197. (A) The quote is an adage that can translate to "it is better to shame a man than kill him." The context before the quote provided makes it clear that it is better to shame a man because it is possible to awake his courage through his shame. If the man were killed, there would be no possibility of redemption.

198. (D) The "it" in "it is," or "'tis," refers back to "death." The sentence says that "it" (death) should be feared as an option by those who committed the offence. According to the writer, death should be feared as an option because disgracing the offenders may make them desperate and then enemies and the threat that they could pose should be controlled by the fear of death.

199. (E) I, II, and III. The passage appeals to ethos through its ethical issues of men's faults and the presentation of the writer's background knowledge to establish him as credible. The passage appeals to logos with its wealth of historical information, including dates, names, etc. The passage also appeals to pathos with its figurative language, provocative concepts, and emotional diction, such as "having awakened their courage by this open shame."

200. (C) Although the writer is not indifferent, his tone is objective throughout the passage as he is not personally involved or subjective. The writer provides an objective account of the issue of the punishing of cowardice and then provides historical examples. Not until the final sentence of the passage does the writer make clear his opinion on the subject.

Chapter 5

Passage 5a

201. (D) The writer sees the ideal beauty of the wood-cutters' lives in spite of the slovenly nature of their huts. In the next paragraph, she speaks of the job of the poet, which is to add beauty to the normal lives and jobs of people and to leave out the dirt. As such, the writer's mentioning of their slovenly huts is an example of the dirt that would be left out.

202. (E) The last choice, "Men who must be at the full expense in describing their position," describes poets of the present time (when the passage was written), while the other choices describe men with the three listed positions that lived in slower times, etc.

203. (A) The first answer choice is the only option that speaks generally of poets. All of the other choices use the first person to describe the particular feelings of the writer. Also, the other choices are not direct results of the more rapid growth.

204. (C) The second paragraph analyzes the effects of more rapid growth on the lives and jobs of poets. Because of rapid growth, the poet must describe the lives of workers, since workers don't have the time to find the moral and meaning of their lives.

205. (D) "Mushroom" is used metaphorically to say that the growth is fast. Mushrooms are rapidly growing fungi. To say something is mushrooming is to say it is growing rapidly.

206. (B) In context, the writer is saying that she will not be so open to the West as to confuse ugliness with beauty, discord with harmony, and to praise and be happy with everything she sees.

207. (E) Metaphor is found in the line "I come to the West prepared for the distaste I must experience at its mushroom growth," with mushroom used figuratively. Simile is found in the line "In older countries the house of the son grew from that of the father, as naturally as new joints on a bough, and the cathedral crowned the whole as naturally as the leafy summit the tree." Alliteration is found in the phrase "mighty meaning." Allusion is found in the sentence "I trust by reverent faith to woo the mighty meaning of the scene, perhaps to foresee the law by which a new order, a new poetry, is to be evoked from this chaos, and with a curiosity as ardent, but not so selfish, as that of Macbeth, to call up the apparitions of future kings from the strange ingredients of the witch's caldron."

208. (B) Irony is expressed in the line "The march of peaceful is scarce less wanton than that of warlike invasion." One would not expect the march of the peaceful to have the same disastrous results as warlike invasion. It's ironic because one would expect the opposites of war and peace to have opposite effects, but according to the writer, they have the same results.

209. (C) The passage relies heavily on natural description and alludes to Shakespeare, mythology, history, etc. It begins with the description of a place and carries through its argument using descriptive imagery and allusions.

210. (A) The tone of the passage can best be described as bittersweet, because the writer does seem to mourn a simpler time and regret the effects of the rapid growth of the present; however, she ends on a hopeful note, saying that she will be a part of a new body of poetry, a new intellectual growth.

Passage 5b

211. (A) "Verity" most nearly means "truth," in context. In the sentence, the sentiment is that although the phrase is inelegant, it has a brilliant truth to it nonetheless.

212. (B) The use of the word "sucker" provides a humorous and informal tone to the passage. The writer uses this word at the end of the first paragraph in order to establish his tone as he moves into the second paragraph of the passage.

213. (E) The writer does not provide an anecdote in paragraph two. He speaks generally about the French and the American. Syntactical inversion is present in the line "of Yankee sneer and bitterness containing not a trace." A simile is present in the sentence "They cast it as one casts a coin into the hand of some maundering beggar." One colloquialism is "oh-wells." The allusion is to the author Zola, by whom the children are reading books.

214. (B) The Frenchman views the American with pity, as can be seen in the line "he yet, detesting, sorrows for them, sees them as mere misled yokels."

215. (D) The Frenchman is said to view the American as inexperienced in the characterization of the Frenchman as an old understanding professor who shakes his head at his young and innocent student, the American.

216. (E) The American primarily sees himself as worldly, or sophisticated, as being called from his New York apartment to the city of Paris to find romance.

217. (E) Romance is not uncurtained to the American. In other words, romance is curtained, or hidden from, the American. Although it may cross his path, it will be unseen, unfelt, and unknown by him.

218. (C) The style can best be described as unorthodox, or unconventional, in that the passage is humorous, informal, and colloquial, as well allusive, complex, and sophisticated. The writer uses different languages and shifts perspective throughout the passage.

219. (D) The writer is lightly humorous and full of high spirits as he explores his subject of the American in Paris. He doesn't take the topic too seriously and seems to enjoy writing about this subject.

220. (B) With his playful tone and unorthodox style, the writer's main purpose is to entertain his audience with his observations about the American in Paris.

Passage 5c

221. (E) "Affinities" most nearly means "resemblances in structure" in the context of the phrase "reflecting on the mutual affinities of organic beings." While the other options are synonymous with "affinities," only E is the scientific (biological) definition being used here.

222. (B) The conclusion is problematic because it is a hasty generalization, meaning that it is concluding something without sufficient evidence. Begging the question assumes something true in the writer's thesis that has yet to be proven. Ad hominem is attacking the person making the argument rather than the argument. Post hoc is a fallacy in which the event before something happened is assumed as a cause; it mistakes following in time as having a causal relationship. Non sequitur means that the conclusion does not follow as a logical conclusion from the evidence presented.

223. (A) The writer provides the counterargument, which is the belief of the naturalists he refers to. He provides their view as possible but then provides an example that shows the limitations of their argument. A warrant is a shared assumption, a rebuttal is a response disagreeing with an argument, data is the evidence used in making an argument, and a claim is the thesis of the argument.

224. (C) The writer is in awe of the woodpecker and the misseltoe, which can be seen in his diction; for example, his use of the phrase "so admirably" to describe the adaptation of the feet, tail, beak, and tongue of the woodpecker for catching insects.

225. (D) The main clause of the sentence is "it is equally preposterous to account for the structure of this parasite with its relations to several distinct organic beings, by the effects of external conditions, or of habit, or of the volition of the plant itself." Therefore the subject and predicate are "it" and "is" in this complex sentence.

226. (A) In the last paragraph, the writer paves the way to present his findings. He explains reasonably that his studies involved domesticated animals and cultivated plants, and that although the knowledge gained is imperfect, he believes these studies to have afforded valuable information.

227. (C) In context, the problem is mysterious in that the answers are unknown. The other synonyms for "obscure" are more physical ("dark," "faint," and "remote") or a mismatch in terms of connotation. "Ambiguous" means that it can have more than one interpretation, which is not a good fit for this sentence.

228. (D) "Coadaptation" refers to the changes in a species that result from the species' relationship with other species and its life. The examples of the woodpecker and the misseltoe are presented to prove that their modifications must be a result of how they interact with other species. The other options are seen as limited by the writer.

229. (A) The writer is forthright, or straightforward and honest, in the last paragraph of the passage. He admits that it "seemed to [him] probable…" and that the knowledge he has gained is not perfect. He admits that his process is not perfect and that he is not completely certain. He's being honest.

230. (D) The writer sets himself up as credible by being honest and careful in this passage and points out the logical fallacies and shortcomings in the arguments of the naturalists. He is appealing to the audience's sense of ethos and logos.

Passage 5d

231. **(A)** The antecedent for the pronoun "they" is "advocates." The advocates of bringing science into regular education have been "pooh-poohed" by men of business and classical scholars.

232. **(C)** "Pooh-poohed" is an informal colloquialism meaning that something, in this case, the idea of bringing science into ordinary education, has been disparaged and dismissed.

233. **(B)** The writer describes the classical scholars as "Levites in charge of the ark," using a biblical allusion. If students don't recognize the "Levites," they should recognize the ark as an allusion to Noah's ark, in which he saved the animals. Here the classical scholars are in control of culture.

234. **(D)** Rule of thumb is an inexact form of measurement and here, a symbol of practicality, as the practical men worship it as an idol.

235. **(E)** When the writer describes the practical men as a species that has not been "extirpated," the closest synonym is "exterminated," or made extinct. The word "species" is a context clue in that one would describe a species as being exterminated or made extinct.

236. **(C)** "Milton's angels" is a literary allusion to John Milton's *Paradise Lost*, a poem in which the brightest angel of God turns on Him in frustration and hubris and becomes the Devil.

237. **(D)** The sentence provided includes a metaphor, "logical weapons," and simile: "may be as deep as a well and as wide as a church door," but there is no personification.

238. **(A)** The tone of the sentence is exasperated, meaning that the writer is very annoyed and irritated. This can be seen in his declaration: "I will not waste time in vain repetition of the demonstrative evidence of the practical value of science." He finds the practical men hopeless and stubborn.

239. **(B)** The writer has contempt for the practical men. He refers to them as a "species" and repeats "practical" in order to mock them and their practicality as being foolish and limited. He views them with disgust and scorn.

240. **(E)** Although the topic is science, the writer does not rely on scientific data to make his claims. Instead, he proves himself to be literary, learned, well rounded, etc. It seems that in developing himself as an expert on the topic, he shows himself to not be limited by science in his education. While he does allude to Darwin when he discusses the struggle for existence, it does not qualify as "scientific data."

Passage 5e

241. **(C)** The first paragraph is defining "geology" and does so in part by using etymology, looking at "ge" and "logos" as meaning a discourse on the earth. It also provides two questions that help define the subject of geology.

242. (A) The paragraph's claim is that the mineral kingdom was previously thought of as the subject of geology but that further study shows that changes in the earth, including the animals and plants, are also part of the subject of geology.

243. (D) The sentence enumerates, or lists, the various substances and then uses parallelism in the last part, "in their present form, and in their present position." The sentence doesn't use metaphor, or any other figurative language.

244. (E) The sentence is a cumulative sentence because the main independent clause ("he can show that they have acquired their actual configuration and condition gradually") is in the beginning of the sentence and additional details are accumulated afterward.

245. (A) "Artificial" is used to mean "made by humans rather than nature" when describing excavations. This means that the miner finds things that are not revealed by natural forces but rather that are dug up.

246. (D) The meaning of "just" when used to describe the remark is "accurate." The writer is saying that although the remark is accurate, that the earth's crust is small, it is also big and in fact huge in relation to man.

247. (C) The last paragraph defines "earth's crust." It provides denotation, boundaries of the definition, measurements. The last portion of the paragraph ruminates on the scope of the definition, reacting to both its enormity and its relative smallness.

248. (B) Because of both the enormity and relative smallness of the earth, the geologist views it with awe (of its hugeness) and humility (at its smallness in comparison to the universe).

249. (B) The paragraph primarily appeals to logos with its measurements and further definition of "earth's crust."

250. (A) The primary purpose of the passage is to inform the reader about the study of geology. The writer seeks to clear up some misconceptions about the field. It defines geology, which is further evidence of its intention to inform.

Chapter 6

Passage 6a

251. (C) The line uses "she" to refer to Spain. It reads, "On the western side of the Mississippi she advanced in considerable force, and took post at the settlement of Bayou Pierre, on the Red River." Spain is being personified as a woman advancing in force.

252. (A) The first paragraph of this state of the union address is meant to inform the listeners of the present situation in foreign relations, especially with Spain. While Jefferson does try to persuade his listeners later to stay within the law, this paragraph is meant to inform.

253. (B) The sentence provides the number of volunteer cavalry and is analyzing the writer's reasoning for providing the commanding officer with this number. Because of its factual information and its analysis of reasoning, this sentence appeals most to logos.

254. (C) The sentence uses the emotions and values of honor, accomplishment or entitlement, confidence, camaraderie, strength, and determination. It relies on the appeal to pathos to persuade the listeners that these volunteers are outstanding citizens and that they are worthy of our help and protection.

255. (B) The root of the word "promptitude" is prompt, which should help readers figure out that the word is used to describe the quickness with which the citizens responded.

256. (E) The sentence provided has more than one independent clause and several dependent clauses attached. As such, it's a compound-complex sentence.

257. (A) The last sentence repeats "it was due to" in the beginning of two successive clauses. Repetition of a word or group of words in the beginning of successive phrases, clauses, or sentences is anaphora.

258. (C) "Efficaciously" most nearly means "effectively" in both of these sentences. "Expeditiously" is describing something done effectively, but with quickness, which is not mentioned in these contexts.

259. (E) The last paragraph's primary purpose is to defend the writer's choice to disarm the people who were taking matters into their own hands in terms of fighting the Spanish.

260. (A) The tone of the last paragraph can best be described as "fervent," meaning that the writer is showing intensity. This can be seen in the closing line, especially "should be promptly and efficaciously suppressed," which expresses the writer's intensity.

Passage 6b

261. (A) The first paragraph ends with the phrase "conflicting conceptions of what political institutions are," meaning that the writer is introducing the two different definitions of political institutions. Nothing is said of their uses, origins, causes, and effects.

262. (B) In context, "contrivance" most nearly means "clever plan." The sentence states that the first idea of government is one that involves invention and contrivance, which can also be thought of as inventing and planning government.

263. (D) The three sentences referred to are analyzing, or breaking into stages, the process of setting up a government, according to the first school of thought. This can be seen in the phrases, "the first step" and "the next," which show the ordering of the steps.

264. (E) Government, according to the first school of thought, is not fated because it is decided and created by men. It is neither inevitable nor natural.

265. (E) The sentence provided is declarative in that it declares something. It is not demanding or asking anything. It is also not a fragment or a simple sentence, because it is a full sentence with many clauses.

266. **(B)** The last line is an analogy comparing the way that these thinkers look upon government and the way they would look upon a machine, namely a steam plow or a threshing machine.

267. **(B)** Because government, according to the second school of thought, is a natural product of the life of the people involved, it is not purposeful in that it is not intentional. It is organic and discovered, not planned with a purpose in mind.

268. **(C)** The two paragraphs are classifying the two types of conceptions of government. The writer is using binary classification to categorize and discuss ideas about government.

269. **(A)** The writer doesn't judge one conception as better than the other and his primary purpose is not to call them valid or absurd. Ultimately, the writer wants to persuade us that if we temper the claims of both conceptions, we can find and use the truth in them.

270. **(D)** The tone of the passage is primarily impartial, because although the writer classifies the two major conceptions of government, he does not choose one side over the other.

Passage 6c

271. **(C)** In context, "confounded" means confused in that some writers have confused society with government and as a result have not seen any distinctions between the two.

272. **(D)** The mode of composition of paragraphs one and two is primarily definition, as the main purpose of those paragraphs is to define society and government. There are many constructions that are variations of "society is . . . ." and "government is . . ." Both are defining.

273. **(D)** "Encourages and creates" are used to show the actions of society and government, but they are not opposites. They both mean "to bring about."

274. **(E)** Society is personified as a patron, while government is personified as a punisher. They are provided human actions and attributes.

275. **(B)** The line "for when we suffer, or are exposed to the same miseries BY A GOVERNMENT, which we might expect in a country WITHOUT GOVERNMENT, our calamity is heightened by reflecting that we furnish the means by which we suffer" makes the claim that causing our own suffering makes it worse.

276. **(A)** The sentence is a biblical allusion to the Garden of Eden, a paradise. When Adam and Eve eat from the Tree of the Knowledge of Good and Evil, they realize their nakedness and have the capacity for shame, or a loss of innocence.

277. **(D)** It's a paradox because it is seemingly contradictory, but true nonetheless, that the man should have to give up his property in order to protect it.

278. **(D)** The sentence is imperative because the construction "let us suppose" is a command.

279. (E) The third paragraph is developed by examples in order to illustrate what men can do together and their need for each other to survive. It illustrates the positivity of society.

280. (A) Government is necessary because men are inherently bad. Once their needs are met by society, they will turn on one another. So while government is bad, it is a necessary evil to provide men security.

Passage 6d

281. (B) In context, "prodigious" most nearly means "great in size or force." The word is describing the influence that equality of conditions has on all of society and it is clear from the context that the writer is struck by the impact that equality has over society.

282. (C) The word "it" is referring to the influence of this fact, this fact being the general equality of conditions in America. The influence of this equality "creates opinions, engenders sentiments…"

283. (D) The tone of the paragraphs can best be described as reflective, in that the writer is reflecting on his observations in America. He uses words and phrases like "attracted my attention," "perceived," "observations," "my thoughts," "I imagined," and "conceived the idea." All of these words and phrases point to the reflection that the writer is doing in these paragraphs.

284. (E) The author refers to "our own hemisphere" and the rising power of equality in Europe. While he is reflecting on his visit to America, the United States, or the New World, he is seeing the influence of equality on his home, Europe, and writing a book on the topic. Because he "turned his thoughts to" his own hemisphere, it is also clear that he was turning his thoughts away from America.

285. (E) The word "hence" is a context clue that shows the conclusion that the writer decided to write the book being discussed follows the reason before it, which is that democracy (equality of conditions) is "rapidly rising into power in Europe."

286. (D) The sentence is both imperative, beginning with the command "Let us recollect," and cumulative, as the main independent clause of "Let us recollect the situation of France seven hundred years ago," comes first and then many details are accumulated after that that elaborate on that first main clause.

287. (A) The major difference between the two opinions is that democracy is new, or novel, as stated in the sentence vs. old, or ancient, permanent, etc.

288. (B) The paragraph is developed by example, in that it discusses the specific details of France seven hundred years ago to show the shift into democracy. This proves the second opinion that democracy is ancient.

289. (E) The fourth paragraph traces the causes of the rise of democracy, or equality, and the decline of aristocracy, or the privilege of nobility.

290. (E) The last sentence is the major claim because it states the overall point of the paragraph that there were new ways to gain power and because of that possibility of advancement, the value of noble birth declined. The other sentences provide examples and are too specific to certain groups, like financiers, or are minor claims leading up the major claim.

Passage 6e

291. (E) All of the provided statements are true according to the first sentence of the passage. The writer refers to "sorrowful indignation," which points to both sadness and anger as a result of the difference between people that is either a result of nature or their unequal treatment that is a result of civilization.

292. (A) In context, "solicitude" most nearly means "attention." The writer refers to herself as watching the world with "anxious solicitude," meaning that she is watching the world events with an anxious, concerned attention.

293. (D) According to the writer, "the neglected education of my fellow creatures is the grand source of the misery I deplore." The rest of the passage discusses the problems of women as a result of flaws in their education.

294. (B) The sentence develops an analogy between women's minds and flowers that are planted in too rich a soil. The comparison helps clarify that women are educated to be pleasing and that this flawed approach to their education proves detrimental.

295. (C) The writer does not point to the education of women as being self-inflicted by women on themselves. It points to the writings and prejudices of men in not treating women as equals.

296. (A) One of the surprising facts about this passage is that the writer, a woman fighting for the improvement of women's education, discusses what she believes to be the natural inferiority of women in comparison to men. This may be considered ironic by current-day readers, who would expect the opposite from this writer.

297. (E) The last word of the passage is "society," and it most nearly means "company or companionship" in that the claim is that women do not seek to be friends with the fellow creatures (men) when in their company.

298. (C) The writer's purpose is to persuade readers that women's education needs reform and that this education should not be limited to the goal of making women more alluring. It should instead seek to make women respectable.

299. (D) The passage is an argument. It seeks to persuade readers of the need to reform women's education. The passage addresses possible counterargument that others would argue that the writer is dealing with the issue of equality between the sexes. The writer has a clear stance and she wishes to persuade her readers.

300. (A) The tone can best be described as measured indignation because the writer is angry about the education of women. However, she expresses this anger in a limited amount. She is frustrated and angry, but she does admit that she sees women as inferior, which limits her anger.

Chapter 7

Passage 7a

301. (B) Ironically, the only way that being liberal can be positive for the prince is if it is enacted with dishonesty. It must be done in a way to secure a reputation for liberality without the true honesty that liberality should be characterized by.

302. (C) The first paragraph is mostly developed by cause and effect. The paragraph analyzes the effects of being liberal as a prince. The paragraph begins with the cause of exercising liberality and displays all of the effects and results of doing so.

303. (A) Ironically, being liberal leads to being poor, despised, in danger, and having a reputation for being miserly. Although liberality is synonymous with generosity, according to the writer, it does not lead to being loved.

304. (D) "Odious" most nearly means "detestable" in that being liberal will soon make the prince run out of money and he will have to spend the money of his subjects, arousing their hate and displeasure.

305. (E) The pronoun "it" is referring back to the antecedent "danger," which appears before the semicolon. The prince wishes to draw back from danger and so he runs away.

306. (E) This paragraph is developed by example. After developing his major claims about the disastrous results of being liberal and the conclusion stating princes should therefore not fear a reputation for meanness, the writer uses paragraph three to provide historical examples to prove the validity of his argument.

307. (A) Paragraph four is developed by counterargument. The writer provides possible objections, or counterarguments, and then refutes them.

308. (B) The major claim of this passage is paradoxical in that it is seemingly contradictory that liberality would make a prince hated, but according to the writer's reasoning, it is true nonetheless.

309. (B) The passage as a whole relies on the appeal to logos because the writer's argument can be offensive to feelings and morality. His argument is counterintuitive to our feelings toward conventional morality and the treatment of people, and therefore, he relies heavily on logic to persuade his readers.

310. (C) Above all else, the writer's tone is forthright in that he is being completely honest about the realities of being a prince. He reveals the truth behind doing good things for reputation's sake and divulges how a prince can use this information to his benefit.

Passage 7b

311. (B) The first paragraph praises selflessness, claiming that true pleasure comes from the knowledge of knowing that the good man has sacrificed his own advantage for the good of others, putting himself last and therefore being selfless.

312. (A) The pronoun "he" refers to "a good man," mentioned before the semicolon.

313. (D) Nature is personified as teaching us to delight in true pleasures, if we follow our natural appetites. Nature is given human actions and, as such, is personified.

314. (B) The pronouns "us" and "our" refer to all people. Because "they" refers to the residents of Utopia, "us," which includes the writer, must be a different group. The group is not gendered male or female and minds are not people. The paragraph is discussing human nature—that is, all of us.

315. (E) Nature leads us to true and pure pleasures, not to the delights that are mistaken for the pure and true pleasure.

316. (D) Paragraph two is primarily defining pleasure. It defines pleasure as "every motion or state, either of body or mind, in which Nature teaches us to delight."

317. (B) In context, "perverse" means "directed away from what is right or good." The appetite for what is forbidden leads people astray from what is right or good.

318. (C) The primary rhetorical device in paragraph three is the rhetorical question, which is used many times to make the reader consider the writer's points for himself or herself.

319. (E) Perverse appetite is said to be our reason for indulging our taste for forbidden objects. Perverse and forbidden are not discussed as opposites in the passage.

320. (A) The passage primarily appeals to ethos, because of its use of "us," its rhetorical questions, and its topic of morality in a perfect society, a Utopia.

Passage 7c

321. (A) The end of the paragraph, stating that mankind cannot "do the same," refers back to the beginning claim about certain creatures, which is that certain creatures live sociably with one another.

322. (D) The statement says that creatures "want that art of words," meaning that they lack the ability to speak.

323. (E) The first "their" refers to others and the second "their" refers to men, because the statement is that men say things about the appearance versus reality of good and evil to others, and in so doing, men trouble the peace of others for their own pleasure.

324. (B) The statement made is ironic in that it is the opposite of what one would expect. One would expect man to be least troublesome when he is at ease, not most troublesome then. This is an example of situational irony, not verbal irony.

325. (B) The creatures are not ambitious because they have no differentiation between private and public good and as such, always do what's best for the group.

326. (B) The structure of the passage is accomplished by enumeration, or listing, complete with a numbering of examples. This can be seen in the beginning of each paragraph, except the first, which presents the claim of the passage.

327. (C) The passage as a whole is comparing and contrasting men and the certain living creatures that are capable of living sociably with one another.

328. (B) The numbered listing, or enumeration, and the mode of carefully comparing and contrasting men and the creatures capable of living sociably together, contribute to the appeal to logos. The writer is relying on a logical structure and logical mode to make his points.

329. (A) The passage relies on informing readers why men can't live sociably with one another (in contrast with certain living creatures that can). This can be seen in part by the fact that the writer claims men may desire to know why men can't do the same (live sociably with one another). He is not arguing or refuting; he is just informing those who may desire to know, not those who are arguing otherwise.

330. (E) The tone can best be described as learned, in that the writer is knowledgeable and informative about nature, Aristotle, human nature, politics, etc.

Passage 7d

331. (B) The writer creates an analogy between books and food saying that God created us as omnivores to make decisions as to what we read and eat.

332. (D) The paragraph compares meat and food in order to claim that some of each is good and some is evil. The difference is that bad meats cannot be nourishing even in good conditions, while bad books, if judiciously read, can lead us to the truth.

333. (B) The claim is that just as God created us as omnivores in body, expecting us to follow the rules of temperance, he also created us as omnivores in mind. Therefore, a very mature man will exercise his own judgment.

334. (D) The writer is praising, or lauding, the virtue of temperance. He says temperance is wonderful; however, God entrusts man with reason to judge material for himself.

335. (C) "Prescription" here is being used as a word meaning "rule and principle being laid out." It is used as the opposite of God trusting us to make choices as mature people. Instead, it is the idea that God would keep us perpetually like children, giving us rules to follow. The writer refutes this idea of God setting out such rules.

336. (A) The only technique not present is anaphora. The allusion is to the Garden of Eden in Genesis; the simile is "as two twins cleaving together"; the personification is of both Good and Evil and vice; and the rhetorical question is "what continence to forbear without the knowledge of evil?"

337. (D) With its use of figurative language, emotional diction, and allusions to the Bible and mythology, the paragraph appeals to pathos. Also, with its use of the topic of good and evil and its use of rhetorical question, the paragraph appeals to ethos.

338. (E) The writer uses the word "adversary" to refer to the opponent, evil, that virtue should come face-to-face with. Virtues shouldn't be fleeing, secluded, unused, or not living.

339. (B) The overall purpose of the passage is to argue against the censorship of books considered bad. The writer argues that even books that are considered bad can help lead us to the truth.

340. (A) The passage as a whole can best be described as complex and allusive as it incorporates many different modes, complex sentence structures, different devices, etc., and its reasoning is complex. Aside from that, it contains allusions to myth, the Bible, other works of literature, theologians, etc.

Passage 7e

341. (D) "But, Lord!" is an exclamation or an interjection. The use of the exclamation point helps make this clear to the readers.

342. (A) The sentence provided is a fragment because there is no subject. The question it raises because of its incompleteness is "Who is jealous?" Because the writer is writing in his diary, he probably does not feel the need to provide himself as the subject in each sentence, but for the reader, the subject is missing.

343. (D) The phrase is not figurative; it is repeating the first consonant sound of "M." It is an example of alliteration. Assonance repeats the internal vowel sound.

344. (B) Stating that Captain Cocke is the greatest epicure and eats and drinks with the greatest pleasure and liberty ever is an example of hyperbole, or overexaggeration.

345. (E) In context, "repulsed" most nearly means "repelled," or "driven back." The writer of the passage is referring to the fleet being driven back by the Dutch East India ships when the fleet attacked the ships at Bergen.

346. (D) The entry for August 16th refers to the Great Plague of London and the Second Dutch East India War. It does not mention any personal turmoil or troubles.

347. (B) In the line "embarked in the yacht and down we went most pleasantly, and noble discourse I had with my Lord Bruneker, who is a most excellent person," the writer uses three compliments (pleasantly, noble, and excellent) to praise his evening, discussion, and company, respectively.

348. (D) The writer uses more conjunctions than necessary, repeating "and," which makes this an example of polysyndeton.

349. (B) "Her" refers to the ship, which is named the *Nore*. The *Nore* is personified as a woman and the writer refers to her readiness in preparing for the next leg of the journey.

350. (A) In his diary, the writer is primarily narrating his days' events. He does comment on the events and sometimes describes the people and things around him, but mostly he narrates. This can be seen in his time markers and transitions, such as "thence," which provide the next event.

Chapter 8

Passage 8a

351. (E) The passage is structured by enumeration. It is listing, with the use of Roman numerals, the causes of the ruin of Rome.

352. (B) The paradox is that the art of man is described as both permanent and fleeting, which are opposites. This is true in a relative sense. The art of man is more permanent than his life and fleeting when measured against all of time.

353. (A) The footnote is elaborating on the claim that the pyramids' age is unknown. It provides two different theories on how old the pyramids are.

354. (C) The pyramids are used as an example of a simple and solid edifice of which it is difficult to know the duration.

355. (E) Footnote 10 elaborates on the image of the dropping leaves of autumn. The footnote mentions that this image is peculiar to Homer (an allusion) and describes this image as natural and melancholy.

356. (A) In this context, "propagated" most nearly means "spread." In discussing the destruction of fire, the writer says that the mischief of fire can be kindled (or started) and propagated (or spread).

357. (B) The date of November 15, A.D. 64 refers to the persecution of the Christians, not for the major fire of Nero's reign.

358. (D) The title of the work cited in footnote 12 is *Annal*. *Histoire Critique de la République des Lettres* is the work cited in footnote 11.

359. (D) The portion of text contains personification in "fresh beauty from her ashes," asyndeton in "every wound is mortal, every fall irretrievable," enumeration when it numbers the two causes which render fire more destructive to a flourishing city, and alliteration in "state of solitude and safety."

360. (C) The primary mode is cause and effect as the writer is analyzing the four principal causes of the ruin of Rome. This passage is analyzing in detail the cause of injuries of time and nature.

Passage 8b

361. (A) The sentence uses anaphora in that it repeats "to be" in the beginning of the three successive clauses.

362. (C) The primary form of figurative language is personification because Learning and Genius are personified as pressing forward to conquest and glory and bestowing smiles.

363. (B) The structure of the first two paragraphs is a movement from the general to the specific. The first paragraph makes a claim about those who toil at the lower employments of life and the second more specifically discusses the writer of dictionaries.

364. (C) Overall, the job is characterized as being thankless in that the best one can hope for is being free from blame. The writer of dictionaries is described as a "humble drudge," clearing the way for Learning and Genius.

365. (B) Our speech is described throughout paragraph four using parallel structure, with the repeated constructions of "to be . . . without."

366. (E) Paragraph five is developed using the mode of process analysis as the writer goes through his steps of working on the dictionary. This can be seen in his past tense descriptions of having gone through the steps, such as, "I applied myself . . . " and "I reduced to method . . ."

367. (C) "Fortuitous" most nearly means "happening by accident" because it is being used to modify orthography, or spelling, and we are told that the spelling is unsettled and happening by chance. This definition is also clear through the context that irregularities of language are from ignorance and negligence of writers, which can be two examples of accidents.

368. (B) The tone can best be described as resigned because the writer accepts that language is imperfect and must be treated as such. He admits it is inconvenient, but he is accepting of the truth about language.

369. (A) "Visible signs" are letters because in context we read that words were unfixed by visible signs (letters) when language was oral and therefore not written down.

370. (D) The last paragraph is analyzing the causes of the different spellings that he is faced with when writing his English language dictionary. The major cause is that language was first oral and sounds can be caught imperfectly and as a result, written down differently.

Passage 8c

371. (D) The mode of composition of paragraph one is definition. The paragraph is defining "natural liberty," "freedom of men under government," and "freedom of nature."

372. (D) The evidence used in the paragraph is a direct quotation from Robert Filmer. What is in italics is directly quoted and this can be seen by the use of citation in the paragraph, which is the providing of the title of the work (*Observations*) and the section and page (A. 55).

373. (C) The evidence, or direct quotation, provided in paragraph one is being used as counterargument. This can be seen because the writer says, "Freedom then is not what Sir Robert Filmer tells us." He provides the quotation, which is a definition, but disagrees with it and goes on to argue against it, making it counterargument.

374. (A) To mirror the overwhelming will of another man on a man, the writer uses asyndeton, meaning that he omits conjunctions between the adjectives that modify "will."

375. (B) In context, "arbitrary" means "determined by impulse or chance." This meaning is clear from the other words used in the list that show the random nature of the will of another man.

376. (D) In the second and third uses of the word "arbitrary," it most nearly means "not limited by law or despotic." It is used as a close synonym for "absolute" and is used to modify "power."

377. (A) The irony is in the first claim because one would think that a man without power is someone who could easily become a slave, which is a state of powerlessness. The claim that a man without power cannot enslave himself is an example of situational irony because it is the opposite of what we would expect.

378. (A) The first sentence of the paragraph offers a definition of slavery, which is "the state of war continued, between a lawful conqueror and a captive." Although other parts of the paragraph are italicized, only "slavery" is defined.

379. (C) The last paragraph is set up as an exception to the claims made in paragraphs two and three. The example of the Jews does not fit the earlier discussion because the master did not have the power to kill the slaves he kept, which does not fit the earlier definition of the master-slave relationship.

380. (C) "*Exod.* xxi." is evidence that the content of the paragraph is a biblical reference. It stands for the book of Exodus, chapter 21.

Passage 8d

381. (A) As seen by the placement of the most important concern in the topic sentence, the chief occasion is the fact that people walking through the streets find the begging they witness sad. It's ironic that the concern is not for the mothers, nor their children, but for those walking around that wish to avoid unpleasant sights that are melancholy.

382. (B) The purpose (as stated) is that the speaker would like to offer a practical and informed solution to the problem of the overwhelming poverty in the nation. Because this is a satire, the stated purpose is not the actual purpose.

383. (C) The only phrase that is neutral is "may be supported by her milk;" all of the others are negative, disparaging, and insulting in some way. While the speaker pretends to be caring and compassionate, his disparaging diction toward women belies his false concern.

384. (B) The primary appeal in paragraph six is to logos in that the bulk of the paragraph is calculations. Besides that, the diction is clinical when discussing employing children and in the line "is utterly impossible by all the methods hitherto proposed."

385. (C) "Towardly" most nearly means "advantageous" in context, meaning that children normally don't steal until they are at least six unless they live in favorable, or advantageous, places. This definition is ironic because we would consider places in which children steal before the age of six dangerous or bad, not advantageous.

386. (E) After claiming that we can do none of the other proposed ideas in the answer choices, the speaker of the piece finally gets to his "modest proposal," which is to cook and eat the children.

387. (D) The tone of the passage can best be described as pragmatic in that the speaker is trying to propose a practical solution. This can be seen in the calculations in paragraph six and the line "I propose to provide for them in such a manner, as, instead of being a charge upon their parents, or the parish, or wanting food and raiment for the rest of their lives, they shall, on the contrary, contribute to the feeding, and partly to the cloathing of many thousands."

388. (D) The piece is a satire, which means that it is a piece of writing that points out vice or folly in society for the purpose of drawing attention to the problem through the use of irony, derision (mocking), or wit.

389. (A) Because the piece is a satire, the actual purpose (or the writer's purpose) differs from the speaker's stated purpose. The actual purpose is to use humor, including absurdity and wit, to bring attention to the real problem of poverty.

390. (B) The sentence before the proposal to eat the children is an example of understatement because to say he hopes it will not "be liable to the least objection" is quite the understatement considering how people would react if this suggestion were a serious suggestion.

Passage 8e

391. (B) The stated occasion of the passage is a letter written from a man in the country that thinks that the writer of the passage needs to define the terms that he uses in his writing.

392. (A) The intended audience for the passage is country readers, because the writer of the letter is a person from the country and he is asking for definitions of terms used by the writer in his narratives.

393. (A) "Appellations" most nearly means "identifying names." All of the other terms are too limited. The titles presented are not only careers, nor do they only apply to men.

394. (B) According to the second paragraph, the most important thing is being inoffensive to the people around the gentleman. It is a product of good breeding, but the breeding is not the important characteristic.

395. (B) Sophronius is provided as an example of a gentleman. He is a skilled conversationalist and he never appears to be cunning.

396. (C) "Office" most nearly means "a function or duty assumed by someone." In this statement, Sophronius is described as doing a good job in handling all types of conversation—that is, he is skilled in doing all functions or duties in conversations.

397. (E) Writing that Sophronius's conversation "is a continual feast" is an example of a metaphor. It does not use "like" or "as," so it is not an example of a simile, and it does not provide human characteristics or actions, so it is not personification. It is figurative language and qualifies as a metaphor.

398. (B) Jack Dimple is provided as an example of a Pretty Fellow, which is a poor substitute for a Gentleman. Jack Dimple is an artificial imitation.

399. (D) The perfect mimic is Jack Dimple, who is a Pretty Fellow, which is an imitation of the Gentleman. The Gentleman is referred to as a man of conversation and an agreeable being.

400. (D) The passage is primarily using the mode of definition as the writer is defining what a gentleman is.

Chapter 9

Passage 9a

401. (D) The passage's primary mode of composition is definition as it sets out to define poetry, the poet, and imagination. The rhetorical questions in the first paragraph help make this clear.

402. (C) The rhetorical strategy that is used twice in the first paragraph is the rhetorical question. These questions help achieve the purpose of exploring the definitions of poetry, poets, and imagination by introducing the questions to be answered with the extended definitions to follow in the next paragraphs.

403. (A) "Subordination" is "the treatment of something as less valuable or important." In this context, the poet brings the soul of man into activity, and each faculty is ranked below another according to their worth.

404. (E) The poet is described as first bringing the soul of man into activity (bringing to life), then subordinating (separating and ordering) the different faculties (abilities), and then joining them (blending or fusing). Paradoxically, it is the poet's job to both separate and join.

405. (C) The writer says that he would "exclusively appropriate the name of Imagination" (i.e., he would call Imagination) "that synthetic and magical power."

406. (E) "Novelty" and "freshness" are synonymous in the pairings and are set up in opposition with "old and familiar objects." Both "novelty" and "freshness" are about being new, which is in opposition with what is old.

407. (B) From the list, only nature is seen as superior to its counterpart, art. The manner is seen as less than the matter. This can be seen from the construction that begins this list of three pairs. It states, "still subordinates art to nature" (i.e., art is placed under nature in importance or value).

408. (E) There is no apostrophe in the poem. There is personification of the soul, imagery of fire and wings, simile comparing the soul's power of conversion to fire and food, and an ABAB rhyme scheme throughout the three stanzas.

409. (B) The writer of the passage includes the poem, which is about the soul, to characterize the Imagination. Before providing the poem, the writer says, "and his words may with slight alteration be applied, and even more appropriately, to the poetic Imagination." In other words, the poem can be used to describe the Imagination.

410. (A) The final paragraph relies on personification of poetic genius as a body and uses metaphor throughout to figuratively describe Fancy, Motion, and Imagination. This reliance on figurative language is an appropriate way to conclude his points on poetry.

Passage 9b

411. (A) The problem with developing a theory on Private Judgment is that it leads "different minds in such different directions." The other answer choices come from descriptions of "religious truth," which follow in the next sentence.

412. (B) The statement proposes a response to the problem of finding a theory on Private Judgment, but this conclusion is unsatisfactory in that it is "intolerable to those who search," as stated in the third sentence.

413. (C) The major claim, which is introduced with the word "therefore" to signal the coming of a thesis to be proven throughout, is that people who feel the need to search for a theory on Private Judgment have an obligation to explain how it is a duty, an advantage, and a success. The other answer choices either come before this major claim or are subordinated to it.

414. (B) All of the techniques are there except asyndeton. Polysyndeton is used in paragraph one, in the lines "a duty, and an advantage, and a success," and "the Church of Rome, or in the Wesleyan Connection, or in the Society of Friends." Anaphora is used with the repetition of "or" in successive rhetorical questions, and repetition is used with the repeated terms of "good" and "evil."

415. (C) Toleration is brought up to state that private judgment must show why it should be tolerated. All of the other choices are presented as qualities that make private judgment questionable.

416. (D) Defending what is established is the path of least resistance in that those who are proponents of tradition do not have to suffer because they are not trying to change the way things are.

417. (C) The sentence uses anaphora to repeat "considering" at the beginning of the successive clauses.

418. (E) The sentence is periodic as it holds off its main independent clause, "we consider that when Private Judgment moves in the direction of innovation, it may well be regarded at first with suspicion and treated with severity."

419. (D) The passage concludes with epistrophe, as it repeats "disadvantage" at the end of the two successive clauses in the final sentence.

420. (A) The passage, with its use of "we" and discussion of morality, responsibility, and duty, most relies on the appeal of ethos to persuade its readers of it claims.

Passage 9c

421. (B) Including both the time and the place, the first sentence of the passage simply presents the setting of the passage, which is elaborated upon in the rest of the paragraph.

422. (D) In context, "outfits" here means "sets of equipment or articles for a specific purpose," which is here for traveling to Santa Fe. It's not a shipment because it is traveling with them in their wagons.

423. (A) "One of these" is a steamboat. The one being presented is called the *Radnor*. The sentence before states that "almost every day steamboats were leaving."

424. (C) The boat is personified as a woman starting with the sentence "The boat was loaded until the water broke alternately over her guards."

425. (D) The statement mostly appeals to the reader's sense of adventure in discussing the long and arduous journey and it flatters the reader by praising his persevering nature.

426. (C) The writer enumerates all of the many things and people carried on the *Radnor*, but he does not use anaphora, epistrophe, asyndeton, or polysyndeton.

427. (B) The fourth paragraph relies on description, a description of the Missouri River.

428. (A) The paragraph, with its vivid depictions of the Missouri, has a tone of awe as it impresses upon the reader the power of the river.

429. (B) In context, "treacherous" most nearly means "marked by hidden dangers" because the shallows are described as having secrets (something is hidden) and the next sentence discusses the frightful results, hence the danger.

430. (A) The passage narrates the trip from St. Louis on the *Radnor* up the Missouri.

Passage 9d

431. (B) "Expedient" most nearly means "a means to an end." In context, the writer is saying that government should help people achieve a desired goal, rather than get in the way—that is, governments should not be inexpedient, meaning they shouldn't get in the way of men's goals.

432. (C) Comparing the standing army to an arm of the body of a standing government is a metaphor. It is not personification because the standing army is not given human characteristics or actions.

433. (C) The sentence is imperative, commanding the writer to "witness the present Mexican war."

434. (C) The point is that the American government is trying to remain unimpaired throughout time, but that it is changing, because it is losing its integrity.

435. (D) The three sentences use anaphora, as they repeat "It does not" in the successive independent clauses.

436. (D) The use of the "I" stresses the writer's value of independence and the power of the individual, and it appeals to pathos in that the writer makes clear his impassioned tone. However, these claims are not personal in nature. They are about government.

437. (B) Overall, the passage is an impassioned proposal because it is proposing that men make known what they want of their government in order to begin to make a better government a reality. The writer uses "I" to show his personal and passionate feelings.

438. (C) The writer values independence above all else. He uses first person to make his individual voice heard and he continually stresses the value of the man over the group, or the government.

439. (A) Primarily, government is characterized as an obstacle. It is not wholly good or bad, but it gets in the way of what could be further progress for the American people.

440. (E) The tone can best be described as zealous because the proposal for men to make known their desires for a better government is full of passion and fervor on the part of the writer. He uses "I" and he also uses anaphora to stress his passionate claims.

Passage 9e

441. (C) The paragraph does not use synecdoche, which is a form of figurative language in which the part stands for the whole. While it is full of figurative language, it relies on metaphor and personification. It does also contain sentence variety, starting with a bunch of simple sentences and moving into more complicated constructions. It also uses polysyndeton when "and" is repeated in the line "we eat and drink and lie down and pray."

442. (B) Primarily the writer is describing sorrow and his particular experience of sorrow in his prison cell. This is seen through his use of imagery.

443. (B) The writer repeats words at the beginning of the sentences and throughout, including different forms of words ("brute," "brutal" and "fools," "folly"), and he uses parallel structure and figurative language ("dragged it through the very mire"). He doesn't repeat words at the end of his successive phrases, clauses, or sentences, so he doesn't use epistrophe.

444. (C) The writer is using "it" to refer to his family's name, which he feels he has disgraced through the behavior that has led to his being imprisoned.

445. (A) In context, "tremulous" most nearly means "exceedingly sensitive," because the writer is saying that a leaf of the most sensitive gold would register direction, probably due to the wind, that the eye cannot see, but it is less sensitive than sorrow, which is the most delicate and sensitive of all things. "Having little substance" is a close meaning, but it ignores the sensitivity that the writer is describing.

446. (C) The final paragraph uses the mode of composition of definition as it defines sorrow. This can be seen in the construction "sorrow is the most sensitive of all created things," which defines what sorrow is amongst other things.

447. (E) The writer is a husband, writer, and prisoner. He refers to his wife, calls himself a former "lord of language," and mentions the calendar outside his door that has his (prison) sentence written on it.

448. (C) While this line refers to the specific sympathy provided to the writer, overall the passage is a musing on sorrow, especially on its ability to stop time and to be more powerful than anything else. This line does not describe nor define sorrow, and defining and describing sorrow is the major purpose of this letter.

449. (C) The passage mostly appeals to pathos. With its use of figurative language, imagery, and sad content, the passage is meant to be emotionally moving for its readers.

450. (A) The tone can best be described as plaintive as the writer is sad, mournful, melancholy, etc. He discusses his never ending sorrow, his shame at disgracing his family's name, and his grief upon losing his mother.

Chapter 10

Passage 10a

451. (D) The writer uses "one" to refer to a person who is asked about the obstacles that confront young writers. We can assume that a writer would be asked and that the writer falls into that category as she answers the question in the next sentence, beginning with "I." "One" is the general pronoun, while "I" is specific to the writer.

452. (A) "Novelty" most nearly means "newness" in the context in which it is used. This is most clearly seen in the construction "now that the novelty upon which they counted so much is gone," meaning that the newness inevitability wears off.

453. (C) "They" refers to "the dazzling journalistic successes," which is also renamed as "stories that surprised and delighted by their photographic detail."

454. (C) The author twice uses the dash in order to set apart her conclusions. One example is "novelty—never a very important thing in art," and the other is "They . . . —taught us to multiply our ideas instead of to condense them."

455. (B) The tone is ironically disparaging because the beginning of the sentence seems to be praising the merits of a good reportorial story, but ultimately the sentence is saying that these stories are useless after their one relevant moment in time.

456. (D) Millet's *The Sower* is provided as an example of simplicity in composition as the painter had hundreds of sketches but finally edited his work down to one picture that was simple.

457. (C) In the portion of the paragraph that discusses writing, not the writer, the primary mode of composition is classification, as the writer separates writing into the two categories of business and art.

458. (E) The sentence uses repetition of the word "old": comparison of the writer and his public, metaphor of vision being blurred by memory, and personification of the artist being married to old forms, etc.

459. (C) The primary mode for the whole passage is argument with the major claim of "Art, it seems to me, should simplify." The problem posed is: what are the difficulties facing young writers? Then the author of the passage offers her opinionated response, which is an argument.

460. (A) Above all else, the writer values works that are simple. She disparages detailed works in this context as just "lively pieces of reporting" and equates all of the other qualities with writing that is successful in the moment but ultimately fleeting.

Passage 10b

461. (B) The first sentence provides the setting of the passage, which is also elaborated on in the next sentence. We learn that the scene of the passage is in the country, far from the writer's home, on a dark Sunday night.

462. (C) The paragraph begins and ends with first-person point-of-view, so a switch is not in the paragraph. The paragraph begins with repetition of "far" and "home"; asyndeton in "soft, thrilling, powerful"; imagery of sight and sound in describing the prayer; and a simile of "shrieked like a lost soul."

463. (A) This sentence provides the structure of the rest of the paragraph. After this sentence, the writer discusses the preacher in the rest of the paragraph, then discusses the music in the next paragraph, and discusses the frenzy in the last paragraph.

464. (C) The writer uses asyndeton to characterize the preacher as being many types of men. It provides the effect of a rapid list of many different types of people.

465. (E) In context, "plaintive" means "expressing sorrow." This can be seen in the body of the paragraph in phrases such as, "expression of human life and longing" and "expression of a people's sorrow, despair, and hope."

466. (D) The tone of the sentence can best be described as laudatory, as the writer is praising "the Music of Negro religion" as being the best expression of "human life and longing yet born on American soil."

467. (A) "It" refers back to "the Music of Negro religion," introduced in the beginning of the paragraph, in the topic sentence. The rest of the paragraph describes it.

468. (D) The writer uses climax to structure the passage and in the sentence that provides the outline of the passage. It moves to the most important, "the Preacher, the Music, and the Frenzy." In the last paragraph, the writer writes, "Frenzy . . . was the last essential of Negro religion and the one more devoutly believed in than all the rest."

469. (A) The sentence uses alliteration of "s" in "the stamping, shrieking, and shouting" and of "w" in "wild waving of arms, the weeping" to mimic the frenzied noises of the shouting heard at church.

470. (B) The writer is in awe of the "air of intense excitement that possessed that mass of black folk," but also is slightly frightened. He uses words that show fear, such as, "terror," "demoniac," and "awful."

Passage 10c

471. (C) The first paragraph relies on the mode of composition of classification, as the writer classifies the subjects of feminine literature into cooking, children, clothing, and moral instruction.

472. (C) The claim is made in the first paragraph, specifically the last sentence of the first paragraph, through the use of rhetorical question. The question is posed so that the reader will think for himself and then arrive at the conclusion presented in the opening of the next paragraph, "None!"

473. (D) The second paragraph, which is quoted to be in the voice of someone other than the writer, presents counterargument. The counterargument is that there is no men's literature because men are people and women are distinguished as the opposite sex.

474. (A) The writer puts the two terms in quotation marks to distance herself from speaking them, as an indication that she does not agree with these categorizations.

475. (E) In context, "construed" most nearly means "understood." In this sense, the sentence means that men are not put into a strictly understood category of what it means to be a man; however, women are put in such a category.

476. (E) The portion of the sentence in parentheses is an allusion to the Bible. It alludes to the fact that Eve was made from the rib of Adam—that is, she is a "side-issue."

477. (C) Maleness is personified as monopolizing and disfiguring literature, described as a great social function.

478. (C) Paragraph seven is developed by the mode of composition of cause and effect as it analyzes the causes that led up to literature and its effects.

479. (B) The sentence is in parallel structure to make its claim about the uses of literature through time.

480. (C) The final paragraph introduces the examples of masculine literature that will be discussed in the next paragraphs. The writer will begin with the examples of history and fiction.

Passage 10d

481. (C) The claim that progress depends on things remaining the same is paradoxical in nature, because it seems to be contradictory, but is true nonetheless.

482. (E) "Plastic" most nearly means "malleable," or "adaptable." The writer claims that men who learn from experience and are adaptable to new ideas are most successful in terms of making progress.

483. (B) Paragraph one uses an analogy to compare progress to life stages, or growing up. This can be seen in the initial comparison to infancy through to the writer's comparison to old age.

484. (D) The sentence uses personification as it describes old age as being forgetful and having a memory. It also uses simile as it compares old age's instinctive reaction to a bird's chirp, with the use of "like."

485. (C) The second stage, described as manhood, is labeled the stage of true progress, because in this stage, man uses the lessons from his experiences while he also is flexible enough to make changes to improve himself.

486. (D) The statement serves as a qualifier because it is qualifying, or modifying, the original claim. It tempers the claim by saying, "not all readaptation . . . is progress."

487. (A) The purpose of the simple sentence is to show the realistic, and perhaps shocking, effects of when ideal identity is lost. He uses the simple sentence to show the starkness of the failure, which is different from the rest of his complicated sentence structures.

488. (B) The sentence uses polysyndeton, by repeating "or" between "generations," "languages," and "religions."

489. (E) The style of the passage does not depend upon enumeration, while it does use different type of sentences, figurative language, an extended analogy between progress and the aging process, and a paradoxical thesis.

490. (D) The tone can best be described as contemplative, because the writer is thinking through the issue of progress. He is being thoughtful and using complex reasoning.

Passage 10e

491. (A) "Clamour" most nearly means "loud continuous noise" in context. The sentence states that beneath the clamour (continuous noise), a keynote can be heard.

492. (C) The sentence is imperative as it is making a demand, which is to give women labor and training.

493. (C) The sentence uses anaphora as it repeats "we" in the successive clauses that display all of the many tasks that women did to serve humanity.

494. (E) The statement is a rhetorical question, but it also relies on anaphora, with its repetition of "while" at the beginning of the successive clauses and it uses periodic structure as it holds the main independent clause (in this case a question) until the end of the statement.

495. (D) The paragraph mostly appeals to ethos and pathos. Some of the techniques that achieve these appeals are rhetorical questions and repetition of "we" for the appeal to ethos; and the content, which is full of suffering and toiling, as expressed through emotionally charged diction, appeals to pathos.

496. (D) The purpose of the sentence is to level the different types of women, be they wives of men of status or not, and to express that all women had work to do regardless of their class distinctions.

497. (A) The tone can best be described as resilient as the writer discusses how women, even after all of the changes that have altered their role, continue to have work to do and how they continued doing such labor as was needed.

498. (E) The passage moves from the distant past into the more recent past; therefore, it's chronological in sequence. This can be seen in the time-marking transitional paragraphs, such as, "Then a change came" and "Then again a change came."

499. (A) The primary mode of the passage is narration because although the writer is making a claim about how women's work has changed over time, the way in which the writer expresses her points is in the form of narration. She is telling the story of woman's labor over time.

500. (B) The purpose of the passage is to narrate how women's labor has shifted according to the changes in the types of society over time. The chronological structure helps readers to see her narration.